THE SHTETL THAT WAS

THE SHTETL THAT WAS

Ralph Jaffe

VANTAGE PRESS
New York

FIRST EDITION

Published by Vantage Press, Inc.
516 West 34th Street, New York, New York 10001

Manufactured in the United States of America
ISBN: 0-533-12061-6

Library of Congress Catalog Card No.: 96-90467

0 9 8 7 6 5 4 3 2 1

In memory of my father, Shiya Leib, my mother, Rochel, and my sister, Neche Minna, who all perished in the Holocaust.

In memory of my relatives, friends, and all the Jewish people from my shtetl Kavarsk, who were murdered by the Nazis and their sympathizers.

In memory of my dear uncle, Louis, and aunt, Lena Jaffe, and their friend, Jack Levine, who together sponsored and brought me to America. To them I owe my life.

In memory of the ORT in Kovno, its students, teachers, and director, Jakob Oleiski. To these people I owe my success in life thanks to the early training I received from them.

Contents

THE SHTETL THAT WAS

ONE
Kavarsk (Kavarskas)

I was born in Kavarsk. My father was born in Kavarsk. My father's father and mother, I believe, were born in Kavarsk. This was the place where, my bones tell me, my grandparents and my father spent their youth. My father grew up in Kavarsk before he married my mother and, of course, before my sister and I were born.

Kavarsk was always there. Where I will be after I die I do not know. But I do know where I was before I was born. It was in Kavarsk.

For me, this tiny town was the oldest spot in the world because it was on this earth even before history began, meaning it was here before I was born.

As a child, the question of whether there was a Kovno (Kaunas), a Paris, a London, or even an America was arguable. Maybe they did exist; maybe they did not. But when it came to Kavarsk, it was not a matter of believing or not believing. It was a fact. I knew it firsthand. As a newborn baby, I had already lived there many generations, through my father and mother and, as I imagined, those who came before them.

I felt Kavarsk in me as a child. And now, as an older man, I still feel Kavarsk inside me, even while being the proud American that I am.

To me, Kavarsk was—and is—more than a tiny town in a faraway country called Lithuania. Like my blood and bones, it is a part of me—a part of me from which I had to separate myself in order to leave for America.

Do you know what it is like to tear a piece of yourself, a precious priceless piece of yourself, from yourself? I had to do it; I did it. And the doing of it is what I remember most about Kavarsk.

I remember the last long hug and kiss from my mother. Her golden tears ran down her cheeks as she struggled to avoid breaking our embrace on that July morning in our cozy house. Together we walked up the hill where she watched me depart with my father in a bus. He went with me to Kovno, where he saw me off on a train.

(As I write these words recalling my mother's parting embrace, tears stream down my face as they streamed down her cheeks. I feel it now, years later, as I've never felt it before.)

This Kavarsk is where I kissed and said goodbye to my sister, whom I loved so very much and whom I miss terribly to this day.

This Kavarsk is where, from my early life, I loved—I really worshipped—my dear father, a very special father and a very special human being. His love for my mother, my sister and me was unmatched. He was the kindest and most loving human being I have ever known.

It was not just his family. He approached life and everyone with thoughtful kindness. He left his mark. The way in which I have lived my life and the things I have tried to do have all been influenced by what I saw, felt and experienced in our home.

I loved my father as a son loves a loving father. But I was not alone. My father was loved and admired by everyone in Kavarsk. They held him in high regard. They all respected Shiya Leib.

Kavarsk—this is where I parted with my relatives, my friends and the townspeople, each of whom I knew by name—never to see them again. All were murdered at the hands of the beastly Nazis and their Lithuanian collaborators. My people were all slaughtered for the unforgivable crime of having been born Jewish.

Kavarsk—in the winter when blizzards would cover it with a blanket of snow and ice. The delightful, gurgling brooks would freeze. The surrounding fields and forests would become enshrouded in deep snow. Our wooden houses would be half-buried in deep drifts. When you left the cozy comfort of the home, having been warmed by burning wood in a brick stove, you faced a fierce fight against the mercilessly cold air.

You knew another human was near only when you heard crunching footsteps in the dry frosted snow. Also, you could hear the sleigh bells on the horses as they galloped past your house.

Then came the spring to Kavarsk. The white meadows would smile with green. The once silent streams would gurgle again and lovingly rush to feed the Shventa (Shventoya) River. And soon came Pesach (Passover), a time when the muddy streets would turn dry and allow you to run in bare feet again, released from the woolen boots *(volekes)* and galoshes.

I remember, too, the swimming hole. We ran through the meadows for a swim in the clear, cool, refreshing Shventa. Hip deep in water, we would watch the log pontoons as they were deftly piloted down the Shventa to the big river, the Neman (Nemunas), some one hundred kilometers (sixty miles) northwest.

We looked forward to market day in Kavarsk. It came every Monday. We would slip around the peasants' wagons and look for white horses with long tails. When a peasant was busy with a customer, we would sneak behind the horse to pluck the long white hairs from the horse's tail, always praying that we would not get kicked by the horse nor caught by the peasant.

We enjoyed the mischief. But we were also practical. We put the long white hairs to good use by braiding them in a special way to make a fishing line that we attached to a long flexible branch. It was our way of converting a horse's tail into a fresh fish.

This is the Kavarsk I remember. This is the town where my dearest dreams are buried in its deep, cursed black earth.

Who knows how many of those who are buried in that accursed ground, had they been allowed to live, would have ended up in the 1978 edition of *Who's Who in World Jewry*, or in the 1980 edition of *Who's Who in American Jewry*, alongside my name.

In the town where they lived and loved and longed and labored, there remains no memento, no memorial, no reminder of their lives. It's all covered over with the black, blood-soaked earth. Still, in my heart they are inscribed forever.

TWO
Remembrance of Things Past

For many years I have been toying with the idea of recording my past in writing, and of doing so in some comprehensive form. From time to time I have shared some incident, some circumstance or other, with family and friends, but somehow or other, these scattered pieces lose their meaning unless they are part of the larger mosaic that makes up a life—a life, in this instance, that I, alone, know in its entirety.

Letting these stories stand alone is like looking at disconnected portions of some great artistic masterpiece without ever having an opportunity to look at the whole canvas. The result is a jumble, especially if the distinct segments are viewed independently over many years.

To bring the bits and pieces together into a meaningful whole is my aim in these pages. My purpose is to pass on to my children, my grandchildren, and their children a legacy—the story of my life—with the hope that it will add depth of meaning to their lives. I—and I alone—am in a position to pass on the rich tradition of the generations that came before me to the generations that came after me, and are still to come.

These pages are my humble attempt, dear children, to tell you how I felt about those who shaped my life, and how, through me, they affected and affect your lives to this very day. My story is the story of my roots—and of your roots and the roots of those to come.

I am now seventy-two years old. Fifty-six years ago, at the age of sixteen, I left Kavarsk with the full expectation that we would all be reunited in America. It did not turn out that way. Yet, over the course of more than half a century, not a single day has passed when I did not think about them or recall something about them. After all these years I still miss them terribly, and I try to fill the emptiness with my remembrance of things past.

I could have recited these recollections to a machine that would turn out a tape. I chose not to; it would have been out of character for me. I am more introvert than extrovert. I am someone who prefers to convey his thoughts and feelings in a contemplative mode, slowly and deliberately writing my pages in longhand. I am, in a sense, talking to myself while simultaneously allowing you, my children, to eavesdrop on my private, internal conversation.

I can say quite honestly that I remember my past vividly, going all the way back to the time when I was a mere six-year-old. The recall is so stark and strong that, occasionally, it scares me. I close my eyes and see my life passing before me, as if it were some foreign movie with English subtitles running from left to right. There they are, crowding the giant screen—my parents, sister, grandmother, grandfather, cousins, the dear friends with whom I played, the shtetl (town) where I was born.

Had I been an artist I would have painted the scenes on a colorful canvas. I guess that is why I love Chagall's paintings so much, especially those depicting small towns such as my own Kavarsk. Since I am not an artist, however, I have done the next best thing: I made a map of my shtetl. I have also a picture of my early shtetl, taken in 1928. As I look at it, I am repeatedly moved by the beauty of it all—not by the superficial glitter of material riches, but by the lasting luster of the love we had for one another.

Therefore, after much toying with the idea of writing my life story, I finally decided to get serious and do it. There are two reasons:

First, I am seventy-two and not getting younger. I have all my faculties and would like to put them to work while they are still in good shape. Second, I felt a compulsion to respond to the active interest in my life shown by Rochelle and Lenny.

Every so often Rochelle would say to me, "Daddy, why don't you write about your life?" On other occasions when I would relate some episode, while she might not have repeated the sentiment in words, her eyes spoke silently—"Why don't you write it?"

Lenny showed the same intense interest in the events surrounding my family and myself. While Lenny never urged me to "write," as Rochelle did, he showed the same eagerness to learn about my past that his sister had.

So here I am, beginning to recall and write down everything I can remember from the age of five or six, especially the period up to age sixteen and a half. This, as I suggested earlier, is not my first start, but this time I have resolved to stick with it to the end. I owe it to those who came before me, to those who will come after me, and to myself.

Fortunately, the bits and pieces I started in the past to write down have not gone lost. In particular, I refer to something that happened to me twenty-four years ago, on August 3, 1970. I wrote about it then, put it away, forgot about it, and then rediscovered it. I am including it verbatim as it was written then.

I am writing in my small basement office that I built for myself in our house, one of 144 homes in a beautiful condominium development known as the Estates of North Hills, in Manhasset, Long Island, New York. Here I keep all kinds of records pertaining to our transactions that, in my semiretired state, I need to keep track of. Periodically, I ruffle through these files and destroy old bank statements, business correspondence, and other materials that now are of no relevance, in order to make room for current and pertinent documents.

But the papers and the memorabilia of personal and sentimental character I keep and have kept over many years. They are stored in metal fireproof cabinets. My occasional return to these scraps of paper rekindles the memories that give me a sense of solace and consolation.

In the course of making these periodic returns to the past, I came across six letters written in Yiddish. When I finished reading them, I broke down; I wept uncontrollably. Fortunately, my wife was out shopping, which meant that she did not have to witness her man melting away in tears. It also meant that I could spend the rest of the afternoon sitting back, eyes closed, reliving the pains and pleasures of the past.

It was at that moment that I made my resolve, a vow I shared with no one—not even my wife—to put pen to paper and, in the old-fashioned way, write out in longhand the story of a person that, by inference and indirection, is part of the long story of a family and the much longer story of a people.

Since the six letters in Yiddish were the goad that prodded my resolve, I should like to begin with an English translation of each. Two were from my father; one was from my sister, one from a girlfriend, and the final two were letters I wrote to my parents. (I had written my parents regularly every week from the day I first arrived in America.)

The two letters I wrote to my parents were returned to me, marked with a German postmark (a swastika). They had apparently been opened by the Nazis who had, by then, occupied Russia and Lithuania.

After reading these letters, I believe you will understand why my rereading of them years later drove me to write these memoirs. I am not certain that I can convey my sentiments as clearly on paper as they are inscribed in my mind; but I will do the best I can.

The last letter written to me by my father was dated June 3, 1941. The Germans entered Lithuania just a few days later, on June 22 of the same year. The letter was addressed to me and to my Aunt Lena and Uncle Louis, with whom I was living at the time:

My dear son, sister-in-law, brother and nieces,

I wish all of you to be well and to have a happy life. We received three letters from you today. It has been a long time since I last wrote to you. Today, however, I can reveal to you the reason for not writing. Minka, your sister, is well now.

Through you alone, my dear ones, can I find encouragement and hope. Minka was very sick this winter. She became ill with a throat infection; after that she had the grippe; then later on she became deathly ill. Her condition almost killed all of us. It was Purim when she became paralyzed. For five weeks she was unable to speak. She also suffered from convulsions.

I had taken her several times to the biggest professors in Kovno. Thank God, she will be well again and she will be the same beautiful and clever Minka she has always been.

She is already able to write and she is sending you a short letter today.

My dearest Ruvalle, today we feel much better. You and all our dear ones will be happy to know that, as soon as she felt better, the first thing she asked of us was that we give her pictures of Sandra. When we did, she just kept on kissing the pictures and would not let go of them.

We wish all of you over there the best of health and we wish the same for all of us over here.

Ruvalle, I want to thank you very much for the pictures you sent us. We do like very much the girl you are with. She is much more beautiful than the picture of the girl you sent us a while back, the one with the Negro girl standing beside her.

There is nothing new I have to write to you in regard to politics. I'm sure you know better than I do that the situation today is very tense and it isn't good. I am, however, full of expectation and hope that Hitler will get his *mapola* and downfall at the end.

By us it is quiet. I make a living and I have no need for money from you.

Ruvalle, when you write to us, don't say anything bad about our government. Don't look at what the newspapers are writing. Write only about the good things.

I have nothing new to write. However, you should never forget Lena and Louis for what they have done for you. We are most appreciative and grateful to them. May we all be well.

Give our best wishes to the entire family.

From your loving father, mother and sister.

Leib Jaffe.

The second letter read:

Today, I was thinking that perhaps it would be nice to go away to our dacha [a small bungalow in the Pine Forest not far from town]. Unfortunately, it is very cold at present. We can not recall ever such a cold month of May.

About our village, there is much new I could write to you. But, we are not permitted to write about everything. Minka will write to you about all the news that we are permitted to write as soon as she will get a bit stronger.

Elka (my father's sister) doesn't feel better. Dearest Lena, write and let us know how Louie is feeling. I hope that he is well by now.

When I received your letter I was in no position or condition to send you a reply. We had a bad situation here. (Minka was ill.)

We must never lose hope. The time will come, someday, when we will be together again. We will then happily be able to talk with each other and to talk about everything.

Reizel (a cousin) from Kovno was with us. She came to get a birth certificate. You would never have recognized her because she has become so skinny. It is a reminder that onc should not be envious of the once-rich.

In my next letter I will tell you more. May all of you stay well.

Leib Jaffe

This is my sister Minka's last letter. It was the first letter she was able to write after her recovery. Minka was fifteen years old at that time. The letter was dated June 3, 1941:

My dearest brother Ruvalle,

How are you? Thank God, I am well. My dear brother, I will not write much now, as our father wrote to you about everything.

Early tomorrow morning, we are driving to Vilkatanzie to spend time in a dacha. I will not write anymore, because in Kavarsk there isn't any new thing to write about. May you all be well. From your sister Minka, who misses you very much. Best regards to my uncle, aunt, and cousins. Send us pictures of everyone. Be well. Adieu. We received your pictures.

This letter was written just three weeks before Hitler entered Lithuania on June 24, 1941. Two years before, on September 1, 1939, Hitler had overrun Poland—part of a deal he'd made with Stalin to divide Poland between the Nazis and the Communists. The same pact turned Lithuania, Latvia, and Estonia over to the Soviets. Since all letters were opened, my father discreetly self-censored the news he sent us.

The next letter, also in Yiddish, was written by a girl who was graduated with me from the only public school in our town, which went up to the eighth grade. The graduating class consisted of six pupils.

Our families were very close. Her parents were my parents' closest friends. We lived in the same house and shared a big kitchen. This letter, mailed from Kaunas, was dated May 11, 1941:

Dear Ruvin, I received your letter and, with great joy, I read all the news which you had written. First, I must apologize for not answering you sooner, but this is not entirely my fault. You could never imagine how involved I have been.

First of all, I brought over my sister Nechamke to Kaunas. Also, because I am very much involved with what goes on in the factory, I had to run here and there. Now that four of us children are here in Kaunas, things are much better.

Nechamke and I are working in the same factory and we are earning each as much as three hundred rubles a month. The times when I worked for Dobke for five Litas a month are behind us. Now we earn much more and are able to buy things and dress well.

My dear, I am happy to know that you are having a good time. We, too, are enjoying ourselves nicely. My sister Nechamke, together with another girl, have their own room and every evening entertain many friends. That makes us quite happy. I live in a separate place, since we could not find a place where we could all live together.

We have made an application for an apartment, with the hope of getting one so we would be able to bring over our parents from Kavarsk to live with us. We do hope we get one.

Now I will give you the names of the friends that we have. Perhaps you will know some of them: Moishke Vilek, Moishke Bar, Meilachke Lafer from Anyksht, whom you must know because he was an ORT student, and Benke, who is also working in Kovno. Also there is our Berl, who is going out with one of my girlfriends. They visit us with a friend of his who comes to visit me. We go to the movies together; he likes to spend lots of money. And, in the meantime, I squeeze the *neshome* out of him.

As you can imagine, many *khevre* [comrades] come with whom I play around as I also do with him. Since I ignored him a bit this week, he was angry with me and didn't show up for a few days. This Saturday, however, he dressed himself up and came over. So we all went to the movies.

My brother Berke says, "In the meantime go out with him. Pleasure he provides you. Money he has and he is not stingy with it. So what do you care?"

So, in the meantime, I go out with him because, anyway, in the next few months he is due to go into the army. I am reconciled to the fact that he will leave soon.

Well, enough of this. I prefer to write to you about how things went with us on May 1. We celebrated that day in Kovno with a great parade. Every evening we enjoyed ourselves—more and more. I went to two Night Balls in Cafe Monico. We had four days off—no work.

Ruvalle, today your sister Minnale and your father came to Kovno. I was so happy to be with them. It has been a long time since I have seen them. The last time was *Rosh Hashanah* [the Jewish New Year], and they told me that my younger sister Yentke received a book for being a good student.

The news from Kavarsk I am sure you know. Also that Sorke (a girl in our graduating class) married Itzky. I can imagine what's happening there with them. She is lucky. In general a girl has to be crazy to get married so young, but for her, Sorke, it is good, as she is lazy and doesn't like to work.

I think it is time for me to finish this short letter. (Who knows whether you will have the patience to read a long letter.) But you know what? It is very easy for me to write to you. It comes very naturally to write to you, because you are my closest and dearest *khaver* [friend], with whom I feel so free and with whom I can share my pain and happiness. Ruvalle, I don't understand why we are so close to you. Well, as to you personally, okay. But with your parents and with Minnale, you can't even imagine how close we have been in the last few years.

When I left for Kovno, only sixty miles away, your mother cried as though it was her child who was leaving her house. I think of Minnale as my sister. There is no difference between my natural sisters and her.

Dear one, I have to bring this letter to an end. Please write to me about everything and send me your picture. That I may not be in debt to you, in the next letter I will send you my picture.

Dear one, a hearty regards from me to your aunt and Sandra;

Nechamke, Nochemke, and Berke send their best regards. Stay well. From me who misses you. Your girlfriend, Yochele.

Ruvalle, you know what? I think we are going to see each other. So I am going to say, "Until we see each other." My dear Ruvalle, you know what I would like to do now? I would love to walk together with you for a while by the river Neman.

It is such a beautiful day. The sun is shining. And my heart longs so much for you.

Enough of the romantic. Let's talk about some serious things. I forgot to answer you about some of the things you mentioned in your letter, such as your saying that in America you have to be rich to be able to satisfy a woman. I think that, in your case, you won't have to look too far for one who would be satisfied with less, because you already have her right now.

I don't think that I have to be your advisor. You know full well what you have to do. So, please, stay well—for me.

The final two letters in Yiddish were written by me to my parents. The first was dated June 5, 1941:

To my loving parents and sister!

How are you? We are all well, thank God, and we hope we will hear the same from you.

Your letter did not arrive yet this week. I believe it now takes much longer for the letters to be delivered.

My dear ones, I don't have any special news to write to you. The world situation is a very serious one. But what can we do? We have to accept what is. They have thrown us about and scattered us to the winds for the last four thousand years. Maybe this is the way it was fated to be. However, to everything there is an end. Let's just hope that it will not take too long.

We must never lose hope. No one knows what the next minute will bring, especially at the present time. If man did not live with hope then the world could never exist and there would be nothing of interest in the world for which to live.

No human being is ever happy with what he possesses; we are always looking for something else. I think that perhaps I have wandered around too much in philosophical pursuits. So, I will end my writing now. From your son and brother who wants to hear only good things from you—Ruvin.

The uncle, aunt, the children, and the family send best wishes to you. Please give my regards to Aunt Elke and family. How is her health? Give my best wishes to Leib and family. My best wishes to all, good night.

The second letter was dated June 12, 1941:

To my dear loving parents and sister!

Hopefully, my writing will find you in happiness and health. My dearest, I received a letter from you this week that was written before Passover.

My dear ones, from my writing to you every week you must now know very well that there isn't much that is new that one can report in every letter. There is much going on in the house. There is much going on with the upcoming wedding this Sunday, when we will be making a trip to Yosef's [Uncle Joe's], whose daughter is getting married.

The *simche* would have been complete if we had all been there together. Stay well and do not lose hope. The day will yet come when we will all be together in good health. We will then be able to make up for the bitter times, the lost days. So, here's wishing you the best from your son and brother who wants to hear only good things from you.

Ruvin.

There is still another letter written by my Aunt Lena that was marked "opened" and was returned to her. It was dated June 6, 1941:

My dear ones, how are you? We are all well. It's been a long time since we received a letter from you. In a previous letter I told of the news that I am going to become a mother-in-law. My elder daughter is getting married in three months from now, and she has also written a letter to you and to Elke. But because not all the mail has been received I'm writing to you again. I wish you well and hope that you will live to enjoy *naches* from your children.

My dear ones, I am growing old. As the saying goes: When one becomes a mother-in-law one is not young anymore. But today I feel as if I am sixteen years old. I start thinking to myself that it wasn't long ago that I got married. Yet, it is now twenty-four years. That's how life goes by.

Two weeks from now will be the wedding of Joe's elder daughter. I had hoped that you would be with us this summer, but it did not happen. What we think and hope is not always what comes to be. This is all I have to write to you. Be well. May we only hear good things from each other and from every one of us. Good night.

I just arrived from visiting Shmulke [Sam]. He moved into another flat. Irving had a girl, a brilliant child. He, Irving, is a much better worker than all his brothers. Be well. From your friend, Lena Jaffe.

Everyone sends regards. Louie is sleeping already. So are the children.

Sarale works in a hospital; she has been working there for two months. She visits us twice a week. Nattie went over to see her intended in-laws, who live not far from here. "Good night," that means a *gute nacht.* I send my regards to everyone and to Elke and her family. I wrote a letter to her. Please write and tell me how is her health. And how is Yankel and the children? Did the son come home yet? Good night.

Yours, Lena.

These letters in Yiddish, with their warm and repeated references to family and friends and their daily doings, moved me profoundly. I knew that someday I would have to share my feelings with my children and grandchildren.

And then on Monday, August 3, 1970, something strange, scary, and startling happened to me, an unplanned event that gave further impetus to my resolve to write an autobiography.

Driving in my car to Staten Island, where I had a plumbing contract to oversee, I approached the Verrazano Bridge. It was a routine matter for me to make such trips in my work on some new developments that were going up on the island. To amuse myself, I would listen on the car radio to the *tumler* Art Raymond on station WEVD, or to Bob Grant on WMCA.

I enjoyed Raymond's Yiddish songs and comments. I was intrigued by Bob Grant's highly controversial attitudes. I identified with Raymond; I respected Grant, not because I necessarily agreed with what he said, but because he showed some real guts in his outspoken critique of liberals. Although I generally disagreed with him, his direct mode of expression held my attention.

Occasionally, while listening to him, I would murmur to myself and break into a loud laugh. I am sure that if some passing driver saw me doing this, he would simply conclude I was some kind of a nut.

On this particular day, not really different from any other day, I was driving along engaged in my customary form of self-amusement. When the big blue and white sign signalled the entrance to the Verrazano Bridge, I made the sharp right turn off Belt Parkway and toward the bridge.

Suddenly a strange feeling of anxiety came over me. I felt nervous, tense, scared. I started to get cramps and a nervous stomach. I broke into a cold sweat and my heart started to pound rapidly. I was certain that I was being hit with a coronary.

My instinctive first reaction was to pull over to the side of the road and just rest. I checked my rearview mirror. The traffic behind me was heavy and fast-moving. For me to come to a halt would be impossible. If I dared do it, the other cars would come crashing down on me.

Having no choice, I pulled myself together as best I could and began to ascend the bridge. My prayer was that, somehow or other, I would be able to reach the toll booth, then pull over to the side and pull myself together.

As I reached the crown of the bridge, the midpoint of my crossing, I glanced out the left window of the car at the vast expanse of sky and water. There I saw the wide gaping mouth of the mighty Hudson River that, before emptying into the great Atlantic Ocean, moves through the Sea Gate on one side and Staten Island on the other. I'd made the crossing many times before, but this time what I saw shook me. I heard a voice within me crying out, *Do you know why you are feeling the way you do?*

You're not physically sick, said the voice within. *Think, think. What made you feel the way you did?*

My thoughts turned to the past. What could have happened to me at some point in my life to make me now, at this moment, lapse into such a fit of anxiety and tension? For a while there, as I pursued my fruitless search for an answer, I really thought that I was going nuts. I was glad there was no one in the car with me; had there been, that person might easily have concluded that I'd simply gone bananas.

Through all this turmoil I continued to drive with my eye on the road, broken only by an occasional glimpse of the awesome waters below. My eyes were in the here and now, but suddenly my head was alive with vivid visions of events and things past. The voice within, like some divine power, commanded me to think, to think hard about that past, because hidden within it was the answer to why I was feeling the way I did. I knew that this day was no ordinary day, and that this moment in time was no ordinary moment. There was something special about the place, the time, and the coming together of past and present in a boy, now a man, out of Kavarsk.

What was it? The question pursued me. The answer eluded me. The tension heightened.

To momentarily escape my dilemma, I decided to turn my attention to the agenda for the day. I reached for my appointment book, which was at my side. A leather marker made it easy to flip it open for the day and I did so. The day was Monday, August 3, 1970.

There was the answer! As past and present merged, things began to fall into place. Thirty-two years ago, on Monday, August 1, 1938, I'd crossed the waters under this bridge. (The bridge had not yet been built.) There I was, a scared, bewildered, lonely sixteen-year-old boy, his red hair cut short before his exit from Europe, not knowing what was in store for him in America and what would happen to his parents, sister, and family in the frightening future.

There I was, a wide-eyed teenager, sailing up the Hudson on the French liner the *Normandie*, gaping in awe at the skyscrapers reaching up prayerfully like steel and concrete hands toward the blue heavens.

Now, once again, I am here crossing the waters on this famous bridge, the longest suspension bridge in the world. I see the bridge as a friendly handshake between Brooklyn and Staten Island. I am reenacting my earlier passage—the initial bewilderment, the subsequent wonderment, and the ultimate attachment to a new home across the waters.

I am the bridge. At sixteen, I spanned the ocean from one continent to another. Twice sixteen years later, I am spanning the Narrows from one island to another. *I am the bridge and I am the bridge builder.*

Here I am, in my comfortable Cadillac, in pursuit of my trade: to install plumbing in still another new development in the New World. To get to this point—in my profession, in my adopted homeland, in my life—I had to cross many bridges.

I now realized, however, that there was one more bridge to cross; it ran from one generation, through me, to another generation. It did not run from place to place but rather from person to person, from my father and mother to my son and daughter and, perhaps, beyond. Smiling, I thought to myself, *If I were a bridge, I would be the longest suspension bridge in the world, from the grassy turf of Kavarsk to the brassy towers of Manhattan.*

By the time I crossed the Verrazano I was on a high; I had solved a mystery and confirmed a resolve. My body was at peace.

When I got to the tollbooth and tossed in my two quarters, I felt that I had crossed a threshold in my life. To collect myself, I pulled the car over to the side where it was safe to park, turned off the ignition, and just sat there looking into space.

Soon that space began to fill up with places and people, with noises and voices, with food and drink, with the quiet of the shtetl and the hubbub of the city. My whole life raced before my eyes. My sixteen years as a youth, my twice-sixteen years since my arrival in America—scene after scene flashed vividly before me, all in a matter of seconds.

They say that in the last moments of a dying person's life, his entire life is replayed for him. If so, I must have died on the other side of the Verrazano Bridge. And, since I am here to tell the tale, I must have been reborn.

I knew the purpose of my rebirth: To tell a tale that only I could tell, because only I knew the full story about me.

I knew I had to do it, but I was apprehensive. If I could have immediately written down everything I saw in that revealing flash, then writing my story would have been easy. But I knew it would not come that simply. I knew it would take days, months, and even years to complete this self-imposed assignment.

I also knew that autobiographies written by men and women of advanced age are not always to be trusted as accurate. In old age memory plays tricks, and what one imagines to have been may not necessarily have been so.

I decided there was no time to waste. What I had seen I'd envisaged so clearly that it might have happened only a few minutes ago. Those images should not be allowed to be tarnished by time. I had to take pen in hand and capture them—*now*.

Even as I sat in my car, in lonely and deep revery, I knew that reciting my odyssey would not be all fun. There would be moments of pain, as well as of pleasure—moments when I would recall my joys in America, and moments when I would recall the death of my beloved ones in Lithuania, who were killed for no other reason than that they were born and lived as Jews.

I do not expect that my writing will be a great literary masterpiece. My prose is not as good as my plumbing. I am writing for those who know me and for those I love. I am writing to share me with them. I am writing to be a bridge between past and future, between the world of the shtetl and the world of the west, between a centuries-old culture and new cultures in the making.

I do it less because I want to than because I have to.

When I got home I hastened to jot down the above and signed it "Ralph Jaffe, Monday, August 3, 1970."

THREE
A Big Family

Were it not for the Holocaust, ours would be a large family—much larger than it is today. As you know, I was born in Kavarsk in 1922—on February 13, to be exact. My father, Shiya Leib, was also born in Kavarsk, at the turn of the century in the year of 1900. His father, my grandfather Yakov (in English, it would be Jacob), was also born in Kavarsk, as was my father's mother, my grandmother Neche Minna. Her maiden name was Heiman.

Unfortunately, I never got to know my grandparents on my father's side, since they both died at a relatively early age. The remarkable thing is that, although my grandmother on my father's side died prematurely, she managed to give birth to ten children; one of these, named Hayim, died when he was only two or three years old. Her last child was my Uncle Irving, who lost his mother when he was still an infant of two or three.

As to the death of my grandfather Yakov (also called Yankel), I heard the story on many occasions. What happened reveals much about the kind of man he was.

He died shortly after Yom Kippur. He was a fanatically religious man. On Yom Kippur, he would habitually go to *shul* in the evening for Kol Nidre. He would remain there, in the synagogue, all night and all the next day, praying while standing all the time.

On this particular Yom Kippur the temperature was abnormally hot. The windows in the *shul* were not open. And, as you know, in those days there were no electric fans, no air conditioning; in fact, there was no such thing as electricity. The *shul* was lighted up with kerosene lamps and candles that burned and threw off added heat all night long.

After the blowing of the *shofer* that concluded the observance, my grandfather, who had not eaten for twenty-four hours and had not sat down during all that time, started to wend his way home—hungry, tired, perspiring. On the way, he stopped in at the house of his brother Ruvin, my great-uncle and the father of Morris Jaffe. The house was close to the synagogue. He drank a glass of milk before starting out for home again.

A few days later, he fell sick with pneumonia and died shortly thereafter. I did not personally witness any of this, but I'd heard the story many times from members of our family.

My father had five brothers. Four of them left for America: Yoske (Joe), Lazke (Louis), Shmulke (Sam), and Shrolke (Irving). The fifth brother, as I mentioned earlier, died as a child.

My father also had four sisters. One of them, Friedka (Frieda), went to America. One sister, Elke, who lived in Kavarsk, was married to Yankel Hochman. They had four children, named Hirshka, Chaim Osher, Neche Minna, and Beelka.

A second sister, Dinka, was married to Rafael Segal and lived in Roguva, about eight miles from Kavarsk, with her seven children; I do not remember all their names. I do remember one son, Leibke, who went to South Africa, and a daughter, Neche Minna, who was married in Roguva and then went with her husband to Paris to pursue her studies. She lived there until the Nazis took over, at which time they returned to Lithuania, where they ultimately suffered the same bitter fate as the others who were exterminated by the Lithuanian and German anti-Semites.

There was another daughter, Yentke. I knew her very well. She, too, had moved to Paris, but had returned to Lithuania in order to become a nurse in Kovno. As it happened, I was, at precisely that time, at an ORT school in Kovno, and although she was older than I was we spent many happy moments together.

Then there was Yankele, the sole survivor of our entire family. He now lives in Kazakhstan.

There were three other children, whose faces I recall but whose names I can not now remember.

I do, however, remember still another sister, whose name was Peshka. I remember her name but never saw her. She was married and lived in Vitebsk, Russia; she had four children. My father corresponded with them, and I recall that in the 1930s he sent food packages to them. They were living through hard times, days of austerity decreed by Stalin during one of his five-year plans.

The letters my father received from his sister had to be read not only line by line but also, and mainly, in-between the lines, because all mail was censored. My father knew how to decipher their unwritten code. I remember him telling us that their stomachs and feet would swell up for lack of food. (They did not have to tell us that they were starving; they merely had to say they were suffering from swollen stomachs and feet.)

I do not know the name of her husband or the names of her children. What happened to them I can only surmise. I believe that they, too, were victims of the Holocaust.

My mother, who was the same age as my father, was born in a very small village called Gelez (Geleziai), about thirty miles from Kavarsk. Her name was Rachel Norwitz (Norvic).

My mother's father, after whom I was named, was Ruvin Gavriel. He died when he was very young. I don't know what happened; I heard very little about my grandfather on my mother's side.

As I look back on those times now, I regret that I never asked my mother about her father. In the normal course of events in Europe in those days, very little was spoken in our small towns about those in the family who came before. I'd venture to guess the reason was their total preoccupation with the daily chores that had to be performed simply to ensure their survival.

My grandmother's name on my mother's side was Etta. I knew her well and loved her very much.

My mother had two brothers and one sister. One brother, whose name was Shneika, married a girl from Gelez. She was a redhead with a face full of freckles; her name was Dobka. In 1929, her husband took off and went to South Africa. His wife followed shortly thereafter.

The second brother's name was Shmulke. He lived with my grandmother and her second husband, Shiya. In the 1930s, they moved from Gelez to Subatz (Subacius). I remember it well because I used to spend part of every summer there with them. Gelez was about seven miles from Subatz.

My mother's sister's name was Keilka. She was married and lived in Kupishok (Kupiskas) with her four children. Keilka was gorgeous; people who met her would repeatedly refer to her as "the beauty."

Her husband left for South Africa with the announced intention of settling and later bringing his family there. I do not know what happened subsequently. He may have lacked the means to bring his family to South Africa; perhaps there were other reasons.

I do recall my Uncle Shmuel and my grandmother talking about my Aunt Keilka and her husband. They thought there was something wrong with him. He would write to Keilka and accuse her of infidelity, believing she was involved with a man in Kupiskis who owned a flour mill.

He returned to Kupiskis around 1935. The family disappeared in the Holocaust.

FOUR
The Homecoming

It was a sunny summer Sunday in July 1929. I was playing with a few other children in a small straw-roofed barn behind a friend's house. The interior of the barn was divided in half by a partition built out of wooden logs. Each log was carved lengthwise to take on the shape of a V. That made it possible to pile the logs tightly on one another. Whatever space remained between the logs was packed with moss to keep the cold out in the severe Lithuanian winters.

Part of the barn was used as a stable for horses and cows. The wagons and straw were kept in the other part of the stable to feed the horses and cows. The straw was also used to cover the section of the floor where the animals were kept, so that when they lay down they would not be befouled in their own excrement.

Every spring the stable would be cleaned. The straw, which had piled up layer on layer throughout the winter, served a double purpose. First, as we mentioned, it helped to keep the animal clean. Second, and more important, the straw mixed with animal excrement became manure, the fertilizer we used in the fields to prepare the soil for spring planting. (In those days there was no chemical fertilizer, as there is today.)

It was in such a barn that we kids were playing the game of Doctor and Nurse. (We had to invent games because there were no toys available to us.) In thinking back to this and similar moments, I have often—even to this day—wondered how we could play Doctor and Nurse, since none of us ever saw a doctor or nurse in our town.

Although I was enjoying our game, I suddenly announced to my playmates that I would have to leave. I explained that I had to go back to my grandmother's house in order to join my mother and sister in welcoming my father, whom I loved and had missed very much. He was returning from a trip to Mexico.

My grandmother—my mother's mother—was then living in a very

small village, called Gelez, with a Jewish population of about thirty families. It had one main street, a dirt road with wooden sidewalks.

My grandmother's house was located on this street. As you arrived from Subatz, which was about seven miles away, the house was on your right. Subatz was a prosperous, modern town that even boasted a railroad station, located on a major line that ran from Panyvez, the county capital, to several other fairly prominent towns and cities.

Diagonally across from my grandmother's house was the one and only church, a big beautiful structure with the peak of the cross thrust high in the air, glittering in the sunlight.

My grandmother's second marriage was to a very wonderful, soft-spoken man with a dark black beard; his name was Shiya. With her first husband—my grandfather, after whom I am named—my grandmother had four children. I believe my grandfather died prematurely. My grandmother had no children with her second husband, both of them being fairly well on in years when they were married.

Earlier I mentioned the redheaded girl with many freckles who was married to Shneika, one of my grandmother's children. The home of this young lady was our designated synagogue. It was there the Torah was kept and our services conducted.

The house in which my grandmother lived was made of wood. The logs were shaped and fitted together in the manner I described earlier. It had a straw roof. The front of the house, which faced the main street, was about twenty feet wide. It then ran back for about sixty feet, with a door in the middle.

Internally, the space was divided—and for a very specific reason. The rear portion of the house was a small workplace containing spinning machines. Farmers would shear their sheep and bring the raw wool to town; it would then be processed so the wool could be used as thread.

The machines were hand-operated by the person who brought the unprocessed wool. He would turn a handle on the machine that, in turn, would engage several gears. The wool would come out on big rollers. I remember helping my grandfather lift the heavy rolls of wool.

Here's the way the operation ran: The farmer would bring in a big bag of sheared wool. He would then carry it to the machine—a machine that to me, at the age of seven, seemed monstrously huge. The rollers on the machine were covered with a wiry brush, which looked like belts about four to six inches wide and about ten feet long. These strips were wrapped around and nailed to the rollers. I still remember helping my grandfather replace the strips when they were worn out.

Let me see if I can give you an image of this little workplace and the way it worked. I can see it almost as if it had happened yesterday. Here's the way it was:

In front of the machine, about three feet above the floor, was a canvas feeder table. It "fed" the machine. It was about five feet wide and three feet deep. It was used to feed the rollers to which it was connected. We used to take the raw wool, all twisted and knotted, out of the bags, and would separate the clusters of wool by hand as best we could so that the clumps were smaller and the machine could handle them easily. We placed these smaller pieces on the canvas, which became the feeder for the machine.

Now the person who brought us the raw wool would begin to crank the handle; that started the process. As he cranked away, the rollers next to the canvas would pick up the wool and start to feed it to the machine's interior. As it moved from roller to roller, each with its wire brushes, the wool grew steadily more refined.

Finally the wool, now combed many times over, was fed into a big wooden drum-type roller, which was about five feet wide and three feet in diameter.

When this multiroller operation was completed, the wool would come out soft and fluffy. The processed wool was then lifted from the drum by my grandfather and grandmother and placed on a scale, where it was weighed. The scale had a very long arm that extended from the ceiling. On one end of the scale was the wool; on the other were weights, clearly marked with numbers to show how much the wool weighed when the scales were balanced. The charge for the service was based on the weight—so much per pound.

From our point of view, the job was done. From the peasant's point of view, what we did was only a first step: Now the fluffy wool had to be converted into usable form. That was the responsibility of the woman of the household, as a rule.

Winters were the perfect time to take the next step. The outdoors were forbidding. Indoor work was welcome. The women would place handfuls of the refined wool on a wooden foot-operated spinning wheel that would turn out yarn that could be—and was—used to knit a variety of woolen things.

Personally, I loved the whole business. To me it was a wondrous wonderment. It was also an experience that brought me closer to my grandmother and my step-grandfather. We were joined by blood and marriage, and also by the work we did together.

In the background there was always the pleasant obligato of the machine. It was a safe workplace. No electricity and no danger of an electric shock. To me, the experience was an exciting, exhilarating, enlivening sort of play. It was a pastime that made the time pass faster in Gelez, a sleepy little town where otherwise, at age seven, I would have practically nothing to do.

Please remember, dear grandchildren, what we did not have; we had no TV, no radio, no computer, no VCR, no movies, no Nintendo, no Toys R Us, and no shopping malls. Imagine that!

Yet, even without these things, my three-year-old sister and I did not find life boring. We had things, *real* things, to do.

Among the other delights of summers in Gelez, aside from our occupation with the wool machine and the hospitality of my grandmother, was the respect paid to us by the other children. They looked upon us as "big town" folk—which indeed we were when set alongside of Gelez, with its population of thirty families—so we never ran out of children with whom to play. In addition, my sister and I brought a few toys of our own from Kavarsk that were novel to the kids in Gelez. We were the centers of attention, surrounded by friendly faces in children's play.

The particular summer day in Gelez that I now recall most vividly was full of excitement and anxiety. My father was returning to us from Mexico. Two years earlier he had left for this distant country that, to me, was another world. I did not know why he went, but I was sure he'd be returning a disillusioned person. I could not wait to see him again. With each passing moment I grew more and more tense.

In anticipation of the great event—my father's return—my mother and grandmother had scrubbed every little nook and cranny in the house. The air was filled with the mouth-watering aroma of freshly baked bread and cakes. Father's return was an event to celebrate.

My mother was the essence of elation. She was young, she was beautiful, and my father loved her dearly and tenderly. My father was a handsome young man, about twenty-nine; my mother loved him very much. As the old saying goes, "absence makes the heart grow fonder," and today was to be the day when my mother and father would once more embrace after a separation of two years.

My father came by train to Subatz (Subacius), which was about seven miles from Gelez. My Uncle Shmuel, who had a horse and wagon, went to meet him at the train station.

My first glimpse of my father was a cloud of distant dust as the horse and wagon kicked up the dirt of the unpaved road. As the vehicle came closer, I was able to distinguish two human figures on top of the wagon. I could not yet see who they were, but my heart told me that it had to be father and Uncle Shmuel. When the wagon drew still closer, my eyes confirmed what my heart felt. I raced back into the house shouting, "Father is here!"

In an instant, my mother, with my little sister in hand, my grandmother and I were running down the road to meet my father and celebrate his homecoming.

I see him now, right before my eyes. I see him leaping off the wagon. To me, this was more than the return of a parent; this was the coming of the Messiah. He looked so big and strong as he ran toward us. Since I outran everyone I was the first one he embraced. He lifted me high in the air, held me tight, and kissed me. Hand and hand we ran together toward my mother. He threw his arms around her in his strong embrace as my mother, panting away, tried to catch her breath. Taking my sister from my mother's hand, he lifted her high in the air, hugging and kissing her. Then all four of us, my father carrying my sister in one arm and fondly touching the shoulders of my mother with the other, moved joyously toward our happy house.

By the time we got to our house it was surrounded with people. News travelled fast in this small town. And the arrival of my father from a faraway land was big news in Gelez. There were some who, no doubt, came just to greet my father. There were others who must have come out of curiosity to hear about a distant world and how people lived there. Undoubtedly some of the younger folk were thinking about the possibility of one day emigrating to Mexico. Many of the young people were, in fact, constantly on the lookout for a way to leave the limited and sometimes imperilled life of the Jews in Lithuania, dreaming of relocating to the promising land across the Atlantic.

I do not recall whether or not my father brought any toys for my sister and myself. But I do remember one memento, which I cherished and guarded with my life. It was a small folding pocket mirror. No one had ever seen anything like it. I was very proud of it; I showed it off to my envious friends every chance I had. They had never seen such a wondrous contraption before.

We spent an unforgettable week together in Gelez celebrating the return of my father. But happy as we all were, as we gathered in my grandmother's house, we still felt that this was not quite home. Gelez was fine and fun, but we wanted to get back to our roots, back to the place where my grandfather and my father and I were born and grew up. We wanted to return to Kavarsk.

As usual, my Uncle Shmuel made his horse and wagon available to us for the trip home. We loaded ourselves and our belongings into the wagon and started out on a beautiful sunny morning in August. On an elevated bench in front of us sat my father and my uncle, the driver. On a bench that was lower down and behind them sat my mother, my sister, and myself. We waved our happy-sad farewell to Gelez. Uncle Shmuel was now in command. Tightly he seized the reins, which were attached to a bit in the horse's mouth. By pulling on the right-hand rein, the horse veered to the right; by pulling on the left-hand rein, he veered to the left. The reins were used like the steering wheel on a car.

To get the horse started, my uncle made a strange clicking sound. Somehow the dumb creature knew what it meant, and off we went. The horse and wagon galloped out of Gelez as we, with a trace of a tear, waved good-bye again to that dear little *shtetl* and to all those who came to bid us bon voyage, on our long journey to Kavarsk, which was sixty kilometers, or thirty-five miles, away.

In a modern vehicle, on a modern road, the distance could be traversed in half an hour. It took us a whole day. As we wandered on dirt roads, through forests and meadows and small towns, the peasants would pause from their labors, their summer harvesting, to gaze at us. By the time we arrived in the vicinity of Kavarsk, night had fallen. Everything was enshrouded in darkness. As we got closer we were able to detect the flickering light of kerosene lamps, casting their thin rays through the windows of the humble huts.

All this was happening in the dead of night. All was silent until we approached our house, when the quiet was suddenly and noisily broken by the ominous obligato of some howling dogs. It is only years later that one dares to wonder, in retrospect, whether those barking beasts were giving us a welcome for the present, a warning for the future, or both.

At last, after a long journey, we were home again in our wooden cabin, with its thatched-straw roof and dirt floor. We lit the kerosene lamp and brought our baggage in from the wagon. So—here we were, our family with our bit of worldly goods, reunited again and so to remain until the time I left for America.

It was a simple life. A small cabin with no plumbing, no running water, no heating, no electricity, no bathroom, no designated kitchen, but packed with a togetherness and love for one another that sustained me over many years and continues to do so right down to this very day.

This little house, I believe, was part of a complex which belonged to my grandfather. He and my grandmother, as we noted earlier, had ten children. They lived in a brick house in front of our cabin; it faced the main street.

In between this larger brick house and our little wooden cabin were stables, which accommodated horses, cows, wagons, hay, and straw. At the very end of these stables lay our cozy little cottage.

It was after the death of my grandfather that some of his children left Kavarsk. Joe, Louis, and Frieda left for America. Peska married and lived in Vitebsk. Dinka married and lived in Roguva. My father, Uncle Sam, and Uncle Irving remained in Kavarsk, living in the small house. Sam left for America just before my parents' marriage. Irving continued to live with them until he departed for America. (I was then about four years old.)

The brick house on the main street, which had a small store attached to it, was inherited by my Aunt Elke. I believe that it became part of her dowry to her husband, Yankel.

The log cabin in which we lived was divided into two rooms, separated by a brick oven. The oven served as a partition between the bedroom, where my parents and sister slept, and the all-purpose room that served as the dining room, living room, family room and kitchen. That's where I slept.

The oven had a double purpose: one was to cook our daily meals, heat water for tea, bake herring wrapped in paper, and the like. The other was to heat the house in the winter.

The oven was on your left as you walked into the house. Its opening and hearth faced the all-purpose room. Every Friday night, it was used for baking *chaleh* and bread in preparation for *shabat*.

On the bottom of the oven was an opening that we used as a chicken coop. We did raise our own poultry there. As a consequence, we could count on fresh eggs daily. When the hens could no longer lay eggs they were taken to the *shochet*, where they were appropriately prepared for the next day's chicken soup.

The oven, as noted, also provided our heat in winter. There was a brick ledge in front of the hearth. That was where, in the summer, most of the run-of-the-mill cooking was done, either on wood or on a kerosene Primus.

Alongside this oven was my bed. It consisted of a wooden bench that curved up at one end; the curve served to hold a bag of burlap material filled with thrashed straw. This bit of homemade furniture served as a place where I could sit, where I could place my pillow, and where I could—and did—sleep.

In front of this bench was a large wooden table surrounded by wooden chairs. Above the table was a kerosene lamp suspended from a wooden ceiling beam. Along the wall, facing the small oven, was a wooden clothes closet and a linen dresser. On the wall above the dresser was a mirror. Along the wall to the right, as you entered the house, was a small low bench with a bucket of fresh water and a bowl for washing. The interior of the walls was plastered and whitewashed.

The bedroom had two beds where my parents and sister slept. We did not have the kind of mattresses we have in America. My parents and sister slept on what we called a *shenek*, a strong mattress cover stuffed with shredded straw.

The lower portion of the large oven used for baking extended into the bedroom. In the wintertime, in very cold weather after my mother was done with her baking, I would climb up on top of the oven and, perched there, I would sleep through the night.

It must be clear from this description that our house was not pretentious. We were far from rich in material things. But in our spiritual lives—the respect and regard, the love and understanding we had for one another—we were very rich indeed.

It was a richness further enhanced by our concern and care, not only for the members of our family, but for all members of the larger human family. When someone was in need and we had the means to help we felt it was our part to do so, not because it was a religious *mitzvah* that would be rewarded in *yenner velt*, but because it was the humanitarian thing to do.

Because my father and mother nourished me in this kind of caring environment, I am thankful to them. Out of that *menschlich* milieu, I developed a sense of belonging—a sense of being part of something outside my own skin, a sense of purpose that has served me well and has sustained me throughout my life. I learned, in my home, that to give to others is, in turn, to receive. For teaching me that lesson by the way they lived, I am eternally grateful to my father and mother.

FIVE
Learning and Earning

In time, the excitement over my father's return from Mexico subsided. My Uncle Shmuel returned to Subatz *(Subacius)*. Things began to settle down as we returned to our daily chores and endless hardships, which were the norm for the Jewish inhabitants of our town in those days. Also, vacation time was over and the hour had come when we had to return to school.

I was to enter my second year in our school, which was located five houses away from us. To get to it, you walked a short distance down a hill. The school was located in a private dwelling owned by the Millner family. Next door to the school was a government-run store that sold vodka. Our school was a temporary installation, pending the construction of a real school with funds sent to us from America.

Our makeshift school had two classrooms to accommodate all the Jewish children in town. We had two teachers. One taught Yiddish, Lithuanian, and other studies in a curriculum prescribed by the government; he was paid by the government. The other taught Hebrew and the Bible; he was paid by the parents.

When our second school year ended, we rejoiced. We could now look forward to the joys of summer—playing with our friends, swimming in the river, visiting the forest with our family and friends. But, above all, we were looking forward to the next term when, at long last, we would have a real school with a real school building.

The new school had four rooms: two classrooms, a recreation room, and a dwelling room for our teacher, Haim Lurie, who was the teacher designated by the government. The school also had a large football (soccer) field, gymnastic bars, and a basketball hoop.

It was at this school that I spent the next six years in the elementary grades. This was, of course, the one and only Jewish elementary school in town, with a student body of about fifty-five to sixty in attendance. There was also a Lithuanian public school in town, which served gentile kids from Kavarsk and the surrounding areas.

The school hours were long and the work was arduous. We started at 8:00 A.M. At noon, we all went home for lunch. We returned to school at 1:00 P.M. and continued to 4:00 P.M. When we got home, we were faced with two hours of homework; in the final two years, with three.

During the school year you were not allowed to roam the streets on school days. Our teacher, Haim Lurie, policed the streets on foot to make sure that you were not out there. If you were caught out in the streets before 6:00 P.M. you would be punished the next day in one of several possible ways: you would be made to stand in the corner in front of all the kids; you'd be locked up in solitary in the recreation room; or you'd be made to clean up the quarters of the teacher who lived in the same building. The school week consisted of six days.

To be graduated and get a diploma it was necessary to pass the government exams, which lasted for two days. My graduating class consisted of six pupils—four girls and two boys. Their names were Yochke Shmukler, Sorke Ziskind, Yudishke Delatski, Keilke, Velvke (whose father was the hat- and cap-maker in town), and myself. To prepare for our finals, the six of us studied together for a solid three months. We would get up at five in the morning and meet in one of the houses that had an attic, or in one of the houses that had a barn. We would sit or lie on the hay and study. Sometimes we would go through the night, especially as the deadlines for the exams approached. The method of grading the exams and our papers was as follows: we were ranked from two to five, with a *two* listed as a failure and a *five* listed as tops.

When the day of the exam arrived, we were all quite naturally nervous. A government monitor was present during the two-day examination. We came to the exam all dressed up in our finest. The six of us were seated in this large classroom. On the first day we were given tests; on the second day there were more tests, plus oral exams.

Five days later we made our appearance at the school, where the government official bestowed the diplomas upon us. I was glowing with pride. I brought the diploma and my grades to my parents. I had four *fives* and two *fours*.

While we were busy doing our exams, my father was busy trying to make a living. While our standard of living was below the standard of living in America today, it was quite substantial when measured by the standard then prevailing in Kavarsk. My father was determined to live up to our modest expectations.

My father developed an unusual business. He would buy wheat and other things directly from the farmers who brought their produce for sale at the weekly market days on Monday. Then he would transport his purchases to the larger cities, such as Vilkomer, Kaunas, and Panyvez, where he would try to sell them at a profit.

The business depended heavily on our horse and wagon. Up until 1930, it was the only way to get things, and even people, from here to there. The only alternatives to the horse and wagon were a bike or one's feet.

My father knew his way around; he had been around. *He* certainly knew how to get from here to there, and, in his handling of farm products, he was quite astute.

He had been abroad. In 1925, he, together with Uncle Irving and Morris Jaffe and others from our town, decided to go to America. The first step in their journey was to go to Berlin, where they were supposed to get a Lithuanian visa and a ticket for a ship to America.

Until 1922, anyone who was in good health and wished to go to America and had the means to pay for the trip could do so. Until that year everyone, except for the physically disabled, would go to Ellis Island, where they would be processed. They would be medically examined, mainly to halt the importation of endemic and epidemic illness. All seemed to be going reasonably well.

In 1922, however, Congress enacted legislation to stop this free and easy entry of immigrants into the United States. Quotas were imposed—nation by nation. The nations of Western and Northern Europe were favored; those of Eastern and Southern Europe were not.

When my father and the others made their application for visas to America, they were informed that the Lithuanian quota had already been filled, so they had to find a way around the regulations.

At that time in Berlin there were all sorts of travel agents who knew how to play the game. They knew, for example, that there were Baltic nations, such as Estonia and Latvia, whose quotas for emigrants to America had not been filled. One of these agents induced my father, among others, to buy tickets from him to America. He promised to supply them with passports and visas credited to the other Baltic states. The operation was, of course, strictly illegal.

It appears that someone found out about the scheme and informed the German authorities. Some of the agents and their customers were rounded up, including my father. They were sent to jail for a month in Berlin.

Upon their release, however, Irving, Morris, and some others managed to travel to Canada, and then through Canada into the United States. Others went to South Africa. My father and several others returned to Kavarsk.

Then, about two years later, my father, together with a few friends and family members, went to Mexico. As a consequence of these wanderings and adventures, my father acquired the reputation in our small town of being a "world traveller." While he hardly deserved the title, he did become well versed in the ways of the world.

Feeling somewhat at ease in the realm of travel, in 1930 my father went into the travel business—not international travel, but rather confined to Lithuania. He and three other contemporaries in Kavarsk formed a partnership. They all had experience in transporting people from town to town by horse and wagon. Now they decided to modernize their operation. They chipped in and bought a 1930 Chevrolet, which could seat six passengers and also store some luggage and cargo. A highly visible sign on the front of the vehicle notified the public that they could get to Kavarskas, Ukmerges, and Kaunas.

The van made daily trips from Kavarsk to the capital city of Kaunas, and did it in three hours. It was possible to make the trip from Kavarsk, spend several hours in Kaunas, and then return to Kavarsk—all in one day. The same trip would take five days by horse and wagon.

To us kids, this magical machine was frightening; we were afraid to get near it. On several occasions, when the car raced past a horse, the creature would bolt and break into a wild gallop. Sometimes, as a result, the wagon would be overturned and its contents scattered. Several times the riders were injured.

I shall never forget one such terrible accident involving the Chevrolet and some horses. It grew out of a custom in our town—a ritual meant to be filled with exciting enjoyment. When a wedding was to take place and the groom came from another town, the people in the town where the wedding was to take place got dressed up, harnessed horses to wagons, and raced to greet the groom on his way to our town to wed his bride-to-be.

When I say they "raced," I mean that literally. It was a contest to see who would get to the groom first. Whoever did was the winner, on whom would be bestowed the honor of being allowed to escort the groom back to the town where the marriage was to take place.

It happened on a Friday. The groom lived in Ukmerges. My father's Chevy van was to pick him up and bring him back for the wedding. Many people were eager to make themselves part of the event, especially since my father's novel vehicle was involved.

Two houses away from where the bride lived there was a young man who was madly in love with the bride-to-be. But, for reasons I did not know at the time, she was marrying someone else—it was an arranged marriage. This fellow, whose name was Simon, did not want to participate in the traditional race. But under pressure from his family, he reluctantly joined in the exercise. He got all dressed up, donning his patent leather shoes, and, along with a relative, he mounted his wagon to participate.

I was riding with my cousin Shmulke Rapshonsky and his father. All of us assembled in the marketplace and set out through Vilkomer Street to meet the groom, who was being brought to town in my father's van. In the distance, we saw a cloud of dust rising from the ground. We knew that it signalled the coming of my father's car. To us, that meant the race was on. Who would be the first to meet the car with its honored guest, the groom?

Our wagon was third or fourth in line. Since the road was narrow and many wagons participated, the line extended for quite a distance.

As my father's van drew closer and grew more visible, we began to race our wagons faster. We tried to pass one another on this very narrow road. Some of the horses broke into a gallop, becoming uncontrollable.

In this wild confusion, the wagon of the young man who had not, in the first place, wanted to come to the event, slipped off the road into a ditch, capsizing. He was hit on the head by the axle of the front wheel. Many of the drivers tried to stop their wagons, but they were unable to do so. The horses acted as if they were in a stampede. Everything was covered with blood.

We finally managed to get to the victim. He was moved on to the truck and hurried into town. There being no doctor available, however, it was decided to take him to Ukmerges, where there was a hospital.

Since it was a Friday night, it was necessary to get the consent of the rabbi to make the trip. Unfortunately, on the way to Ukmerges, just a short distance from town, the young man died. He was brought back home and stretched out on the floor, where he lay until Sunday.

It was truly a tragedy. I believe the wedding was postponed until after the family finished sitting *shiva.*

The following year, my father and his partners bought a passenger bus that made daily trips between Kavarskas, Ukmerges, and Kaunas. The most popular and exciting of these daily trips was the one from our town to Kaunas. It was an especially thrilling experience for the children, once we got used to it, although it did take time for us to overcome our fear of the huge (as it seemed to us) motor-monster.

For while the bus seemed huge in our eyes at that time, we would, today, call it a minibus, since it held only eighteen passengers. We did not understand what made this horseless thing move. When it was about to come to a stop we would hold our breath, waiting for it to stand still. We looked upon the entire operation as something miraculous, rather than as something that would become a common convenience in the daily doings of the evolving twentieth century.

The bus used to depart at 6:00 A.M. from the marketplace in our town, which is where the passengers, who came from our town and from the surrounding towns and farms, would gather. Some travelled for social or business reasons; some went out of curiosity. Some gathered in the marketplace just to stand and stare, perhaps envious that they themselves were not making the trip.

By 9:00 A.M. the travellers were in Kaunas, capital of Lithuania. They'd go about their business and be back in our town by 7:00 or 8:00 P.M. There was always a little crowd in the marketplace to greet the lucky folk who had, in so unbelievably short a time, been to Kaunas and back.

I would go to the marketplace often. And I would puff up with pride when my father descended from the bus and opened the door for the passengers. It was as if this bus were a giant ocean liner that had returned from a voyage with my father, the captain of the vessel, in command. While the passengers were disembarking he would ascend a small iron ladder, climb to the top of the bus, untie the ropes, and unload the luggage. The "cargo" consisted either of items bought for personal use or things that had been bought in the big town of Kaunas to be sold in our smaller town of Kavarsk.

To those of us who were the children of the partners who owned the bus, a special privilege was extended. After the bus was emptied and the baggage removed, we would pile into the vehicle with the driver and enjoy a short trip to the place where the bus was parked overnight. This little routine was repeated every evening, except on Saturday *(shabat)* and on the Jewish holidays.

When fall would come, with its nights that came earlier and stayed longer throughout the winter and on into the early spring, we would play a game. We would gather in the marketplace at about 7:00 P.M. We would look down the street on which the bus was to arrive and peer out at the horizon, straining to catch the first glimpse of the car's headlights. Then we would try to figure out how far the bus was from town and make bets on just when it would arrive in the marketplace. For us kids, the bus was not a business; it was a center of joyous activity in our daily lives.

But for my father and his partners it was a business—indeed, an expanding business. Eventually they bought a second bus with greater capacity for both passengers and cargo. Townsfolk who saw the buses constantly coming and going might have concluded that this was truly a very lucrative and profitable enterprise. Whatever they thought, however, we knew otherwise. Our life-style did not change. We were barely able to make ends meet.

My father was constantly in debt. He would borrow from one person to pay what he owed to the next person. In this process, I was often the carrier pigeon. My father would send me to one person to borrow and then would send me to another person to make a payment on a debt.

I recall conversations in our household between my father and my mother when they talked about the money they owed this relative or that relative and others as well. It was only in later years, two or three years before I left for America, that our circumstances grew more comfortable.

We might earlier have come upon easier times, were it not for a little business war that broke out within our family. In those days, transportation was not regulated by government. There were no franchises, no controls, no limits. If you could buy a truck, van, bus, or car, you were in business.

As luck would have it, my father and his partners ran into unexpected competition from my Aunt Elke, my father's sister, and her husband, Yankel, who was a brother of one of my father's four partners. After my father and his partners bought their second bus, the new company bought a bus and began to compete for customers.

This sparked a price war between my father's company and my Aunt

Elke's company. My father's advantage was experience; he knew the business. He also knew how much it would cost to meet the payments on the bus and to hire a licensed chauffeur. He knew the idiosyncracies of his passengers; they knew him and he knew them. He had established a reputation for reliability. As a consequence, after a short "war" between the two companies, Aunt Elke's bus service collapsed. Since she could not maintain the payments on her bus, it was confiscated by the supplier.

SIX
Aunt Lena Visits

The date was 1931. We were preparing for the arrival of my Aunt Lena from America. She was coming with her daughter Margery to visit us.

Aunt Lena had been born in Poland. Her mother, brother, and married sister were still living in Poland when she came to pay us a visit. This was the first time we had met. Lena was married to my father's brother Louis. Although separated by an ocean, my father and his brother and Aunt Lena developed a close relationship—by mail. They would correspond often, Aunt Lena doing most of the letter writing from the American side.

They would periodically send us packages with used clothing. I remember our excitement when a package (a *posilke*, in Yiddish) would arrive. My father would go to the post office to claim the package, bringing it back to the house, where people gathered around the table to see what the latest delivery would bring. They would watch my father almost ceremonially draw his knife and proceed to cut the thick thread, which held together a heavy durable cloth cover containing the contents.

Most of what was in the package was for women. This was to be expected, since these were hand-me-downs from Louis's three daughters as well as from his wife. There was, of course, always something for my father, not only from Louis but from the other brothers too.

On one occasion, my father received a sheepskin-lined leather jacket. Through many wintery years, he would wear this three-quarter-length coat. As for myself, I always ended up disappointed. There was never anything for me, since Louis and Lena had no sons to outfit me with their hand-me-downs.

In anticipation of Aunt Lena's arrival we were doing a special housecleaning. My father borrowed an extra mattress from the bus company's bookkeeper. He used this special mattress to replace the regular stuffed-straw mattress that my parents normally used.

In our house, there were many prominently displayed pictures of my aunt, uncle, and their daughters. From those photographs, I knew that Aunt Lena was a good-looking woman. I suppose, too, that the fact she was coming from America infused her appearance with a special aura, for we thought of Americans as the richest and most beautiful people in the whole wide world.

I don't know just how my parents felt about the visit. How would this woman from America feel about our home and the way we lived? And how would she manage to get to our town at a time when it was not easy to do so? Although Lithuania and Poland are cheek-to-cheek neighbors, they were not, at that particular moment, on speaking terms. They had, in fact, broken off diplomatic relations, because Poland had seized Vilnius, which was the Lithuanian capital after World War I. In light of this Aunt Lena had to travel to Germany to get into Lithuania, after which troubling trip she would finally get to our little log cabin, with its dirt floor and no running water, indoor toilet, or bathroom.

My guess is that my parents were quite apprehensive about the whole experience. As for myself, then a nine-year-old boy, I had no notion of what was going on; I was simply elated to know that my *Amerikanske tante* was coming to stay with us.

My aunt and Margery arrived in my father's van from Kaunas. We were there in the marketplace to welcome them to our town. As my aunt got off the bus I felt as if I was beholding some queen, for Aunt Lena had the beauty of royalty and dressed accordingly. And there, at her side, was Margery, looking for all the world like Shirley Temple.

They stayed with us for several weeks. We had dinner at Uncle Ruvin's house. Many pictures were taken. My father's bus took us to Aunt Dina's house in Roguva, where a dinner was held in honor of Aunt Lena and her daughter Margery. More pictures were taken. During the week, my mother, Aunt Lena, and Aunt Elke visited the cemetery where my grandmother and grandfather were buried.

There are no pictures, however, of one situation I shall always remember. Since we had no indoor toilet in our cabin, we had to use an outhouse. We had given it an extra scrubbing in order to accommodate our distinguished guests. Despite this, Margery refused to use the outhouse. How she managed, I am not quite sure.

During Aunt Lena's visit I was exposed, for the first time in my life, to grapes and bananas she had brought with her from Kaunas. I liked the grapes; I did not like the bananas. Years later, after I came to America, I did develop a tolerance for bananas; but it took time.

As a result of Aunt Lena's visit, we developed a much closer relationship with her, and, through her, with the rest of the family in America. She became our link to our American relatives—a relationship that continued through correspondence to the last letter of June 1941.

SEVEN
A New Home

In the group that went to Mexico with my father was a family of some four or five adults. Their family name was Promer. They owned a large wooden house, which consisted of some nine rooms with a large kitchen and a large brick oven. The family also had a small smokehouse for curing and smoking meat, salami, and fish; it was also used as a laundry.

The Promers did not wish to put the house up for sale. When my father returned from Mexico, they gave him power-of-attorney and other legal instruments giving him the right to live in their house. He was also empowered to rent part of the house in order to get the necessary cash to pay taxes, meet maintenance expenses, and the like.

A couple of years after his return, we moved into this larger house, which was next door to my aunt's brick house. We were separated by a driveway. We were located on the middle of a hill on the main street that ran from the marketplace down to the Shventoya River, and beyond to the forest.

We occupied three rooms facing the main street in the front half of this large house. We now had wooden floors and a cellar beneath our apartment. As in our old house, we had a large living room; that is, a dining room with a small oven that served as a partition. It was also a source of heat, and, for me, a place to sleep in cold weather. Also as in the old house, there was a bedroom that was shared by my parents and sister. There was yet another room, on the other side of the oven, which was used for storage; we also washed there. This room contained a large galvanized bathtub used almost exclusively by my mother.

My mother suffered with rheumatism. My father and I would bring buckets of water from the well we had dug behind the house and fill the tub. The tub had been outfitted with a small wood-burning stove to heat the water. A flue pipe ran from this stove to an opening in the oven's chimney so there would be no smoke in the house. We would then add coarse salt to the heated water. Since we did not have the luxury of hot spring baths, this heated salt water tub was our expedient makeshift solution for helping to relieve the suffering of those stricken with rheumatism.

Although this house was much larger than our previous home and was even equipped with a wooden floor and a cellar, we still had no interior sanitary facilities. We still had no running water, no electricity, and were dependent on the outhouse in back of the stables.

Our family occupied one-third of the house. Another third was rented to the Shmucklers, who were my parents' best friends. Their apartment faced the backyard and had a view of the meadows. We also shared with them a large room with a clay floor and a large oven, which we used for baking bread and *challa* on Fridays.

The oven also had a lower ledge that, once again, we used as a chicken coop.

In our communal kitchen we would keep handy buckets of fresh water. There was, on one side of that kitchen, a storeroom, where we kept things that needed a cool spot. We also used it to store foods that had already been cooked, pickled, or preserved for the winter.

Pickles were one of our staples. We'd prepare them in wooden barrels loaded with fresh cucumbers whenever they were in season. We made sauerkraut by hand, chopping up cabbages and then pickling them in barrels. We also made preserves out of a variety of berries, which grew in abundance. They were cooked and stored in clay pots, and were used not only for ordinary eating purposes but also as a medicine of sorts. If you had a cold, the first thing you did was mix these preserves with some hot tea; you were then supposed to perspire and feel better. The room in which we stored all these goodies was called, as you might expect, the "cool room."

The relationship that my parents had with their best friends, the Shmucklers, was far more than a friendship. It was even closer than a kinship. We—their family and ours—were as one.

Leib Shmuckler and his wife were about the same age as my parents, perhaps a few years older. We felt closer to them and their five children than to any of our blood relatives. Our home was their home, and their home was our home. Our living quarters were joined in our common kitchen, and to get from our apartment to theirs we had to go through that kitchen, so, for all intents and purposes, we found ourselves side by side with them just about all of the time.

One might expect that when two families are living practically in each other's laps, they would soon get on one another's nerves; they do, after all, say that "familiarity breeds contempt," and when you get to know people intimately you do begin to discover their faults. Yet, in all the years that I spent with the Shmucklers in our communal dwelling, I never heard anyone in my family speak ill of them. Quite the contrary, in fact: the ambience was always harmonious. We knew no other way; it seemed to be the natural thing to do. In the many years since, although I have had many friends, I have never experienced the same kind of warmth and attachment as I did with the Shmucklers.

Leib Shmuckler was not born in Kavarsk, and he had no family ties in the town. I do not know exactly when and why he came to Kavarsk. His original home was either in Vilnius or in some town near Vilnius. We do know that he was married to his wife, who *did* live in Kavarsk, some time during the First World War.

All this happened against an intriguing background that fated Leib Shmuckler to separate himself from his home town of Vilnius. He was, so to speak, a pawn in a giant chess game that involved Poland, Lithuania, and even the League of Nations.

I have referred to the diplomatic break between Poland and Lithuania after Poland first claimed, and then proceeded to take, Vilnius from Lithuania. Prior to the war, Lithuania was ruled by the Russian czars. After the war, Lithuania was liberated in line with the principles enunciated in the Treaty of Versailles and implemented by the League of Nations. These policies granted "self-determination" to many nations that had been under the heel of foreign emperors. At the same time, Poland, which had also been under Russian rule, was also granted its independence. Now free to pursue its own agenda, Poland grabbed Vilnius.

The enmity between the two newly free nations was so great that the borders between the two countries were sealed. So, if you were from Vilnius and had chanced, let's say, to visit friend or family in Kovno, you could not return to Vilnius. Accordingly, many Jews, who habitually did make visits from Vilnius to other parts of Lithuania, found themselves separated from their families, unable to return.

It seems that this is exactly what happened to Leib Shmuckler; he found himself shut off from Vilnius. He could not even maintain contact by mail. He ended up in Kavarsk, where my father and he struck up a friendship that lasted until that fateful day, in the summer of 1941, when they were murdered by the Nazis with the help of Lithuanian sympathizers.

Leib Shmuckler made a living in transactions involving the Lithuanian peasants. He had a horse and wagon. He would periodically make a trip to Kovno, where he would purchase enamelware, glassware, utensils, silverware, and china. He brought his purchases back to Kavarsk for sale. The trip would take him, as I related earlier, a full five days.

Our new home proved to be perfect for his business purposes, in that the yard in back of our house was occupied by two buildings, one of which was a warehouse and the other a stable and barn, where Leib kept the horse and wagon.

On Monday, which was market day in our town, he would put his wares on display for sale to the peasants. Some of his sales were in cash; some in barter.

If anything was left over, as generally happened, he would load up his wagon with some select wares and take off on the road, making house calls to peddle his products. Sometimes all he got in exchange were old rags, worn-out clothes, and the like. But Leib knew how to "turn rags into riches," which, while hardly riches in the true sense, nevertheless still added a few coins to the family treasury. He would leave on these trips on Tuesday and return on Friday afternoon just before *shabat*.

I used to watch him on Sunday as he sorted out the rags on the floor of the warehouse. He would quickly inspect each piece, sometimes cutting one piece of cloth from another, and then would assign each piece to its distinctive pile.

For instance: Taking an old coat, Leib would cut out the lining and toss it into a pile together with other linens. Linen was, at that time, looked upon as a luxury fabric, very much in demand. Each part of the disassembled coat would be assigned its proper place. To watch him work his way speedily and accurately through a big batch of "rags" was like watching a great performer doing acrobatics, or an actor playing a well-rehearsed role in a play.

Around these rags he built an extensive business, with much coming and going. If, at some time, there were things he wanted to buy, and if, at the same time, he had accumulated a wagonload of rags, he would take the cargo to Kaunas to peddle his "junk" for the wares he wanted, or to get the cash to buy what he needed.

This is the way this intrepid and tireless man earned a livelihood; he stayed with it, day after day and year after year, without wearying. Through his patience and persistence he was able to provide enough for the family to get by, to eke out a bare living.

As I think back on those years, on our physical and emotional proximity, I have occasionally wondered to myself why, as I noted earlier, we drew ever closer together, instead of flying further apart as a result of the petty irritations that inevitably arise in such an environment. I believe it was the two women, the two true mothers, who made the difference. They were very special, exceptional human beings. They were sensitive, kindhearted, caring, and warm. They knew what was cooking in each other's pots, but they did not deign it proper to tell each other how the broth should really be flavored and stirred and strained. They had respect for each other, and that relationship diffused itself around the house and infused itself into all the members of our families.

As I grew up, I got closer to one of the girls who was my age. We were in the same class in school together. Our close relations continued until we were graduated from elementary school. That school connection, and our proximity in the house, gave us the feeling that we were really brother and sister. And, as you might have guessed, we were constantly being kidded and teased about our closeness. Surely, it was suggested repeatedly, we were destined to get married to each other. Everybody was ready to be our matchmaker, our *shotkhen*.

Her name was Yochke (Yochevet in Hebrew. She was one of the students in the graduation class we mentioned earlier). Because there were no high schools in our town to provide continuing education, it was customary for children, upon graduation from elementary school, to learn a trade, such as shoemaker, tailor, cap maker, and the like. Some would go to larger cities where there were *yeshivas*, schools of religious instruction. If you were a student in a *yeshiva* (a *yeshiva bocher*), you were in a fortunate situation. The tuition was free and, in addition, you lived with some family that would provide you with bed and board—also free.

If you did not learn a trade or become a religious practitioner, the alternative was to become a *luft mentsh*. Literally translated a *luft mentsh* was an "air person." You managed to survive by your wits, in the free-floating style of air in movement. Like Leib Shmuckler, you wandered about, peddling this or that; you bought this and that, then sold it or bartered it.

Even a butcher, master of a skilled trade, could also be a *luft mentsh*. He would buy a cow, a sheep, and a calf; slaughter them; sell the kosher portions to Jews; and sell the portions that were not kosher to the gentiles. In our town we had two butchers. My Uncle Ruvin was one of them.

If one of the kids had parents who ran stores, he would, in all probability, end up working in the store. The occupation was pretty much passed on from father to son.

As for the girls, they had far fewer choices. They would either be homebound, helping out in the house, or become seamstresses. But some broke the pattern. One girl, whose name was Yudishke, decided to go to the Hebrew high school in Vilkomer. She was a very nice girl who limped because she'd been born with one leg slightly shorter than the other. She was also atypical in her decision to continue formal education. Most of the girls who wanted to learn a trade turned to the needle to make a living.

Both Yochke and Keilke chose to become seamstresses. They learned the trade from one of the better seamstresses in our town, whose name was Dobke Kremer. Dobke's establishment, if I may call it such, was right next to our school; I used to go there a lot. Dobke's brother, Arke, was a friend of mine. Dobke was a very nice girl, who was also in charge of the small Jewish library in town. I used to help her with the library and she really liked me a lot.

Another one of our fellow graduates, Sorke, was the daughter of one of the *shochets* (ordained religious slaughterers) in town. She had two "careers" upon graduation from elementary school: She helped out in the house, and she helped out in the family store run by her parents.

Velvke, whose father was the cap- and hatmaker in town, chose to learn his father's trade from his father, of course.

As for myself, I was always drawn to something mechanical; I dreamed of becoming an engineer. I also dreamed, as a young Zionist, of some future life outside Lithuania, of a life in Israel, then known as Palestine.

EIGHT
ORT

Clearly my opportunities for a career were limited in Kavarsk. If I wanted to find employment in a world that was moving out of the rural small-town culture and undergoing an industrial revolution, I'd have to go to a big city for training and, ultimately, to find employment.

My decision to do so did not come easily. My moving to a city outside Kavarsk would be a financial burden for my father. My separation from my family would be a psychological hardship for all of us—father, mother, sister, and myself. I would, at the age of thirteen, have to fend for myself in a strange environment. Although I would have occasion to see my father when he would come to Kovno, where I would be pursuing my training, I would be cut off from the rest of the family and old friends except for Passover and the summer holiday.

Despite all these negatives, I did decide to leave for Kovno; there was no alternative. I did not want to be a shoemaker or a tailor. I wanted to prepare myself with skills more appropriate for the evolving economies of the future, and in this decision I was not alone. An increasing number of young Jewish boys were coming to the same conclusion.

The place to which we were drawn was the ORT school in Kovno. The ORT (Organization for Rehabilitation thru Training) was an international institution founded in the latter part of the nineteenth century to prepare young Jewish children for careers in a changing society.

My father made an application for the ORT school in Kovno on my behalf. A few weeks later, we received a notice for me to appear in person before the director-general, Jacob Oleiski, in Kovno. With my father I rode to the big city for the interview, feeling scared as all heck, although I tried to conceal my frightened feelings from my parents.

The city itself added to the excitement and tension of the moment. I was overwhelmed with the constant hustle and bustle of this metropolis. The streets were paved. Many of the buildings, towering to four and five stories high, appeared to me to be man-made mountains. Some of them had impressive courtyards. I felt dizzy in the midst of the fast-moving commotion. How would I ever find my way in this urban jungle?

My father and I went to the ORT school. We met with the director-general. I was scared. But I did all I could to hide my fear from my father. After the interview we were told that we would be notified by mail whether I'd been accepted.

Meanwhile my father took me to see a woman he knew who lived in Kovno. He wished to make arrangements for me to stay in her house in the event I was admitted to the school. I was to sleep on a high couch in the dining/living room. There were three other boarders in two adjoining bedrooms. In addition, the woman and her two sons, one of whom was in his last year as a student at ORT, also lived there.

It was evening when my father and I returned to our town. We waited for a favorable reply from the school.

After a week or two, we received a letter of acceptance. The monthly fee would be ten Lithuanian litus (or Lit, about $1.00). We were instructed where and when to report, and given a list of tools we would have to buy and bring with us. I was also to outfit myself with a special blue frock, a sort of work apron, to wear over my pants and shirt.

Had I not been accepted at the ORT school, I don't know what I would have done. The likelihood is that I would have learned one of the traditional trades. I could not have been another *luft mentsh.* It wasn't just in me to go out and try to earn a few Lit, as some of the young men had done in years previous when they'd become "merchants" by following in the footsteps of their fathers and grandfathers.

I had witnessed the routine of these "businessmen." They would rise early in the morning. Some would go to an early *minyan* in the *shul.* Others would do the morning prayers at home. Saying your prayers did not necessarily mean that you were truly religious. To pray was the norm, the tradition; your father did it, so you did it. Breakfast consisted of some home-baked black bread and butter washed down with a glass or two of hot tea.

You'd throw a burlap bag over your shoulder and walk to a nearby village or farm, to buy a skin or two or a pound of pig's hair. If you had a horse and wagon, you might buy a bunch of flax or a couple of sacks of wheat. Now you had things to sell; you were in business; you were a "merchant."

If you travelled on foot you would have to start very early and return early. If you had a horse and wagon you could start out later and start home later. But, either way, you had to be back before nightfall in order to do your *mincha* and *mariv* prayers.

What you ate for supper was, predictably, the same old dairy dishes—noodles cooked in milk, boiled potatoes with herring and sauerkraut, all washed down with the customary glass of tea. And you would end the day by reciting the final prayer of *kriyat shma*.

The next day would be like today and yesterday. You would live your life in a rut of endless routine.

On Friday you would accompany your father or your grandfather (or both) to the public bathhouse. There you would get a *pleitze*, a seat on the topmost and hottest shelf of a steam room. A pail of cold water would be poured on hot stones. The steam that was generated enshrouded your body.

While you were in this perspiring condition, someone would rub your body and beat you gently with the branches of a birch. When you were done and got off the shelf (still alive, you hoped), your body was red as a beet. This entire exercise was considered to be very healthful and wholesome for you. But, in order to be the beneficiary of this exhilarating experience, you had to be in pretty good shape to begin with. Some people just couldn't take the prescribed procedure called the *pleitze*.

What I have described was a way of life in the shtetl, the typical small town of Lithuania. It was the routine by which my father and his father before him lived, and which would have been the mold of my life as well had I not chosen to learn a trade at the ORT school.

Earlier, I noted what ORT was and when it was first formed. One of the most important aspects of this remarkable organization, oddly enough, had to do with its initials when read as an acronym. For in Yiddish, *ort* means *place*. The training we received in ORT gave us a sense that we had an "*ort*" in the modern world.

In reading my description of the daily doings and duties in the small towns like Kavarsk, one might get the impression that our lives were an unrelenting round of annoyances, without pleasure. That would be misreading the fact. Although the elements I have been describing indicate the limitations of the *shtetl*, our little town was nevertheless full of energy and high-spirited excitement. We made our own fun as children; we never came running to Papa or Mama to complain that we were "bored." We did not know what boredom was.

For a moment now, I am thinking back to those days in the shtetl. We had none of the elementary amenities that we now simply take for granted in America. Our indulgence, once a week, was the visit to the public bath, which was owned by the community, leased to the highest bidder, and whose proceeds went to maintain the town rabbi and synagogue. In a sense, going to the bath was yet another religious ritual.

Sometimes people seem, perversely, to go on living and raising families despite the fact that, by our standards, they are confined to a very limited style of life. To meet their needs or aspirations, I suppose some would try to improve their situation by moving to a bigger city or to another country—usually America.

As little children we were not, of course, in a position to make any such decisions. We had no choice but to go along with things as they were traditionally ordered. We knew—or felt—the limitations of what was available in our tiny town. And what we were able to get was even further circumscribed by our financial limitations.

But we were not unhappy. We expected little from the world, yet we knew what the world expected from us. There were things expected of us, and we tried to live up to these expectations.

In that framework, our chores were many. And in discharging our obligations we were fully occupied, with no time to be "bored." Boredom was a luxury we could not afford and about which we knew nothing. The word "bored" could not be found in our nonexistent unabridged dictionary.

During the school year, every second was accounted for. We had to study hard, leaving little time for just playing around. At home, we had our assigned chores. There was always homework to do. As I noted earlier, you could not take to the streets to escape homework because the streets were patrolled to catch delinquents. In the summertime, we felt free to follow our fancy—to play with the other kids, to help our parents in their work, to go swimming, to go visiting, to wander about or join in the business with your father or friends and, of course, with the beloved horse and wagon.

NINE
Zionism

As youngsters, some of us were involved in the Zionist movement. In our town we had an affiliate of a Zionist organization called Halutz Hazair. Our participation provided us with a sense of belonging, purpose, and self-fulfillment.

The leader of our chapter was a wonderful fellow by the name of Daniel Charney. Under his guidance, we were indoctrinated into becoming die-hard Zionists. He arranged for us to be visited by *shlichim*, representatives of the movement who came from what was then called Palestine and is now Israel. These visiting organizers would tell us about the beauties of Palestine. They would teach us Hebrew Zionist songs and dances, such as the hora.

We would march into the countryside. The idea was for us to act like pioneers, to get closer to nature, in preparation for the time when we would go to Israel. This exercise, which required us really to act as if we were truly living in a frontier commune, was called *hach shora*. On these occasions, we were uniformly dressed in dark blue shirts accentuated by light blue bandannas bound together by a leather ring. We marched with pride and hope.

The Zionist organization rented the third of our large house not occupied either by our family or the Shmucklers. In that remaining space, there was a large meeting room and a smaller room, which gave us a regular place to hold our meetings. We would gather there together, sing Hebrew songs, do the hora, and listen to lectures.

In the other room our club installed a Ping-Pong table that, of course, provided us with an immediate and handy source of recreation. The table was used mainly by the teenagers. Since I was named to be the spokesperson and leader of our group, since the organization met in part of our house, and since I had the key to the club room, I had ready access to the Ping-Pong table and spent many hours there with my friends.

We mingled education with our recreation. I recall the occasion when a representative of the movement came from Palestine to speak. Young people of the town were invited to come and listen. He spoke with us, not just about Palestine, but also about what was happening in the world; especially the perils of Fascism and Nazism. (The dark shadow of Hitler was already falling upon Europe.) I was chosen to welcome our lecturer, the *sheliach* from Palestine, and I was truly honored. When our visitor spoke we soaked up every word. We did not have daily newspapers in our town; if we wanted to be informed, we had to subscribe to a paper that was published in Kovno. Getting the newspaper from Kovno eventually became a collective enterprise. To subscribe was expensive, but when my father's bus replaced the slow-moving horse and wagon we could get the paper overnight. So we formed a joint venture, in which several families participated. The paper went first to the family that chipped in most. After two days the paper was moved on to the next party, and so on down the line. In that way, one subscription serviced from three to seven families.

My father was part of a group of six subscribers. He chose to be the last person to get to read the paper. His reasons were two: First, if he was the last to receive the paper, it would cost him the least. Second, since we were the last, we did not have to pass the paper on to anyone else; it remained with us. And that was important to my mother. My mother baked bread for sale (more about this later). Since the paper remained with us, she had a handy wrapping for the bread she sold.

My father's decision meant, of course, that some ten to twelve days would go by before the paper that had arrived in our town finally found its way to our home.

When, on one occasion, we read in this paper from Kovno about the appearance of the *sheliach* from Palestine in Kavarsk, we beamed with pride. We were particularly pleased to read that our lecturer was welcomed and introduced by none other than Ruvin Jaffe on behalf of the Halutz Hazair.

By our modern standards, this item would be looked upon as insignificant and stale. In those days, it was a fresh fascination. News travelled slowly then—no radio or TV; no local daily—but, just because news *was* so scarce and travelled so slowly, every item, every word, was precious. For my parents to see the name of their son in print, in a newspaper that came from our capital city, was a source of great joy and pride. They were not alone. The whole town basked in my reflected glory when they saw the item about "Ruvke-Shiya Leib's from Kavarsk."

The news item that made me momentarily famous referred to me as "Ruvke Shiya-Leib's." The "Ruvke" part of the name was based on my formal name of Ruvin. It was the custom, however, to use the endearing diminutive of Ruvin, which was Ruvke, until the child became an adult. The "Shiya-Leib," the name of my father, was added to distinguish me, this "Ruvke," from other Ruvkes in Kavarsk.

We came to look forward to our daily newspaper, however delayed the delivery to our home might be, not only to keep up with the news but also to be entertained by what was then a printed version of our modern-day TV soap operas. The papers would run serialized novellas, commonly called "romances." At the end of each episode we were left hanging with suspense. What would happen next? As we waited for the following installment we would speculate on the outcome. The running "romance" would feed our fantasies and allow us a chance to play the imagined role of the author.

My mother loved these fictional serials. But what with keeping the house in order and baking and selling bread to supplement the family income, she did not have much time for leisurely reading. She did try to set aside Saturday for entering the world of fiction. And if she was unable to do that, she'd set the papers aside, save them up, and devour several episodes at one sitting when time eventually allowed. This was a luxury that we, alone, could enjoy, because we were at the end of the receiving line for the papers—we did not have to hurry them out of our house. In that way, we turned our disadvantaged condition into an advantage.

As spokesman for my youth Zionist group, I had certain assigned duties:

On Rosh Hashanah, it was the custom to send New Year cards to family and friends. Normally, such greeting cards would be sent through the mail. But for any such "mail" intended for the Jewish population in our town, we created our own postal system. Here's the way it worked: We would sell *Keren Kayemot*, stamps for the Jewish National Fund. People would buy these stamps from us. It was a way to raise funds for the Jewish community in Palestine. The buyers would then affix these stamps to their New Year greeting mail. The mail was then deposited in a box that we placed outside our clubhouse. We would then deliver the mail, as would any postal system, to the proper parties. Needless to add, our homemade postal service applied only to mail within our town.

There was still another way in which we raised funds for the Jewish National Fund. It coincided with Purim. On this holiday people exchanged gifts, but customarily the gift was not delivered in person by the gift-giver. It was delivered by a third party—a child, a mutual friend, or even a stranger.

My friends and I set up a service. We offered to be the third party delivering the gifts, and we would, of course, receive tips for our efforts. We then donated these tips to the Jewish National Fund.

In the summer leaders in the Zionist movement would organize outings, where we would receive orientation on our purposes and projects. Both youths and adults would be in attendance. The attendees came from several towns; the leadership came from Kovno, our capital city.

One year we had one of these get-togethers on a farm located between the towns of Kurkel and Anyksht. The farm was about ten miles away from my home. I was then ten or eleven years old. There were two or three others from my youth group and about half a dozen adults. Our leader for the event was Daniel Charney.

We got there on a horse-drawn wagon. We brought along our own utensils and other things we would need. Although, measured in miles, the distance was short, the journey seemed very long to me. We crossed the Shventa River on a raft navigated by a Lithuanian, then resumed our journey on a sandy one-lane road through a pine forest, finally arriving in Kurkel for a seven-day adventure.

When we arrived at this farm with its large house, its large barn and stable, we found that some of the participants from other towns were already there. All in all, some ten towns were represented. We were given our assignments, the heavier work being given to the adults. Our first chore was to dig a round ditch about two feet deep and two feet wide. The circle had to be large enough to accommodate a bonfire and dancers. This was to be, so to speak, our "ballroom."

We also constructed the little outdoor ovens where we did our cooking. For our meals, we gathered around the circle we'd dug and ate our food while sitting on the ground. In effect, we were living in the primitive sort of way pioneers do when they come to some virgin land. We were being intellectually indoctrinated and physically prepared for the communal life we would be living when we would someday be making *aliya* to Palestine.

If we displayed talent for certain kinds of work we were assigned accordingly. I showed some talent for Hebrew calligraphy. Two of us were given the task of making signs and banners with Hebrew lettering on them. (I must admit that my co-worker was much more skilled than I.) As a team, we did well. All our banners and signs were done in our favorite color, blue.

In the evenings, we went to sleep in the barn on a pile of hay. We never once changed our clothing in seven days; we did go down to the river to bathe ourselves, but when we were done we put on the same clothes.

In the evening we lit our barn fire, sang Hebrew songs, and dance the hora. For all of us this was a wonderful and unforgettable experience, through which we found out much about ourselves as persons and as a people.

We also made the acquaintance of young people from other towns. Years later, we rediscovered one another. One such was a good friend called Mendke who came from a small town called Zalmaria, near Malat. We first met at the outing. When I later attended the ORT school, Mendke was a fellow student, and we renewed our friendship.

During the day we would go on marches in the countryside singing our Hebrew songs. In the area of our encampment there was a famous landmark known as the Puntika Stone. I was quite excited when told that we would visit this place, about three miles away. I had heard about it, and about the legends connected with it, for many years. Now I was about to see this wonder of the world with my own eyes.

As we approached the vicinity where the stone was located, I could no longer contain myself. I broke into a run. I had to see this gigantic rock that thrust its peaks above the evergreens. "There it is!" someone called out. I looked; I looked again, and my heart sank.

What a disappointment! True, the legendary rock was larger than most of the pebbles and stones one usually encounters, but it was no massive mountainous piece of stone that would have challenged the skill of veteran mountain climbers. We, unequipped and untrained as we were, scrambled all over this somewhat-larger-than-ordinary stone, which was about twenty feet in circumference and about fifteen feet high. It was a rock slightly larger than one usually encounters, which had been invested by legend with all sorts of magical powers, but to me, I must confess, it was a source only of great disappointment.

I was even more disappointed, however, by the person who, in his way, was also a "rock." I refer to Daniel Charney, who, to me, was a role model. Next to my biological father, Daniel was my chief mentor. He was the ideal *halutz* who would someday make *aliya* to Palestine, and when he did, he would blaze a trail for me and others to follow. I was, therefore, devastated when told that Daniel had left for South Africa. It was rumored he'd fled there to avoid military service in the Lithuanian army.

I was bitter. How could he leave me and the others in our movement? While he'd headed us to Palestine, he, himself, had headed for South Africa! And he was not alone—the family followed.

There was his brother, Motke, a year older than I was, a redheaded kid who did not do well at school. His mother hired me to tutor him. I was paid one Lit a week, the equivalent of ten cents. There was a sister, Chana, one of the most beautiful girls in town. There was a mother who, apparently, had had a stroke. Her body was bent over, her speech slurred, her hands trembling constantly.

The story in town was that the parents were in financial trouble, unable to pay their debts, and that they'd departed leaving their creditors holding the bag.

The departure of the Charney family and the disappointing Puntika Stone were two critical disillusionments from my youth; two crushing blows from which I would never fully recover.

TEN
Winter in Kavarsk

Winter came to Kavarsk in the closing days of November. The luminous white crystals of snow began to fall, and soon the town and the surrounding fields were blanketed with layer upon layer of snow. And there the frigid whiteness would sit until the time of my favorite holiday—Passover.

The winters were brutal, bleak and bitterly cold. Yet they were not depressing. We met the challenge. We conducted our war against winter—with remarkable success.

We did it by looking ahead and preparing for the fearful freeze. The first step was to be ready to keep the house warm; to do that, we bought and stacked piles of birch wood. Sometimes, we would buy the logs and hire a peasant to cut them into suitable lengths for the fireplace. Then we would store them in the barn or stable, or stack them under the extended eaves of our roof where they would not be soaked by rain. We knew the winter would come and we were getting ready for the coming of the cold. We would stack up on food—sauerkraut, potatoes, beets, pickles.

We also needed clothes to keep us warm. We were particularly concerned with keeping our feet warm, since they were the extremities of the body that we could not keep warm with gloves. So, in place of gloves for the hands, we had "gloves" for the feet—woolen boots called *volikes*. And the ones we wore were actually manufactured in our town.

In front of my Uncle Ruvin's house lived a family in a very nice house. The father of the family was called Notel. In back of the house was a small building where he manufactured *volikes*. Notel would sell the boots to people in our town, to farmers and peasants, and to storekeepers in other towns. Both Notel and his *volikes* enjoyed a good reputation.

Notel also took responsibility for two brothers some in our town called *meshugoyim*, literally "crazy ones." Their names were Davidke and

Shrolke. (Every town everywhere, I suspect, has its share of such unfortunates.)

Viewed clinically, the tag was inappropriate. The boys were merely slow-witted. They were also exceptionally gentle; they wouldn't hurt a fly. But people did take advantage of and make fun of them. They were often called upon to run simple errands and were paid a few pennies for their services.

David and Shrolke were supported largely by brothers in America, who would send money to be used on their behalf. The remittances went to Notel, who acted as trustee of the funds. He arranged for the brothers to get food and lodging and other necessary amenities.

Notel employed two or three workers all year round. In the winter he stepped up his work force. The material he used for making the *volikes* was processed wool. I do not know exactly how he went about the business of making the boots, but I do remember that it involved the use of steam.

The *volikes* came in three categories. The most common was medium hard. These would reach up to the calf of the leg and fit into rubber galoshes. There was also a second type, which fit into leather boots. The third type reached above the knee and was made of specially treated hard waterproof material. These did not require galoshes and were the most expensive.

As children, we wore no socks when we used the *volikes.* Older people who wore boots also did not wear socks. Instead, they would wrap their feet in a white strip of cotton cloth about eight inches wide and about twenty-four inches long. These wrappings were called *oitkes* in Yiddish.

As for food in the winter, we had our two basic staples—black bread and potatoes. These were supplemented by a third item, which we called in Yiddish *zoiers*, or "sours" in English. These were made of beets, cabbage (kraut), and *schav*.

The cabbage was harvested a few weeks after Sukkoth. After the first light frost fell on the fields, the growing season would end. The ripe cabbage was now ready to be picked and to be preserved for winter eating. The same was true of the beets.

The process of pickling vegetables was a communal ritual conducted in homes. My mother, for instance, would, on a given day, invite friends and neighbors to pitch in. The joint venture would be called, in Yiddish, *sthelen shetkeven.* The women would get together in the evenings to gossip and sing songs while pickling. With sharp knives they would dice the cabbage and toss it into a wooden barrel as they chatted away at their "pickling party." As I recall the pungent products that came out of these gatherings, my mouth still waters.

Once the work was finished, my mother would serve tea and little cakes especially baked for the occasion. Such collective enterprises were run on a reciprocal basis. When other families had to do their *sthelen*, my mother would go to their homes and pitch in.

After the diced cabbage was poured into the barrel, it was salted and then pounded into a juice under the repeated battering of a heavy log. In between the layers of cabbage my mother would add apples, carrots, beets (to provide a lively color), and a variety of herbs. The heavy work of pounding this concoction into its juicy form was assigned to my father.

After five or six days, the cabbage would begin to ferment. During that time, my mother would regularly stir the contents with a wooden stick to allow the gases to escape. This was a pleasant experience, because the aromas issuing from the barrel were pleasing to the palate.

When the process was completed, the wooden barrels and their contents were removed from the cellar and stored in a special room that kept things warmer in the winter and cooler in the summer.

The "sours" were not cooked; they were eaten raw in their preserved state. Normally, they would be served accompanied by baked potatoes, herring baked on a fire, and bread. Occasionally, if circumstances permitted, something extra would be added. But variety was the exception. Thus did we go through the entire winter.

"Soaked beets" were another staple. But they were not used as commonly as the "kraut" during the winter months. The process of preserving the beets was a variant on the cabbage theme. The beets were peeled and placed in a barrel, which was located in a warm spot. In due time, the beets soured. We looked forward to eating the "soaked beets" as a Passover delicacy.

For that holiday season, we would bring in a fresh barrel of beets and place it under a white tablecloth. We would then heat up a stone in the oven and place it on top of the barrel. The beets, and the juice from the beets (*rosel*), were a mixture that we would relish through the Passover week.

For my mother, life was very demanding. She worked very hard just to provide for our basic needs, in addition to which she made and sold bread to supplement the family income. One of her specialties was a tasty loaf that we called "sweet and sour" bread.

Mother built up a trade with steady customers. On designated days, after school hours, I would deliver the bread to the proper households. Not all the bread was delivered, however. There were customers who came to our home to buy and carry home what they bought. To meet their requests, we had a scale in the house to weigh the orders that buyers would place. If a full loaf was too much, we would cut the loaf down to the required weight. When my mother was not there, my father or I would cut and weigh the bread.

The process of baking the bread involved several steps. First, my father would buy what we called "corn" but in America would be called "wheat." He would then take the raw wheat to a miller to be ground. The output of this operation was known as "once-milled corn kernel flour." Since the mill had no way of separating out the shells from the ground kernels, we were, unbeknownst to us, really working with "whole wheat flour." It had, as a consequence, all the virtues of whole wheat. All the nutritious ingredients and the roughage were retained. The end product was a dark bread known, in Yiddish, as *rozove broyt.*

In the back of our mind there was always a vision of a bread that we would someday like to make and bake. It was called *gebitelte* bread. On occasion we had an opportunity to sample this bit of gourmet baking. Those would be the days when my father would go to Kovno and decide to treat all of us to these palate-pleasing morsels.

Ordinarily, after my father brought home the ground flour, my mother would sift it into a vessel through a homemade screen, and would then add warm salt water. Then she'd cover it with a tablecloth, fortified with a sheepskin coat, a pillow, or anything handy that would keep the warmth inside the vessel. The idea behind retaining the heat was to encourage rapid fermentation.

The next step was kneading the dough. That operation required considerable physical strength, and was, of course, done entirely by hand. My mother was not quite up to it, so she would employ one of the peasant women. This woman would arrive early in the morning. She'd start the process of kneading by adding some flour and water to the fermented dough. Then she would pound and push the dough for a full hour. Her fists and fingers would work their magic on the tough mixture until the dough was nice and firm.

After the kneading was done, the dough in the vessel would be once more covered over and put in a warm spot. There it would sit for four or five hours, the dough continuing to rise.

While waiting for the leavening to be completed, we would prepare the oven. Into it we fed chunks of the dough, cut in portions weighing between ten and twenty pounds.

When father was at home, he helped place the loaves in the oven. When he was not there, I would help. In the winter, the wooden shovels on which the doughy loaves sat were first sprinkled with flour to make sure that the still-unbaked loaves would not stick to them. To accomplish the same purpose in the summer, my mother might lay on the bare shovel a thin tier of scented grasses, which grew near the river; then she would put the loaves on top of the grass. And to accomplish the same objective in the fall, my mother might cover the shovel with a thin scattering of oak leaves. The actual baking took from four to six hours.

Oak leaves were plentiful in our town. There were some people who stacked up the leaves in the fall in preparation for baking all year round. Sharing with neighbors came easily.

Of all the foods we had, we depended most on potatoes. Some people ate potatoes two or three times a day, seven days a week. Potatoes were the staple of small town Lithuanian Jewish families.

We ate potatoes prepared in a multiplicity of ways:

There were potatoes peeled and boiled in water with onions and ground pepper; potatoes cooked or baked with the skin intact; potatoes eaten with sauerkraut, with or without herring; potato pancakes, served with sour cream or sour milk, a dish that was one of my favorites; potatoes with goose fat and *gribenes*, a mixture of sauteed onions and diced chicken skin; and, another favorite, potato *kugel*, a popular Jewish variant of a bread pudding, with the ubiquitous potato pinch-hitting for the bread.

In the summer, Mother would sometimes prepare small potato balls made of grated potatoes and cook them in milk. In the winter she made large potato balls, like the Passover matzoh balls, with a stuffing made of oatmeal, chopped onions, goose or chicken fat. She would cook this for a few hours in a broth of oats and barley.

Sometimes, in the summer, Mother would make what looked like an oversized thick pancake called a "baked bundy." First, the potatoes were grated on a metal grater; then the contents were placed in a linen bag. The water was squeezed out of the potatoes and the bag. Ground chick-pea flour and salt and onions were added. Then the mixture was kneaded a bit, to hold it together, and placed on cabbage or oak leaves before being put into the hot oven, where it baked for about an hour.

We used to eat it with milk. Some preferred to eat it with sauerkraut. When we were kids we were in the habit of eating it as a nosh, but when we were treated to a warm *bundy* with sour cream and butter, the pleasure was multiplied.

If you wonder why so much of our eating revolved around potatoes, the answer is simple. Most Jews in our town had no problem raising their own potatoes, and they raised enough to carry them through the winter. We did have a garden attached to our house, but we used that to grow tomatoes, carrots, radishes, scallions, cabbage, and sunflowers—for their edible seeds. We did not use the garden for potatoes. For growing potatoes, our great staple, my father used to rent a half-acre plot from a nearby peasant. The same peasant would prepare the soil and plant the potato seedlings for us. At the end of July or the beginning of August, we would go to the plot and dig out the plants. We would remove the larger potatoes, which were ready for use. We would replant what remained, so that the smaller potatoes might grow to their full size. Each plant yielded from five to ten potatoes. Through our diligent care, we could nourish a crop to meet our needs through those joyous days when we'd have our hot potatoes with borscht or *schav*.

We continued our planting and replanting of the potatoes up until sometime before Rosh Hashanah. After that date, the peasant we hired would dig up all the remaining plants. We would retrieve whatever potatoes were left, put them in the cellar, and count on them to carry us through the winter.

While winter was always fraught with fear, it was also a time of fun for us kids. We used to go sledding down the street in front of our house, which was indeed a great pastime but also a great peril. The street in front of our house was very steep. When you got to the bottom you had to make a sharp turn, because the road made a sharp and sudden turn. If you lost control, you would hit a stone wall, or, worse, you might go running into a horse and sleigh coming up the hill.

Our parents repeatedly cautioned us not to go sledding down our perilous street. We continued to use the street, despite their warnings, because the snow was packed so tightly and the sled, as a result, moved so smoothly and swiftly. It was a favorite pastime, particularly so on a clear Saturday night when our bodies and spirits felt so in tune with the body and spirit of the world as we sensed it on Shabbat.

After *shul*, the older children—the teenagers—would hitch a horse to a sleigh, ring the horse's neck with bells, pile into the sleigh, cover themselves with blankets, and gallop away across the countryside underneath a starlit sky. Although I was not yet a teenager, I was welcomed into their company; they seemed to have taken a liking to me. (I also believe that being a leader in the Zionist youth group added to my prestige.) Whatever the reason, I was part of the party. In winters, I looked forward to these Saturday night forays.

I came well prepared. I bundled myself up in my warmest coat, and I wore a heavy cap with earflaps that I could tie with a string under my chin. I wore woolen gloves that mother had knitted for me. And, of course, I wore the woolen *volikes*.

Huddled closely and packed tightly in the sleigh with the others, I felt physically and spiritually warm, one of a party who had turned the terrors of Old Man Winter into a terrain for youthful joy. As the galloping horse swayed from side to side, his nostrils emitting steam like some dragon of ancient legend, racing across a white still sea of snow reflecting the glow of the moon, I felt as though I was in some imagined fairyland.

When I got home, our house really did feel warm. The wild winter ride had sharpened my appetite, and the goodies were there. Right after Shabbat my mother would heat up the house and set out our midnight repast.

As I thawed out, my cheeks red as beets, I would gulp glasses—never sips—of real hot tea. Along with it came mother's delicious sweet and sour bread, drenched with her strawberry jam.

At the day's end I collapsed gladly into the arms of Morpheus, there to sleep the sleep of the dead.

Skating was another winter event. Only two or three boys in town could afford real metal skates. The rest of us would buy or make our own wooden skates, shaped to fit the sole of the shoes we wore. Leather straps buckled over the skates to fasten them to the shoes. The skate was shaped like a V; at the bottom of the V was inserted a one-eighth-inch-thick wire, which provided a smooth, hard surface on which to glide across the ice of the frozen river or across the hard-packed snow. To savor the thrill of speedy skating, we would favor the downward slope of hilly areas.

One day my father, on his return from Kovno, brought me a happy surprise—a pair of real metal skates with the front of the blades curled up. They were a present from the children of my uncle Itzek Heiman. He had four children: Eliezer, a writer and teacher who perished in the Kovno ghetto and whose two brothers, Yakov and Naftali, and his sister, Zipporah, had emigrated to Israel.

As I noted, the skates had turned-up noses. That made it easier to glide over ice and hard-packed snow. It would be impossible for me to put into words the thrill and excitement I experienced at having my own real skates. I was the envy of all my schoolmates as I skated off to school with them.

The skates were not permanently attached to shoes made for that purpose. The skates of that time were fastened to our usual shoes. We did not have loafers or sneakers; we wore high shoes, reaching above the ankle and laced to the top.

My shoes had to be modified by the shoemaker to accommodate my new skates. A special plate of 1½-by-1½ inches was inserted in the heel. The plate had a small elongated hole. The back of the skate, likewise, had a small elongated rod that would slip into the hole in the heel. The front of the skate was fastened to the shoe by vise-lock jaws, similar to those once used to attach roller skates to shoes; the jaws, in turn, were tightened or released by the sort of key traditionally used for roller skates. That made it possible for me to remove the skates when I got to school and later put them on again.

In the winter, I would use the skates to make my deliveries as well as run other errands. If I wished to skate on the river I had to get my father's consent, for very often the river looked frozen although it was not truly so. A really deep freeze was needed to keep the ice from cracking and me from falling into the freezing water. So, for me, there was no skating without parental consent.

One of our problems, on the long winter nights, was how to fill the hours. As I noted before, we had none of the modern forms of entertainment—radio, TV, computer games, and so on—to occupy our empty hours. The best we could do was get together in someone's house to talk, play cards, and talk some more.

One of the ways we relieved our boredom was by arranging for the women to gather at someone's home to *flik* (pluck) feathers. Our source of feathers were birds like goose, duck, or—in poorer households—chicken. The host household would let it be known in town that it was plucking time. The women would flock to the feathers (no pun intended).

The gathering served a practical as well as a social function. From a practical point of view, the feathers served to turn pillow cases into pillows; they were also used to convert larger cloth receptacles into comforters (*perenes*), which were stuffed with goose feathers. These comforters, if bought outside, could be quite expensive. Poorer households that could not afford to keep geese or duck used chicken feathers for the same purpose.

In most of the Jewish households the feathers became part of a dowry. A bride-to-be would boast of her collection of bed-things such as pillows and comforters. Some households would devote many years to accumulating this worldly wealth. The *fliking*, in this context, was part of a premarital ritual. The bride-to-be would not come to her husband empty-handed; her "nest" would be well-feathered.

The *fliking* also had its social aspects. It was a chance for the women to exchange news and views. Once they hit a rhythm, they would break into song. When the night's work was done, the host would serve refreshments. The next week, the same thing was done at the same time in another home.

For everyone in our town, including those who were better off, life was tough. A wealthier person might hire someone to collect and cut the wood for the winter. But the more affluent person still had to go out into the bitter, biting winter weather to collect it. It would generally be soggy, so that it would be necessary to dry it. That meant that one had to have some dry kindling available to start the fire, dry out the wood, and get a real blaze going. Along the way, one had to get a breeze going to fan the embers. The most common way of doing this was simply to stand there, getting redder and redder in the face, while blowing away at the stubborn sparks until they burst into flame.

Toilet facilities were primitive. In all seasons one had to go outdoors to the appropriately named "outhouse." In summer this was tolerable; in winter, it was a pain. You had to go out into the cold, ploughing your way through the snow that, as a rule, was piled up super high because the outhouse was located near a barn surrounded with snowdrifts. To open the door to the outhouse was often a struggle, too, because snow piled up against the door as well. When you finally succeeded in getting into the outhouse to do what you had come to do, you had to squat with the piercingly frigid air and winds whirling around you and your exposed parts. The animal comforts that we now take for granted were then unknown and unimaginable to us.

Even the simplest chores, such as getting water from the well, were challenges. To get the water was a dangerous mission. The well would often freeze over at the top because, as we lifted the bucket from the deep well, some of the water would spill over on to the sides of the well, where it would accumulate and freeze. Then, when we transferred the water from the bucket to the pail, more of it inevitably spilled on the sides; and as we carried the pail toward the house, still more would spill and freeze. As a result, the ground became a slippery "skating rink," and many were the times that I slipped and fell, bruising my knees.

In our town, there were certain hardships everyone had to endure—rich, poor, or in-between. There were, for instance, some with enough wealth to pay for electricity, but there were no electric lines running into Kavarsk. Even if you wanted internal plumbing and could afford it, you still couldn't get it because there was no system of running water to supply your home. And if you needed a place to perform certain bodily functions, there was nowhere to go outside the outhouse. For transportation, you still had to rely on a horse and wagon, or on my father's bus when it was operable.

It was inoperable on numerous occasions. In those days, there was no such thing as antifreeze, so we did not dare to leave the bus outside overnight if it had water in it. We would drain the water out of the radiator, and would have to refill it the next morning.

Getting the bus started again was no simple task. Everything was cold, and some things were frozen. Since the bus did not have a self-starter that could be activated by pressing a button, we had to get out there with a crank, which we rotated by hand. Sometimes it would take hours to get the motor going; sometimes we could not get it started at all.

Then there were times when, after we got the bus started, it could not be moved—it was snowed in. I remember occasions when my father, his partners, and hired peasants had to dig us out of our snowbound "prison." They toiled away, shovelful after shovelful, digging through four or five miles of snow to clear the road to the highway. It took days to do.

The men who did the digging did it with hand shovels because we did not have a plough. The task was truly arduous. At times they were digging through snowbanks that were six to eight feet tall. I recall our bus leaving town and rolling through embankments of piled-up snow that were as high as the top of our bus.

Although winter was a harsh season for just about everyone in our town, there were some people who looked forward gleefully to the time when the river would freeze over. These were the people whose businesses were dependent on the ice they could accumulate in the winter, storing it away for sale in the warmer seasons.

One of these two individuals lived right across from our house. On his property he had a soda-bottling plant located in a small building right next door to his very lovely residence. It had an extensive glass-enclosed front porch with a beautiful double-French door.

The "factory" had some hand-operated bottling machines run by the owner and a helper. He would bottle lemonade and seltzer. To keep the soda refrigerated, he had an icehouse. Both the bottling plant and the icehouse were situated right alongside a running brook. In the summertime, when there arose a need for ice for some medicinal purpose, people were able to get it from this place.

The lemonade was quite popular in the surrounding towns and villages, and was distributed on a wholesale basis to these other locations. For me, it was always a treat to cross the street and buy a bottle of lemonade for myself or for guests.

From our house, I used to stare through the windows across the narrow street that separated our home from the residence of the bottling entrepreneur. To me, his house was a thing of beauty. Its large windows were graced with white lace curtains. When, on occasion, I delivered an order of my mother's bread to that house, I was always impressed with its beautiful interior. It had a magnificent living room with made-to-order furniture from Jonava. It also had several bedrooms. My basis of comparison was, of course, our home: Anything that was nicer than our house *and* had furniture made in Jonava, immediately won my respect and admiration.

Jonava was a town located about forty-five miles from Kavarsk, not far from Kovno. It enjoyed the reputation of manufacturing the finest furniture in Lithuania. Anyone who wanted (and could afford) truly fine furniture would order it from Jonava. The city's fame continued for many years. Even after the Soviet Union swallowed up Lithuania, following World War II, the Russian hierarchy ordered its furniture from Jonava.

The second person in town who had a need for ice was Aunt Elke. She was in the business of making ice cream, an enterprise in which I was actively involved. I helped to cut and store the ice, I helped to make the ice cream, and I did it all without pay. We were, after all, like one family, living right next door to each other, working, worrying, playing, and socializing with one another. Aunt Elke had four children—two daughters and two sons. The oldest was Hirshke, about three years older than I; then there was Hayimke, about my age; then came Neche Minka, who had the same name and was the same age as my sister; and then there was Beilke, who was about three or four years younger.

My aunt's husband, Yankel, had little to do with the ice cream business. He was a glazier, who had a horse and wagon and would buy and sell wheat. He would also cart goods from wholesalers in the larger cities to the retailers in our town.

Yankel was a very nice, gentle man. My aunt was of the domineering and aggressive type, quite rough and pushy. Assisted by the boys, the ice cream business was in her hands.

When the river was solidly frozen over, my aunt would hire a peasant, who would cut the ice in two-by-two-foot cubes and place the cubes on a horse-drawn sled. Then the ice slabs would be placed in a cellar right opposite my aunt's house.

The cellar was all that was left of a house that had burned down during World War I; it belonged to my uncle Itzhak Heiman, who lived in Kovno. Uncle Itzhak owned quite a bit of vacant land around our houses. He never bothered to sell it, and it was used by us without any restrictions.

The peasant would begin by cutting a hole in the river ice. He did this with a handsaw. Then he would cut the separate slabs, conveying them by sled to the ice cellar where they were covered with sawdust. My uncle and the boys would pitch in in the later stages of this process.

This operation might extend over the course of a full month or more, depending on the weather. After the layers of ice were removed, the newly exposed water would freeze, forming more ice. And so it went, layer after layer and week after week. When they were finished, nothing was left but a thin layer of ice. When it snowed, the gap made by the ice that had been removed would fill up. During all this, no markers were posted to warn that there were areas of freshly frozen ice that were fragile and dangerous to anyone wishing to cross.

One night, after a heavy snowfall, my cousin Hirshke and I were driving the horse and sled from their house to the river to pick up a load of ice. The distance from house to river was about half a mile. As we approached the river, we saw the men cutting the ice; close by them there was a load of freshly cut slabs.

The river was covered with a white blanket of soft, freshly fallen snow flakes. In the background, on the other side of the river, was the forest with its thick evergreens. The branches were weighed down with the heavy load of sparkling snowflakes. The glistening treetops pointed majestically upward to the gray winter sky. As we drove on, we had the illusion that we were gliding on a wide white meadow leading gently toward an awesome forest. These were our reveries as we moved ahead bundled up in our heavy winter clothes, warm in our bodies and in our thoughts.

Suddenly our horse sank into the river. He'd hit a spot where the ice was thin and freshly frozen; it could not, of course, sustain his weight. We panicked and jumped from the sled.

We called to the peasants for help. They tried and tried, but they could not lift the heavy horse from the freezing water. We ran to get more help. We were afraid that the horse would drown, or freeze, or both. My uncle and others came, and after a long struggle they managed to rescue the poor creature.

We covered the horse with blankets and rushed him to the stable to keep him warm. When I got home I got a good talking-to from my parents, who cautioned me never to go to that place again. Who knows what would have happened if we had followed the horse into the freezing waters?

ELEVEN
Holidays

We knew that winter was half over when Hanukah rolled around. To me this was a signal that my favorite holiday, Passover, was on the way. Hanukah was observed differently in different homes. In our house, for instance, we did not have a Hanukah menorah (*hannukyia*). I cannot recall ever having lit Hanukah candles in our home. I do, however, remember visiting other homes where they did light the colorful candles.

One such home was that of my great-uncle Ruvin. I would look forward to visiting Ruvin's family to enjoy the lighted multicolored candles. They gave me the customary Hanukah *gelt*.

I also associate Hanukah with potato *latkes*, which my mother made, and with our spinning the *dreidel* and playing games with it involving small coins or matches. The *dreidels* were generally homemade out of wood or lead—the lead ones were the most popular—and making them was an art.

We would begin with the branch of a tree about one inch in diameter. We quartered the wood lengthwise. Then we would carve the wood to flatten the pieces, and into the flat surface we would carve the Hebrew letters that traditionally appeared on the sides of the dreidel. These carved pieces of wood became the mold into which we poured the molten lead.

Many bits and scraps of lead were accumulated over a long period of time. Our prime source was the seals attached to the imported textiles we might buy. We would collect the seals, putting them in a spoon that we held over the fire. When the lead melted, we poured it into the wooden mold we'd made.

When the lead cooled we opened the wooden mold, removing any excess lead from the dreidel. We would smooth and polish the lead, and then we were ready to spin the little top and play our little games.

On Hanukah and other wintery Saturday nights my father used to play cards with his friends. The names of the games they played were Sixty-six and *Zoleh.*

Another day to remember was the fifteenth day of the Hebrew month of *Shevat.* It was called *Tu-Bishevat,* and it coincided with my birthday. (On the Roman calendar used in the Western world, that day corresponded to February 13. The year I was born was 1922.)

To the best of my recollection, my birthday was never celebrated, nor were the birthdays of any of the rest of the family, including aunts, uncles, or cousins. The one birthday we did celebrate was the *bar mitzvah.*

The minor holiday of *Tu-Bishevat* was celebrated with the eating of carob (*buckser*), which was imported from Palestine, now Israel. (In the United States, carob is called St. John's Bread.) My *bar mitzvah* was strictly a ceremonial event, without any special festivities or gifts. To the extent that there was any "party" at all, it was a simple affair. After *shul* and after reading the *haftorah* (the appropriate portion of the Torah for the day), my father dispatched me to the local government-run liquor store to buy a bottle of vodka. I brought it home; Father opened it up; he poured the drinks; he made a *lechayim* with our friends the Shmucklers and my uncle Yankel; and that was my *Bar Mitzvah* "party."

My father did present me, the *bar mitzvah* boy, with a pair of *tefilin,* which I carried with me when I left for America.

In between Hanukah and Passover we celebrated Purim, which came some four or five weeks before the latter. The nights were now getting shorter, the days longer. The thaw began to set in, and the snow started melting. The hard, frozen streets turned to mud, and the sun began to reappear in all its golden glory. Spring was on the way.

The river ice would begin to break into pieces, the chunks floating downstream. Sometimes, when they could not negotiate a turn or twist in the river, they would be caught on the banks. Water would back up, raising the river level and flooding the surrounding fields and meadows.

We identified Purim with Queen Esther and that "wicked, wicked man," Haman. It was an occasion to exchange gifts that we referred to as *shalach mones.* Mainly these gift exchanges took place between adults; we children had no possessions to exchange. We were assigned the mission of carriers and deliverers, and for our services we were rewarded with small tips, like a penny or a piece of hard-sucking candy. (We had no chocolate in Kavarsk.)

A common gift for Purim was the *hamantash,* a three-cornered danish filled with poppy seeds. (Symbolically a *hamantash* represented the hat of the hated Haman, which we devoured with delight.) Other gifts were large cooked kidney beans, handkerchiefs, small hand folding mirrors, or combs. A gift would be placed in a plate covered with a cloth tied around the bottom. Grasping the covering at the bottom, we would plod our way through the mud to deliver the *shalach mones*.

Mother used to bake delicious *hamantashen*. We would chop up the poppy seeds in a small brass vessel and would continue to do so until we extracted the white milk from the seeds. A *hamantash* with a tea chaser was a memorable treat; just thinking about it now makes my mouth water. I remember the taste, and I remember the conviviality when relatives and friends would gather at our house, talking, drinking the tea, savoring the *hamantashen* and the large kidney beans that, in Yiddish, were called *bob*.

In *shul*, they read the *megillah*, the long story about Queen Esther. Whenever the name of Haman was mentioned, we would break out with a variety of noises. We would fire very special toy guns that were loaded with powder and cork. We had hand-held noisemakers, with which we used to parade raucously around town. We had other toy pistols that fired paper-loaded powder. All this clamor in the house and in the open was, for us children, a moment of uninhibited juvenile joy.

All these holidays were, for me, just preludes to Passover. *Pesach* was "it," the supreme moment. The holiday, in itself, was a stirring ceremonial, but I do believe that the anticipation and preparation for the celebration were even more exciting than Passover itself.

Part of that excitement must undoubtedly have been due to the changing season. Winter was leaving and spring was coming; joy was in the air. The white winter fields would soon be transformed into green acres of winter-sown wheat. Interspersed were the multicolored dabs of wildflowers. The brooks, which had slept through the winter, were now coming awake and soon would be rushing over the fields and through the valleys, pouring their pure sparkling water into the river.

For a while, during the thaw, the streets would be wet and muddy, but as we neared Passover the same streets would turn dry and inviting. This meant that the time had come for us to go to the shoemaker to remove the *volikes* and be measured and outfitted with a new pair of shoes. We were still growing, and so were our feet.

The shoemaker had no special instrument for taking our measurements. It was all done with brown paper. He would start with a piece that was a bit larger than your foot. He would then fold it several times, making what amounted to a tape measure about one inch wide. He used this homemade "ruler" to measure the length of your foot by putting a mark on the paper measure and then making a cut at that point. In a similar fashion, he would measure your instep by wrapping his improvised tape measure around your foot, marking it, folding it, and cutting it in his skillful way. He repeated this process four or five times. When he was satisfied that he now knew your foot like the palm of his hand, he would write your name on the properly trimmed paper patterns and hang it all on the wall of his combined home and workplace. Before you left, he assured you that the shoes would be ready for the great day, for Passover.

The next stop was the textile store, where mother would choose cloth for a pair of short pants and, if you were lucky, a new shirt. You would go to a tailor, who would measure you with a real tape measure and promise to have the clothes ready for *Pesach*.

For me, the most exciting aspect of Passover, especially as I grew somewhat older, was my involvement in the baking of matzos. When I say, "as I grew older," I am referring to my last three years in Lithuania before I left for America, the years when I was a student in the ORT school in Kovno. I would get permission from the ORT director, the late Jacob Oleiski, to go home a few weeks ahead of the normal Passover vacation time.

I would help my father and my uncle in the baking of the matzos, which we would make not simply to meet our own family needs but also for sale in our town. This seasonal business was yet another way in which we would eke out a living. I looked forward to the event, not just from the standpoint of helping out, however, but frankly because I was homesick for my family and friends. For although I did have occasion to see my father when, in the course of his work on the bus, he came to Kovno, I did not have a chance to see my mother, my sister, our other Kavarsk relatives, and my friends. Passover, accordingly, was a time for reunion and rejoicing.

The school year started right after Yom Kippur and ended in July; the only extended holiday in between was Passover. So, when I came home a few weeks ahead of time to help prepare for the big day, my mother was visibly delighted. Although I was busily engaged in baking matzos, Mother and I saw each other most of the day, since our little "bakery" was right next door to our home.

And now, a few words about the fascinating process of baking matzos in Kavarsk:

The matzo baking took place in the home of my father's sister. The oven in this house had been built with the expectation that, at some time in the future, it would be used to bake matzos. It had been specifically constructed with that thought in mind.

My uncle Yankel was a bit of a jack-of-all-trades. His main business was that of a glazier and merchant. He got about in his own horse and wagon. He also had the reputation of being a good matzo baker and, in that capacity, was employed by other matzo makers in town.

Since my uncle had the skill, and he and my father had the means to get about to make deliveries, they decided jointly to get into the matzo business in a serious way. Their market was not limited to Kavarsk; they also reached out to other small towns with Jewish populations.

The actual making and baking of the matzos took three weeks—six days a week, ten hours a day. The members of the family, together with some hired help, were all given specific assignments.

Making certain the part of the house used for baking matzos was kosher was the first step. This did not normally require the presence of a rabbi. The only time a rabbi might be asked for advice would be on occasions where we were uncertain whether or not what we were doing to "kosherize" our bakery was in accord with prescribed religious practice. But there was never any doubt that to observe *kashrut* was a must; every nook and cranny in the house was washed and scrubbed. The long, wooden worktable used in the process was, likewise, meticulously washed and scrubbed.

Extra kerosene lamps were hung over the table to provide necessary lighting, since we started early and worked late and the days were still short.

At midnight, we fed the oven with birch wood to make certain that it was hot enough to do the baking early in the coming day. This was not only the practical thing to do, it was also the prescribed thing to do in accordance with the *kashrut*.

Throughout the many hours, days, and weeks we spent at our labors, we stayed in an exalted mood. To us, we weren't just baking matzos; we were engaged in a holy ritual, experiencing a very earthy kind of ecstasy.

We started the process by mixing flour with water and then kneading the mixture into dough. This assignment was normally given to a woman we employed. My mother and aunt would pitch in to relieve her. Such relief was definitely necessary—the job ran for ten hours a day, with one break for lunch.

The kneading had to be done in a short time, ten or fifteen minutes. To prolong the process might allow fermentation to set in, and the matzo's distinctive feature was that it was unleavened. Then the kneaded dough, about the size of a rounded two-pound loaf of bread, would be placed on a small table. At this table, a hired hand would cut the dough into small chunks. These, in turn, were distributed to girls, also hired hands drawn from the gentile Lithuanian homes in the vicinity, who would apply their rolling pins to flatten the dough. After flattening the dough, the girls would turn their pieces over to another table, where there were two young boys.

The boys would punch holes in the matzoh using a hand-held metal wheel with teeth in it, rolling it back and forth. To guide the wheel in a straight line, a rolling pin was used as a sort of straight-line ruler. After each row of little holes had been punched into the dough, the pin was rolled on to an adjoining position and the next row of holes was punched. When the entire surface had been properly punctured, the thin slab was placed on a long pole that conveyed the unbaked dough to the oven.

The two boys who punched the holes, known in Yiddish as *redlers*, were my older cousin Hirshke and a hired hand. They were the regular "wheelers." My other cousin, Chayimke, and myself were the "relief wheelers." Occasionally we helped out with some of the other operations as well.

Although this was not an assembly-line operation such as Charlie Chaplin depicted in his movie *Modern Times*, in which the human being is just a cog in a wheel, we were nevertheless very much dominated by the mechanical process. Our pace was set by the flow. We had to move fast so that the dough would not dry out or ferment, and we had to be super-careful that nothing happened that would violate the laws of *kashrut*.

Our two families, the Hoichmans and the Jaffes, worked closely together in this business, and we worked as a team, with each person assigned to his or her special position. My uncle Yankel was the baker. It was a physically demanding job, and he needed relief both during the day and at night.

At night, my father tended to the oven. He fed the logs into the fire and checked to make certain that the oven would be at the proper temperature for the morning. Since my father worked this night shift, it was possible for my uncle to get some sleep during the night. Working the oven was a tiring job—it was important to get relief, and it was doubly important for us kids. Inevitably, the heat of the oven would take its toll.

During the day, my cousin Hayimke and I would relieve my uncle in the matzoh baking. Eventually, I became quite skillful. I had to make sure that the matzoh did not burn, was not too well done, and was not underdone. In an era where there were no thermostats to control temperature and no timers to set the time, you had to operate with your eyes and use your judgment; you had to get the feel and hang of it, and you had to act and react swiftly.

I would take the eight-foot pole to the table and drape it with half a dozen of the prepared and punctured slabs of matzoh dough. I would insert the pole with the matzohs-to-be in the oven. Then I would tip the pole to allow the dough to slide off onto the oven, where the baking would commence.

But now I was confronted with another challenge. The heat in the oven was not equally distributed; if I left the matzohs where they'd been placed, some of them would be overdone and others would be underdone. I therefore had to keep a sharp eye out, in order to redistribute the matzoh dough so that each slab would get the same amount of exposure to the heat. This I would do by using a large wooden shovel, similar to those used in pizza parlors, that could pick up slabs and reposition them. This operation required judgment, speed, and eternal vigilance.

As each matzoh or batch of matzohs was finished we would, after thoughtful and proper rotation, remove them and replace them with a new batch. The finished matzohs were placed on a wooden bench, which was covered with a white sheet, and then we would start all over again. Thus, so to speak, was one "generation" of matzohs-to-be replaced by another "generation." Each came in raw; each matured in the oven; and each would be replaced by a fresh new batch that had to "take the heat." It was just like life!

The table on which we placed the finished matzohs was not their last resting place. From there, we swept them into a large wicker basket, lined with white sheets. We would then place them in another room.

In our town there were only two sources from which to get matzohs, our house and, occasionally, another. We were the main source and more popular, both in our town and in the surrounding towns that did not have their own matzoh-making facilities.

Although it may sound like boasting, we were, despite our humble home, the preferred matzoh bakers. What gave our product its superior qualities was our supervision of the girls; we made sure that they rolled the dough according to specifications. The other factor involved in producing an acceptable matzoh was its appearance, namely the way the rows of holes lined up; they could not be sloppy. They had to be as nearly exact as possible, and also close to one another to make sure the matzoh did not buckle or burn. The idea, ultimately, was to produce matzohs that had been lightly baked, which quality made it easier to use the matzoh to make matzoh meal for both cooking and baking. We prided ourselves on making our matzoh this way.

There was another reason why our matzoh enjoyed local popularity, especially with young people. During matzoh-making time, our "factory" became a hangout for the kids. After the long cold winter, the youngsters found our busy little establishment a place of social and physical warmth. For many kids, it was the only action in town. They would generally come in the late afternoon. Occasionally, they would give us a hand with some part of the operation. They also used the involvement as an excuse to flirt with the Lithuanian girls who worked with us. All in all, at this pre-Passover season, our place was the place to be—to make small talk, to do something that was worthwhile and fun, to help a friend, to start warming up both body and spirit for the days ahead. It was the time when our sleepy little town was waking up.

My father had many responsibilities in our matzoh making. He had to make certain that there was enough flour and water on hand for making the dough. He had to tend to the fire in the oven, as noted. (Since he worked through most of the night on this chore, he did his sleeping in the afternoon.) In addition to all this, my father was also our "outside" man, in charge of sales and distribution. He recorded the orders, which people would place long in advance, when they would also specify the date for delivery.

When families got their shipment, they would generally borrow two companion pieces of equipment from us for use in converting the matzos into *farfel,* or matzoh meal. One part of the equipment was a wooden vessel called, in Yiddish, a *steishel.* It was carved out of a log about eighteen inches in diameter and about four feet long. The section hollowed out for the vessel was about ten to twelve inches in diameter and about fifteen inches in depth.

This *steishel* was accompanied by a round wooden chopper that was about four feet long and about four inches in diameter. Attached at both ends of this chopper were metal plates with metal teeth. One end, with coarser teeth, was used to chop up the matzoh to make matzoh *farfel;* the other end, with finer teeth, was used to make matzoh meal. At the center of this double-purpose pole was a carved-out section, about six inches wide and two inches in diameter, which served as a handgrip. (Some of our customers had their own *steishel* and chopping pole, and did not borrow the equipment from us.)

The orders would vary in quantity, depending on the size of the family, typically running from thirty to sixty pounds. Such seemingly huge amounts were ordered because of the many uses to which the matzohs could be put. They were eaten directly, of course, but they also provided the basic ingredients for making other Passover foods that were not then readily available, such as matzoh meal, matzoh farfel, sponge cake, matzoh balls, matzoh pancakes (*latkes*), and the like.

My cousin and I would make the deliveries. If the load was not too heavy we would carry it in wicker baskets on our back, fastened to our body with ropes. If the load was too heavy, or if we had more than one delivery at a time to make, we would use the horse and wagon. We looked forward to these precious moments because they provided an opportunity for us to make a little money through tips.

Our customers would bring their own wicker baskets lined with white sheets. We would then stack the matzos in the baskets, making certain that we did so vertically and not horizontally so as to prevent the crumbling of the matzos at the bottom of the heap. The matzohs would, of course, be weighed according to the quantity ordered. If the order was smaller and carried by us personally in our wicker basket, we would unload the matzos at a designated place in the customer's home and return with our empty basket. We were delighted with the coming and going, the weighing and stacking, and doubly delighted when we got a tip.

Egg matzohs—a very special item—were generally not made for sale to the public. The religiously orthodox Jews would not eat egg matzohs. In addition, making matzohs with eggs made them more expensive. There were some people, however, who were ailing and required egg matzohs for their diet. There were also some elderly people who found it easier to chew and digest the egg matzos than the hard regular matzos. We baked and distributed egg matzos for these special cases. It was a generally accepted custom and did not require rabbinical approval.

The making of the egg matzohs at the very end of our labors was, if one may use a musical term, the coda to our performance. It came, after the basic operation had been completed, as a sort of encore. We were celebrating what we had done and showing off what we could do. Here's the sequence of events in the making of the egg matzohs:

Once we were done with making the regular matzohs, we would pay all the hired hands for their work. That same evening, those who wanted to have egg matzohs would bring their eggs to us. We would weigh the required amount of flour, and the process would be under way.

We would add the egg to the basic mixture, instead of mixing the water and flour alone; then the kneading followed. After that, the dough would be cut and then passed on to the *redlers* to punch the usual holes, after which the customary process would continue. At each step, as one person's portion was finished, we moved on to the next batch.

The dough for the egg matzohs was handled by young Jewish girls who had volunteered for the undertaking. They rolled the dough, which was then handed over to the *redlers*. After that, my cousin and I would do as we did with the regular matzohs, draping them on a pole, flipping them on to the oven's surface, baking and then retrieving them, placing the finished product in the customer's wicker basket or onto an awaiting white sheet.

The process was continuous. As we completed one stage for one batch, we would start moving on the next batch. And thus it went until the finale, the making and baking of the last egg matzoh. And when that was done we could heave a great sigh, relax, and wait for next year, God willing, for this enlivening enterprise to be repeated.

Once the matzoh routine was finished, we had to apply ourselves to getting ready for Passover itself. In a way, the celebration of the holiday per se was less attractive and exhilarating than the happenings leading up to the seder; the work we did in advance of the ceremony overshadowed the formal ceremony itself.

The baking of the matzoh was the equivalent, in our small town, of a big show taking place in a big town. It involved a sizable cast of players and spectators and, I must confess, was a chance for me to show off my skills as well as add my meager bit to the family income. Baking was our way of "making it," however modest our life-style. My guess is that while my earnings did not go to elevate our way of life, they did, in fact, help to pay off the family's debts to the relatives and friends who had helped us in time of need. Our "bankers" for borrowing were our buddies.

In preparation for the Passover ceremony itself we would rearrange our rooms, moving around the furniture, and we would employ someone to whitewash the walls. Then we would set about converting the matzoh into farfel and matzoh meal, a chore that took my father and myself several days to complete. The pounded products would then be sifted and made ready for use, especially for making matzoh balls for Passover soup. We would store the matzoh farfel and matzoh meal in laundered white pillowcases, and in that way, would have these special Passover ingredients at hand for any other future use.

Just as Passover was characterized by its designated foods, so, too, were we obliged to prepare our utensils for use on this special holiday. This process began two days before Pesach. My sister and I would gather up our pots and pans, our polished silverware and the like, and take them to the public bathhouse described earlier. But this time we went, not to cleanse our bodies, but to cleanse all those things that were involved in our cooking, eating, and drinking during the days of Passover.

In the bathhouse was a large cauldron of hot boiling water. We would dip the dishes, pots and pans, and utensils into the water. We'd repeat this three times to make certain they all were well and truly cleansed. Upon removal, these purified objects would then be rinsed in cold water. Then we'd bring back the "kosherized" objects ready for use at our historic ritual.

All this we'd do in accordance with religious prescription, although I would say that our family was not truly religious in the orthodox sense. I, for instance, did not attend a religious school or go to a yeshiva. My sister and I went to a public school conducted in Yiddish, where we read and studied the Bible as history and literature, but we did not get into religion and *halache* as such. If I were to apply modern measures to the beliefs of my mother and father, I would say that they would have been reasonably comfortable with "conservative Judaism."

Although my parents were not orthodox in their thinking they were, on holidays such as Pesach, followers of the orthodox ways in their practice. Their acceptance of the ritual was motivated more by custom than by law. They were doing what just about everyone else in our Jewish community was doing, with the exception of those who were avowed Communist sympathizers or declared nonbelievers in religion.

As part of our customary observance of Passover we would, on Pesach eve, go through the house and get rid of every sign of *chometz*, such as the daily leavened bread that we ate all year round with the exception of the Passover season, when we were limited to matzoh. We would light candles, carrying them around to every nook and cranny to spy out signs of the forbidden *chometz*. Armed with a feather and a wooden spoon, we would sweep up any of the outlawed crumbs, tie them to the spoon, and then burn the *chometz* in the oven.

On the afternoon of the day before the first seder, my mother and sister would go to the bathhouse; my father and I would go the following day.

I've related a few things about the bathhouse, especially the sort of vigorous rubdown to which we were subjected. That exercise was only part of a larger operation.

This "Russian" bathhouse was a brick building of three rooms. The entrance room was used for disrobing and for "parking" clothes while you engaged in your routine. Then there was a room with a large kettle of heated water and a *mikvah*, through which circulated the ever-refreshing water of the brook. This second room was also commonly used for disrobing as well, especially in the winter when the outer room was quite chilly. The second room was warmed up by the steam coming out of the heated kettle. Then there was a third room, the one used for the "Russian" ritual called the *pleitze* that I described in an earlier chapter.

The bath served as a prelude to Passover week. After the steam room, we would go to the outer room, dry up, and put on our best clothing for attendance at *shul*. That evening the holiday was on its way.

To me, Passover meant eight days of fun—no school, many games to play, and eating the long anticipated Passover foods. My favorite—the tempting taste lingers in my mouth even now—were the matzoh balls. My mother made them, often stuffing them with chopped liver or, my super-favorite, goose cracklings. These *gribenes*, sautéed in the fat of the skin (the word cholesterol was unknown to us) were browned to a crisp and devoured with meat or chicken, or as a nosh by themselves. To get the maximum flavor out of the *gribenes,* we would often cut them open to liberate the *neshomale,* the soul of the dark delicacy. The aroma would whet our appetite and lend added zest to the surrounding dishes.

Another of my favorite dishes was beet soup, called *russel* in Yiddish. I used to break up pieces of matzoh, scatter them in the soup, let them soak a bit, then gobble the well-dunked morsels.

Although *russel* and borscht were both soups made of beets, they did not taste alike, the reason being the former was made out of beets that had fermented. As I've explained, certain foods were allowed to ferment in order to preserve them for the months when fresh food would not be easily available; *russel* was one such food. It was, so to speak, a first cousin to borscht, but it was sharper and clearer, with a bit of a bite and without chunks of beet floating about.

There were two other items that had to be prepared in advance of Passover, both wines, but they were not made of grapes: One was made out of cherries and the other out of raisins. The cherry wine was prepared and bottled in the summer, when the supply was readily available. The raisin wine could be made almost any time, since raisins could be found in stores all year round.

Another alcoholic beverage, which we sometimes drank together with sponge cake or matzohs, was called mead. Although we thought of that word as Yiddish, the same word, pronounced somewhat differently, is used in English to describe a beverage made from a mixture of hops and honey that has been allowed to ferment.

One of our popular desserts was compote—again, a word that occurs in both Yiddish and English with slightly different pronunciations. Compote was made of dried fruits, such as apples and pears, that had been sliced and strung up to dry; to these fruits would be added prunes or raisins, which could be bought in the stores. The mixture was then stewed. Although a dessert, we indulged ourselves by using it as a nosh with matzohs.

As I look back on my eating habits I conclude that I was, without thinking of myself as such, inclined naturally toward being a vegetarian. I never cared much for meat or chicken. I was strongly inclined to favor foods made of potatoes or grains, or dairy products made of milk.

Although we were poor and our house was not furnished with

expensive furniture, there was nevertheless a special Passover warmth, a spiritual aroma in the air, that made me feel that our little home was a palace, the place I wanted to be, especially since it was the first holiday away from school after the cold, gray winter.

The walls glistened with the recent whitewashing, decorated with the framed pictures of our uncles, aunts, and their children we had received from America. We loved to stare in admiration at those photos, concluding with childlike innocence that, judging from the way the people in them were dressed, they must, indeed, be personages of some importance in the land across the sea. Every Passover the photos were removed for the whitewashing, then hung back up again in the same place.

The table shone with its white tablecloth. The small windows were draped with lacy white curtains. In the corner sat the wicker basket filled with matzoh, covered with a white sheet. For eight days I had a sense of an external and internal cleanliness, as though I were some angel dwelling in the home of angels.

The seder service my father conducted was, I must say in retrospect, not quite as formal and ritualistic as it is here, although in our town, unlike in America, it was not customary for families and friends to get together in someone's home for the seder.

Those who were more observant than my father and had larger families would celebrate the holiday in the traditional style. They would read the Haggadah word for word, from the very beginning to the very end, interspersing the readings with songs at appropriate times.

My uncle Ruvin's was one such home. There were eight family members—parents and six children. They reveled in the singing, led by my uncle who was looked upon as quite a good *hazan*, a cantor. The ceremony would last long into the night.

Yes, we would also have our seder. We would—the four of us—gather around the table. Since I was the older child, I was the one who asked the four questions. In response, my father continued to read the Haggadah. He would be the only one to do so; the children did not join in. We could read, but we were not expected to participate in the services beyond asking our four questions.

I do remember scary moments when my father would instruct me to open the door for the angel Elijah. I'd be frightened, because I'd heard stories about how gentiles would wait for this moment to throw stones into the Jewish homes. Relations between Jews and gentiles in the small towns of Lithuania were strained, to put it mildly. There were, for example, the "blood libels," anti-Semitic myths about how Jews killed gentile children in order to get the blood necessary for making matzohs. Gentiles periodically engaged in pogroms, rapacious rioting against Jews often ignited by nothing more than too much alcohol in the heads of those who believed these absurd fantasies.

The Lithuanians were not the only ones who made a mockery of the spirit of Passover; there were young people in town who were antireligious. They, too, would wait for the door to be opened for Elijah, and then they would turn a goat loose into the house. This, of course, was a joke, but the gentile raids on Jewish homes were far from humorous. They were a grim reminder that the life of a Jew was not an easy one, even after many centuries of liberation from Egyptian bondage.

We had our seasonal games for Passover, almost all played with nuts, generally hazelnuts. Since these nuts were quite expensive, we looked upon them as the equivalent of cash. We did not eat the nuts; if we won the nuts in our games, we would sell them.

The most popular game we played with the nuts was one that attracted many players, in fact the more the merrier. To play it we needed some real space—about thirty feet long by fifteen feet wide—and a hard floor made of wood or cement.

We'd draw a line about two feet away from the longer of the two walls. Each player would place one hazelnut on that line separated by ten inches from the nuts placed by the other players, so that if there were six players, for example, there would be six nuts ten inches apart.

The object of the game was for the player to hit the first or second nut at the left end of the line with a little steel ball. If the player was successful, he or she took all the nuts to the right of the one that had been hit. So if you hit the nut at the extreme left, let's say, you then took all six nuts. If you hit the one second from the left, you took all five nuts to the right. If you missed, you had to add a nut.

Another game with nuts involved two people—banker and player. The banker would stand erect; the player would place a hazelnut on the floor next to the outside of the banker's shoe. The banker would take aim by putting a nut to his eye and then dropping it. If he hit the nut, he won the nut from the player. If he missed, he forfeited his nut to the player.

Another game with nuts was called *coopke*. You drew two parallel lines on the floor some nine or ten feet apart. On one of the lines you would cram four nuts closely together and add a fifth on top, creating a little mount that we called a *coopke*. The players would take turns tossing nuts at the mound from the other line on the floor. If you hit the *coopke*, you would pick up all the nuts; if you missed, your opponent would pick up the nut you had unsuccessfully tossed.

Another game involved two caps and nuts. There were two players. One would leave the room; the other, meanwhile, would hide a stipulated number of nuts in one cap, leaving the other cap empty. When the opposing player returned to the room, he had to guess which hat held the nuts. If he guessed right, he won the nuts; if he guessed wrong, he had to compensate you for the number of nuts hidden in the first cap.

Cashing in the nuts we'd won gave us a lesson in marketing. We would generally go to a storekeeper to make the sale. Sometimes the price would be right, but at others it would be wrong, so we quickly learned how to bargain and compromise.

According to tradition, Passover was a time to celebrate liberation from slavery in Egypt. For me it was a time of personal liberation as well, a liberation from hibernation. It was a time to "pass over" from the rigors of school and the iron grip of winter to the joy of friendship and the thaw of spring. I'd feel externally renewed and internally reborn.

In my eyes, Passover was the pleasant pivot around which our little world whirled.

TWELVE
More Holidays

Thirty-three days after Passover came the joyous holiday of *Lag Ba-Omer*. In Hebrew, the holiday is abbreviated by the letters *lamed* (L) and *gimel* (G). In Hebrew, where the alphabet also serves for numbers, the *lamed* and *gimel* add up to the number thirty-three.

Lag Ba-Omer was the one day between Passover and *Shavuot* you were allowed to cut your hair, have a wedding, go swimming. This happy time stood in sharp contrast to the six-week periods before and after *Lag Ba-Omer*, a span of many days dedicated to mourning.

As kids, we observed the restrictions. We mourned, but we did not then know why or for whom we were mourning. Only subsequently did I learn that we were mourning the death of the two thousand disciples of Rabbi Akiva who had died in a plague some two thousand years ago. What we did know was that you did not dare go swimming during this mournful period for, if you did, you would certainly drown. So we abstained from this and other pleasures with no exceptions but for the one day of *Lag Ba-Omer*.

Actually, that day generally fell at a time when it was too chilly for swimming anyhow. So we would wait for the coming of *Shavuot* to jump into the river and splash around. Weather permitting, along with family and friends I would cross the river into the forest for a picnic. And, as noted earlier, when I joined the Zionist youth we would repeat these outdoor exercises outfitted in our natty blue uniforms.

Our holidays were often closely connected with the seasons. Just as Passover signalled the coming of spring, so *Shavuot* signalled the coming of summer. On that holiday we would go to *shul* in the evening and, upon return home, we would have a dairy dinner. As you know, I favored dairy foods, and among these favorites none surpassed the cheese blintzes my mother made with homemade sour milk.

For us, *Shavuot* was a day to relax, a time to commune with Mother

Nature, to embrace the outdoors. We would go to the forest with our family and friends, like the Shmucklers, bearing our picnic goodies. In this I suppose we were continuing the ancient tradition that designated this day as the beginning of the wheat harvest. It was a day to begin to reap the rewards of the hardships we had endured during the winter.

Just as there were days dedicated to reaping so, too, were there days dedicated to weeping. *Tishah B'Av* was one of them. It was a day of fasting in sorrowful commemoration of the destruction of the temple in Israel, first by the Babylonians and, after it was rebuilt, by the Romans.

As children we did not fast. Neither did my parents. In fact, none of the people with whom we customarily associated fasted. There were, of course, some people, usually older and certainly more religious, who did, in fact, observe the fast. Although we were aware that this was a fast day, we did not pay it the same attention we bestowed on Yom Kippur, the Day of Atonement, which was also a day to abstain from food and drink.

Those who did observe *Tishah B'Av* spent most of the day praying in the synagogue. Taking off their shoes, they would sit on low benches or boxes as though they were sitting *shiva* for the dead in their own homes.

From the upper part of the *shul*, where the women sat, one would hear wild weeping and shrill cries. Sometimes these outbursts of anguish were so loud that they drowned out the mournful moans of the men, who were up front facing the east and the site of the holy ark.

The tears these people shed and the painful sounds they emitted were, for them, far more than a mere piety. They knew what had happened. They knew what the Romans had done to the Jews—how they'd burned the temple, slaughtered our sons and daughters, and driven us out of our land, scattering our people like so much dust tossed in the wind.

But we, in our childish innocence, knew none of this. And so, on a few occasions, the day provided an opportunity for juvenile mischief. We would go to the fields, collect some burrs, and hide them under our shirts. Then we would enter the *shul* and throw the burrs at the people who were engaged in solemn prayer. After our first fling we would run away, reload our shirts with burrs, and return for a second foray into the temple. This time we might look for old men with long beards, in the hope that we could entangle their beards in the burrs we tossed at them. For us, it was all fun and games. Then, bored with pestering the worshippers, we would toss the burrs at one another. We did not want to destroy the holy spirit in the synagogue; we were just indulging our unbridled animal spirits.

Before the day was over people would go to the cemetery (the *guten ort*), to pray at the graves of loved ones they had lost.

As in all cultures in all lands, there was a day set aside to greet the new year. Literally translated from Hebrew, Rosh Hashanah means "New Year."

There was not a lot of anticipation and preparation for this holiday, either in our house or in the houses of our friends and neighbors; things ran normally. We'd go to the public baths the day before. Mother would bake a round *challah*, with its symbolic lion's paws.

We did like the fact that this was a day without school, but on the other hand we were expected to go to *shul* to participate in a somewhat disorganized and uninspiring ritual. I say "disorganized" because it seemed, despite the presence of the rabbi, that nobody was really in charge of running the event. There were no prayer books; we each had to bring our own book from home. With our limited resources, we—and many others—could hardly afford to buy new books every time another person was added to the family, so the *sidurim* were handed down from generation to generation with pages crumbling, torn, or missing. There were no announcements as to what pages we were supposed to be reading at a given time.

We did know how to read the Hebrew, but we were not truly conversant with the language. We could barely make an accurate translation, and we were certainly ignorant as to what the passage really meant. And since we generally had to share the prayer book with someone else, we might often find a page turned while we were still in the middle of reading it. The experience was, in short, an exhausting bore.

It was also the custom to assign seats to certain persons, something that was done unofficially but nevertheless quite proficiently. Certain families would have a whole bench set aside for them, and no one dared challenge that fact or invade the turf of the occupant. These privileged pews were passed on from generation to generation within the family.

Some of the elite also had lecterns installed in front of their seats which gave them a place to rest their prayer books as well as a convenient spot to tuck away their prayer shawls. The lectern also served another purpose for the truly devout who would spend hours praying while standing on their feet: They could get some relief by leaning forward on the lectern.

Our seats were located on a bench that we shared with the family of my uncle Ruvin. As you entered the synagogue, our bench was located to your left. From the left wall, it extended to within six feet of the center *bema* of the synagogue. On the *bema,* which was elevated about four feet above the floor, the Torahs were placed and were read aloud when taken out of the holy ark which, of course, was located on the eastern wall.

Seats on the eastern wall were occupied by the dignitaries, starting with the rabbi. Sharing that honored location with him were two of the town *shochets.* They were half brothers, and one of them was also the *Bal Kriah,* the person assigned to reading the Torah. I remember him as a very nice man with a flowing red beard whose rendition of the readings was always flawless.

Other persons of distinction who were honored with benches at the eastern wall either made greater contributions to the synagogue, had the reputation of better understanding the *gemora,* or were one of the *gabais* (lay officers of the temple).

There were several self-appointed townspeople who, during Rosh Hashanah, would lead the *davening.* They would go to the pulpit and pray out loud and clear, setting the tone and tempo for the congregation. One such was my uncle Yankel, the husband of my father's sister Elke. He had a pleasant style and preferred to play the lead role at the morning prayers and on Saturdays.

For the noon, or *musof,* services, most synagogues with the necessary financial resources would engage a *hazan* who would, in a strong and sonorous voice, address himself to the Almighty on behalf of the entire congregation. The same *hazan* would often play an identically chanting—and enchanting—role on Yom Kippur. In our town we did not have an officially designated *hazan,* although we did have a few congregants who, though they lacked professional training, were quite good.

One of them, who would lead us in the *davening* on some holidays, was my uncle Ruvin Jaffe. Ruvin's talents ran in many directions. Apart from being one of the two town butchers, he was also a good bricklayer. He had a good voice; and, since he lived right next to the *shul,* it was easy for him to drop in and lead us in prayer. He would, quite often, alternate with the *schochet* who was the *Baal Kriyah.*

There must have been a bit of a cantorial or a theatrical gene running in our family. My uncle Ruvin (who was really my granduncle) had a brother, Shabseh, who emigrated to the United States and settled in the Williamsburg section of Brooklyn. There, on high holidays, he officiated at the services of the Bialystoker *shul.* When he did, there would be a big sign outside the synagogue announcing the program for the holidays. In large letters it would proclaim, The World Renowned Cantor, Shabseh Jaffe, Will Conduct the High Holiday Services Here.

Yes, it must have been in the blood. The late Morris Jaffe, in his later years, was very much involved in synagogue activities and would lead the congregation in their daily prayers.

On Rosh Hashanah, many women would attend the services, sitting in a separate section from the men. They'd be assigned to the second floor, above the entrance door to the *shul.* The balcony where they sat was walled off from the rest of the synagogue; it was, however, equipped with windows that could be opened into the *shul.* My mother would attend every so often with my sister; I would look up to get their attention.

After the services we would, as young kids do, run around outdoors in front of the *shul.* My sister and I would share a piece of cake that my mother had brought for us. (Jewish mothers considered it a primary responsibility to feed the children at all times; *Ess, ess, mein kind.*) Then we would go home to a standard holiday meal of chicken soup followed by chicken and potatoes. What I loved most, however, was the *challah* dunked in honey.

While Rosh Hashanah was, at best, just a day marking the coming of a New Year, Yom Kippur was a holiday with a very special moral meaning: It was the Day of Atonement. It was assumed that you had sinned, and now was the time for you to admit it and get rid of your sins—to atone.

The way to do so was to *shlug kapores,* which was a symbolic transfer of guilt from a person to a fowl who would be slaughtered or sold. My father and mother would *shlug kapores* by seizing a rooster by the leg, raising it, reciting a special prayer, and whirling the rooster over their heads three times.

As children we did the same thing, except that we used coins instead of a chicken. After the ritual we'd take the money to the synagogue. There we'd find long tables set up for the occasion, each with plates designating a given charity, where we would deposit the money we had consecrated in the *kapores* ritual.

That's what happened with our *kapores* money. The chickens were destined for another fate. I went to the rabbi to buy a ticket from him to license the *shochet* to slaughter the chicken. This was really a self-imposed "tax" through which the community supported the rabbi. Then I paid the *shochet* his standard fee to slaughter the rooster, which I would take home to Mother, who would prepare it for the evening meal preceding our twenty-four hour fast.

This was all done on Yom Kippur eve. The next day we did not eat. The Day of Atonement was a day of fasting, of serious abstinence. It was a day to remind us of the sin of self-indulgence, and of the need to think about what should be done to help others.

Yom Kippur was also a time to pay respects to our departed ancestors. In this ritual, it was my responsibility to get two candles about twenty inches tall. They were exceptionally long because they had to last for a whole day, for twenty-four hours. Since we did not then have *yahrzeit* lights set in glasses, as we now do, we set the candles in a vessel containing sand. One was for my father's dead parents and the other was for my mother's dead father. They were placed on the windowsill close to where we sat. My father would light the candles at an early hour, before the service started.

I was twelve years old when I first fasted. I have observed the fast every year since then, right down to the present.

Before the fast began I would spend part of the day in the synagogue. Restless, as most kids of my age were, I would bounce in and out of *shul*. My sister, four years younger than I, would sit with my mother in the balcony. She would come down at intervals to offer me some honey cake, some *challah* or an apple.

Mother would not stay in the synagogue for any length of time. She had to leave because the air was insufferable. The windows were closed; the burning candles ate up the oxygen. There was no ventilation, because to open the windows would let in drafts that would extinguish the candles. As a result, the synagogue was soon filled with the suffocating odor of the burnt wax. It was too much for Mother, and so she left early—as others did. Nevertheless, there were the truly pious, who went through the ordeal from beginning to end without even sitting down for a moment's rest. To keep themselves going they came with smelling salts, which were passed around regularly.

Yom Kippur, I understood, was derived from a biblical injunction that called upon us "to make atonement before the Lord." That commandment was interpreted by the sages to mean that one should "abstain from food and drink" and like bodily indulgences. Every male of thirteen, and every female of twelve, had to observe this stricture.

According to rabbinical interpretation, Yom Kippur is a day for persons to atone for their sins against God but not for those committed against fellow humans. It was, nevertheless, customary on Yom Kippur eve for pious Jews to seek reconciliation with anyone they might have offended during the year, so that they could begin their Yom Kippur prayers with a clean conscience. I believe that, generally speaking, Yom Kippur is the holiday most commonly observed by Jews, including those who do not habitually adhere to the traditional Jewish way of life during the rest of the year.

Just as Yom Kippur is based on a line from the Bible that calls upon Jews to "make atonement before the Lord," so too is a subsequent holiday, Sukkah, based on the closing lines of Leviticus, which say, "Ye shall dwell in booths seven days that your generation may know that I made the children of Israel to dwell in booths when I brought them out of the land of Egypt." The word, sukkah, means "booth." Our family never had a sukkah. Neither did any of our friends or neighbors. The Jews in our town of Kavarsk had the reputation of being very liberal, more secular than religious. Although there were some families that did build sukkah, I do not myself recall ever reciting prayers in one.

Although we had no sukkah, we did celebrate the holiday in our own fashion. In the synagogue there were a few *lulavs* (the shoot of a palm tree) and *etrogs* (a lemonlike fruit, but much larger). We would join in the morning prayers and bestow the appropriate blessing over the *lulav* and the *etrog*. After my bar mitzvah, I would look forward eagerly to the moment when I could get involved in the Sukkah ritual. I would grasp the *lulav* in one hand and the *etrog* in the other. And then, while making the blessing, I would extend the *lulav* in front of me three times, each time giving it a little shake. Then I would repeat these motions in all directions—to my right, to my left, and behind me.

Sometimes, the *shames* of the *shul* would bring the *lulav* and *etrog* to some of the houses in town to give the women a chance to perform the ritual in their own homes.

In one way or another, all our holidays were history lessons that recalled one or another episode or concept recorded in the Torah. So it should come as no surprise that there should be at least one holiday dedicated to the Torah itself, Simchas Torah, which literally means "rejoicing over the torah." As children we loved this day even though, in our tender years, we did not know what the holiday really meant. All we knew was that it was a joyous occasion.

This holiday, quite appropriately, came immediately after the last passages of the last of the five books of the Torah were read. The Torahs were removed from the ark and given to the congregants in the synagogue. They would parade about (*hakofes*) with the Torahs on their shoulders. Their line of march would carry them once around the *bema;* then they would come to a halt in front of the ark. Having completed their appointed round, they would turn the Torahs over to other congregants who, in their turn, would repeat the traditional course, and so it went until everyone who wished to participate had a chance to be a carrier of the Torah.

We children were not left out of these festivities. We marched with those who were carrying the Torah; we carried flags; and some of us carried little houses.

These wooden houses, resembling birdhouses, were constructed by us under the direction of our fathers. We would decorate them on the inside and the outside. The houses had windows, which we covered with multicolored paper that glowed with a variety of hues. We decorated the outside with blue and white crepe paper. On the inside of the house would be a lighted candle. Proudly we would mount these lighted houses with their sparkling colors on a long, heavily decorated stick, and we'd hold our handiwork aloft as we joined in the march around the *bema* to the ark.

This bit of showmanship served a double purpose. First, it was a chance to show off just who had the most beautiful house, a playful bit of childish rivalry. Second, we played a war game that might have been called Arson. We tried to set one another's house on fire. If you could do it to someone else, you were a hero; but to defend yourself against someone doing it to you, you rode about mounted on your father's shoulders, holding the stick and the house as high in the air as possible.

That's how we celebrated Simchas Torah. It was a moment for merriment and mischief.

When, the next day, we returned home from *shul,* my father and his friends would open a bottle of vodka. I used to wait with bated breath for the cork to pop. The opening of the bottle was, in itself, quite a feat. It was not opened with a cork screw or anything else so mundane. Instead, the bottle was held at a forty-five degree angle, with the nose pointing upward, and hit on the bottom forcefully with a slap of the palm. It was a true demonstration of virility that sent the cork flying. What fun!

Then the men would drink a couple of shots of vodka, with herring and *challah* serving as hors d'oeuvres. When they were done I collected the empty bottles, took them to the government store, got two cents for each returned bottle, and used the money to buy some sucking candy. (As you can see, my talents as an entrepreneur emerged at an early age. They were to come in handy in subsequent years.)

There was one other holiday we enjoyed, although it was not an official holiday and it is not mentioned in the Torah. It came on the last day of June. That, the Lord be praised, was the last day of school. Like the children of Israel leaving Egypt, we were free at last—free to run around barefoot with bleeding toes, to play with our friends in town and from the outskirts of town, free to tend to our many daily chores at home.

In our childhood, in our town, there was a disease from which we never suffered: we did not know about the ailment called boredom. We were never bored. We had no radio, no movies, no TV, yet we were never bored. We had things to do—whether in school or on vacation. There were the things we had to do, the chores that kept us occupied. There were the things we liked to do—our games, our bits of mischief, our picnics, our rivalries and our revelries.

Our town was a world that kept us on our toes, a place of excitement and enthusiasm, of challenge and response. It was a place where we sowed the seeds of hope and looked forward to reaping a harvest of happiness.

THIRTEEN
Our Town

I should like to share with you a few details about the life we lived, a life far removed from the hustle and bustle of the big cities, yet a life that silently spoke to us about the joys of living.

Now that school was out, my sister and I slept late. No need to get up and around to go to class. No need to bolt down a breakfast of bread and butter with a tea or postum chaser or, if we were running behind time, to eat our dark bread on the way to school.

Without the pressure to get to school on time, I did indeed sleep late. When I got up, one of my first chores was to remove and empty the *nacht tepel*, the night potty, which was kept in the house and used by all those who, in the course of a long night, needed relief. To take care of this *tepel* was one of my responsibilities. I would carry it from the house and empty it behind the stable.

Once done with this chore, I would return to the house to have the usual bread, butter, and hot tea. That was followed by errands I had to run for my mother. If the water bucket was empty, I would go to the well and bring back a bucket of fresh water. I would do some shopping at the small grocery store owned by our cousin Sora. There I would buy some things mother needed. My purchase would be charged and entered in Sora's book. At intervals, we paid her in cash, always lagging behind somewhat since we seemed never to have enough to catch up.

I had little time to see my father in the morning. With his partners, he would take turns being in charge of the bus. They would alternate every month, and when my father's turn came, he would leave the house very early and not return until evening. Even when he was not the conductor, he'd leave at the crack of dawn and go to the marketplace to make sure everything was in order. The bus would leave at 6:00 A.M.

After helping with the chores at home, I would get together with my friends for street play. We would run around town chasing a round metal hoop with a handmade wire handle about two feet long, which enabled us to roll and guide the hoop. This homemade toy afforded us hours of entertainment, exercise, and excitement.

We got the same kick out of playing soccer. We used the school yard for our playing field, and although there were few occasions when we had a genuine soccer ball, that didn't bother us; we used a simple rubber ball instead.

Still another game was called "driving the bus." We had one all to ourselves because, after my father and his partners bought a new, more up-to-date bus, they'd abandoned the old bus on one of the partner's property. My friends and I would make believe that this old vehicle was the real thing, simulating the trip from Kavarsk to Kovno.

Since I was the son of one of the owners, I had the honor of being the chauffeur at the steering wheel. Another one of us would be the conductor, whose responsibility it was to announce the time of departure, make certain that all were aboard, and announce the towns through which we were passing.

Since I was the chauffeur, I'd grab the wheel and steer the stationary bus on its imaginary course. I would also imitate the kinds of noises the bus would make on a straightaway and then, imitating the sounds of shifting gears as we climbed a make-believe hill, I would exaggerate the harsh rumbling noise of the engine. In effect, I was both the bus and the bus driver.

We did not have toys, bicycles, tricycles with which to play. But we did have an indispensable sense of invention and imagination that kept our heads and hands busy. No time left over for boredom.

Living in a house quite close to ours was my mother's first cousin, Zelda Rapshonsky. She was married to a man in Kavarsk named Ruvin Rapshonsky. He was the only Jew in town who owned a fairly sizable farm outside the town itself. Their town dwelling was quite comfortable, with stables for horses and cows. The family had two boys, one my age, named Shmulke, and a younger son named Henechke.

One day, Shmulke invited me to come to his house to see a present he had received. I raced to his house and he showed me something I had never seen before: It was a tricycle. Ordinarily this would have been something to take outdoors and pedal through the streets, but that was not possible during that particular season in Kavarsk. The street surfaces were irregular, bumpy, and muddy. But that did not stop Shmulke from finding a more usable terrain for his newfound toy.

The house was large; in my eyes, very large. It had a spacious kitchen, a large living room, a hallway with bedrooms on either side, and a storage room. They were all connected, giving Shmulke a private raceway for his three-wheeler.

Needless to say, the spirit of adventure overcame me and I had to try riding the tricycle. It wasn't easy. First, I had to learn how to mount it. It felt quite uncomfortable; I could not adjust to having my feet straddle the front wheel, to reach the pedals and rotate them. As I tried to do all these things at once—hold firmly to my seat, push the pedals, and simultaneously steer the wheels—I toppled.

But I was undeterred. After repeated falls and several negligible bruises, I mastered the art of riding a tricycle. This, for a kid of eight or nine, was no mean experience. I felt as though I was, in effect, riding a craft imported from outer space.

I earlier described the uses to which the river Shventa was put in the winter. In the summer, it was a fountain of fun as we bathed and swam in its cool waters. It was also a waterway for transporting logs.

Beyond the river, as I have noted earlier, was the forest of pine trees that extended for many miles to the town of Kurkel, located about seven miles away from Kavarsk. To get to Kurkel, it was necessary to travel by horse and wagon through a narrow sand road that wound its way through the forest. A family outing into that fantastic forest with the Shmucklers was something we looked forward to on Saturdays after eating our *cholent*.

The *cholent* I liked best was made of potatoes and meat, mixed with prunes and wrapped in dough for a kugel. The making of the *cholent* was a communal undertaking.

On Friday, after mother had baked the *challa*, Russian *babke* or danish, some friends and neighbors would come to our house bearing potatoes, beans, barley, meat, and *kishkes* in earthenware or clay pots. The tops of the pots would be covered with brown paper. We would place the pots (*shtel arain*) in the oven, and there the content would cook, simmer really, for a full twenty-four hours.

The next day, Saturday, when the men returned from *shul* at about ten in the morning, the pots would be reclaimed by our friends and neighbors. The cooked food was called *cholent*.

After eating the *cholent*, mother would take some cakes she had made. We would also take some soda and lemonade, which we'd bought. We'd make certain that we took along a large blanket to spread out on the ground for our forest picnic. Invariably we'd include a hammock, which we would hang between two trees, and, in anticipation of our frolic in the river, we would put on our bathing shorts.

Now we were ready for our journey to the river and forest. Crossing the river was also a bit of an adventure, as there was no bridge. We'd cross on a raft made up of two boats connected with large, heavy planks across them. The "raft" was attached to a cable that spanned the river and ran through a wooden housing on top of the raft. A man—a strong man—equipped with a wooden hand clamp wrapped around the cable would then pull the raft from one side of the river to the other. This "ferry" had been devised to accommodate a horse and wagon and also to service the people who wanted to visit spots outside our town.

The concession to operate the raft was awarded by the town government, which also fixed the charges for passengers. There were times in midsummer when the river was very low and we could wade over certain spots to save a few pennies.

When, during a picnic, our parents stretched out to get some rest, we would go swimming in the river and go picking wild raspberries, *padjamkes*, or nuts. Picking anything in the pine forest was not an altogether pleasing experience. The forest floor was covered with prickly pine needles and cones and our feet were covered with nothing. Walking through the forest in our bare feet was like walking on pins and needles, but we endured the discomfort and were none the worse for our encounter with nature in the raw.

Some of the older boys had rowboats that they would move and maneuver in the river. My father discouraged me from joining in. There were, at various times, swift currents in the river at unpredictable points, hence it was not always possible for a young boy to control the boat. Indeed, someone from town who was boating did lose control, the boat capsized, and the boater was drowned.

The routine briefly described above was followed Saturday after Saturday, almost as if it was a religious ritual. We would occasionally go down to the river during the week, primarily to wash and not to swim.

There was one particular spot where the river flowed alongside a meadow and a thick cluster of bushes; this spot was the property of the church. It was unofficially designated as the place where men and women could bathe in separate areas, and do so in the nude. Despite these precautions to preserve privacy, some of us naughty boys did, now and then, sneak a peek at the forbidden figures.

Our family would go there to bathe. We would cross the meadow in back of our house and then the meadow belonging to the church. When we got to the river, we passed the section reserved for the women and proceeded past the section meant for the men. When we finally finished the trek to our chosen point we would take our bath. When we were done, Father would give the signal to Mother. We dressed and went home.

My friends and I went there quite often to swim. In the distance, we would see some of the girls we were friendly with swimming in the river. One of us would sneak up behind the bushes where the girls had disrobed and left their clothes. We would snap up the clothes, hiding them someplace where they'd be difficult to find. When the girls came out to get dressed and could not find their clothes, they began to cry. We would holler back to them and blame it on the cows who, we said, had eaten up the clothes. It was real fun, lots of fun.

The river was not just for bathing and swimming; it also played a significant commercial role: It was used for transporting logs. I used to love to sit on the riverside and watch the rafts (*plitens*) float down the river. They were launched at a city called Utian (Utena), destined for Kovno; the distance between the two points was about one hundred miles. It took about a week to float the logs from the point of origin to the point of destination, as the floating timber moved from our Shventa River into the Vileya and then into the Neman.

The logs were jammed closely together to form what amounted to a raft, generally about one hundred feet long by twenty feet wide. It took two people to guide this huge raft down the river, one man in front and the other in the rear.

On occasion they would stop over in our town, staying overnight, buying supplies and food to carry them through the journey. On the raft they would build a small hut, where they would sleep at night, prepare their meals, and keep their belongings out of the rain or hot sun. What fascinated me most was the way in which the two men manipulated their ungainly, giant craft. The lead rafter would signal and holler to the rear rafter, shouting instructions on what to do to steer the logs around a bend and down the river. I would perch myself on the riverbank, rivetted to the procession of rafts, especially when there were fifteen or twenty of them in a row. The men who guided the logs were, in Yiddish, called *plitnikes*.

On their return from Kovno to Utena, the *plitnikes* would pass through our town. They would arrive by bus, sometimes coming in my father's vehicle. We always knew who they were, because they carried their long wooden guiding poles on the roof of the bus. They also distinguished themselves by the songs they sang, half drunk, after they'd gotten paid.

There was a musician in our town whose name was Moishe Zucker. He had many children, and he taught them all how to play musical instruments.

He had a band made up of himself, his children, and a gentile *barebon*, who played the drums. Moishe and his musicians were well known in Kavarsk and the surrounding towns. He was very much in demand to play at weddings, billed as "Moishe's Kavarskan Capelia" (Moishe and the Kavarskan Band). Moishe himself would play the trumpet, but he was able to play almost any instrument, including the violin. In fact, he gave violin lessons to some of the kids in town.

One of his sons, Yoshke, who was my age, was one of my friends. He survived the Holocaust. Together with my son, Lenny, and his wife, Linda, Leibel Barak (my wife's cousin), my wife and I all went to visit Yoshke's family in Kyriat Ata when we were in Israel. This Yoshke provided still another opportunity for us, as children, to amuse ourselves. He would remove the mouthpieces of the musical instruments and distribute them to his friends, including myself, of course. Eight or ten of us would parade through town, blowing on these mouthpieces as if we were a marching band—still another reason why our dictionary lacked the word boredom.

On Sundays during the summer, a regular happening called a *vetzerinka* took place on the church grounds near the river. The young Lithuanian boys and girls would get together and perform folk dances, polkas, waltzes, and tangos. Music was provided by a Lithuanian accordionist. Although this was strictly a Lithuanian event, there were a few Jewish boys from town who would dance with the Lithuanian shikses. No Jewish girl ever danced with a Lithuanian boy, however. As a very young kid, I was a regular spectator at these dances.

Monday was market day, a day that played a significant role in the lives and livelihoods of the Jewish people in town. Most Jewish merchants and shopkeepers depended heavily on market day to make a living by selling and trading their wares.

The peasants and farmers would come to the market carrying their produce: wheat, butter, vegetables, eggs, chicken, ducks, berries, and the like. These products were generally bought by the Jewish and Lithuanian households in town. Fruit was normally brought to market by Jewish peddlers who had leased orchards on an annual basis from peasants or other orchard owners.

Horses would be bought and sold on market day; cows, calves, and lambs intended for slaughter were not. The reason for this was that our town had only two butchers, who dealt directly with the local peasantry and farmers. They would either buy the animals for cash or get them in an exchange through barter. The butcher then took the purchased animal home to be slaughtered and prepared for sale.

At the end of the day, after the marketed produce was sold, farmers and peasants would go to town to make cash purchases at the stores. Done with their shopping, they would relax by visiting certain Jewish homes to indulge in some vodka with herring and bread. Such houses were usually located close to the marketplace.

The private sale of alcohol was legally forbidden, since this was a government monopoly, but the families that sold vodka from their homes managed to do so somehow, perhaps by establishing good relations with the three local policemen.

The illegally sold vodka would be hidden in attics and cellars. When peasants arrived to make their illicit purchases, the vodka would be sold and served to them in glasses. They imbibed the liquor while chewing on mouthfuls of salty herring, fresh out of a wooden barrel, and slices of black bread. Too often, when a peasant got drunk he would pick a fight with a Jew.

Our house was located about halfway down a hill between the marketplace, which was above us, and a small bridge that made a sharp turn over a brook below us. This strip of road was a real hard for a peasant who'd decided to go home in his horse and wagon while in a drunken state. He would start to go down the incline, and since there was no hand brake to check his rolling wagon, it would move forward swiftly on its own and bang up against the horse's rear legs, whereupon the animal would break into a wild gallop. When the wagon got to the bottom of the hill the horse would not be able to negotiate the sharp turn, and the wagon would hit the low wall of the bridge, capsizing and tossing the drunken driver on his head into the stony brook. The water would turn red with blood. Often—too often—this was the finale of a market day.

One of the recurrent festivities was the annual *yerid*, (fair) known as *yohan*. It was a sort of carnival, without the sideshows and rides we have in the United States. The night before, merchants with their wares would arrive from various towns and the surrounding countryside. They would set up tents and booths in the town square (the marketplace), trying to locate them as close as possible to the church. This would be especially true if the merchant was selling religious icons, which, of course, had a natural appeal to churchgoers.

Although there were many objects on sale, such as combs, folding hand mirrors, double-edged razor blades, women's lotions, soaps, and a variety of novelties, which were normally not sold on market day, what predominated were the religious icons. There was no Lithuanian household without them, be it the richest or poorest.

The church around which this annual event revolved was truly a majestic structure. Its steeple with the cross on top could be seen from miles away. Its many bells could be heard regularly peeling their resounding chimes across the countryside. When I returned for a visit to Kavarsk fifty-three years later, in 1991, the church was still there, intact and still impressive to anyone who looked at it, whether Catholic or not.

The bells were rung by men who pulled on ropes. Not all the bells were rung for all occasions. For instance, one bell might be rung on a given day at a given time to tell the hour. But on *yohan* day all the bells would chime loudly and persistently, summoning all the congregants in the vicinity to come to the fair at the church.

Most of the peasants were illiterate and fanatical. They recited prayers from prayer books written in Latin—a language they did not understand. (This would be not altogether unlike us reciting prayers in *shul* in Hebrew without knowing what our mutterings really meant.)

When the bells rang out for the *yohan* the peasants would respond with fearful reverence, as if the toll of the bell was somehow the tongue of Christ calling upon the faithful to come to the *yerid*. The peasants would come to the *yohan* dressed in their finest. This day was a time to pray to God as well as pay for goods.

A processional would begin at the church, with men dressed in white robes carrying a statue of Christ. They would be followed by priests and then by others carrying more statues, icons, and other religious symbols. The entire congregation would circle the church, then reenter. During these proceedings we, as children, were not to be seen anywhere near the church.

The priest in our town was not one who preached hatred toward Jews, as some others did. (I am, of course, speaking of the time when I, as a youth, lived in Kavarsk. What happened after the Nazis invaded Lithuania, I do not know. I even have difficulty trying to recall whether there were many, or any, fights between Catholics and Jews after church was let out. I do recall, as related earlier, some brawls when one of the peasants had had too much to drink.)

Generally, after church, those who attended would go to the marketplace. Among the various attractions were the gypsy fortune-tellers, who set up their booths to read cards and palms. There were also a few hustlers with their card games. They would toss three cards, face down, on a table; you would have to guess the color of the middle card. As a rule, you guessed wrong and lost the bet.

As children, we would walk around the marketplace to see if there was anything to buy that had not been there last year. We would generally buy nothing because we had no money, and so would leave empty-handed, hoping that next year there would be something novel to "buy."

The *yerid* was an occasion not only for you to buy and sell things, participate in religious ceremonies, get your fortune told, be exposed to a card sharp, and dance and sing, it was also the day designated for you to be treated by a dentist.

We had no dentist in our town. If you had a toothache, you simply ached until the dentist came around for his annual visit to the fair. To alleviate the suffering while awaiting that day, you soaked some cotton in vodka and applied it to the sore spot.

At the *yerid* the person declaring himself to be a dentist would set up a tent with a table in it, on which rested several menacing-looking instruments. He also had a special chair for the unfortunate patient. The operator wore a white smock and a professional face, thus establishing the fact that he was in business and that he knew his business.

When a peasant came to him complaining about a toothache, the self-appointed dentist would sit him down and ask him to open his mouth and point to the spot where he felt the pain. The dentist would poke around a bit and then reach for his pliers, grab the tooth firmly, and just yank it out.

Sometimes, he got the wrong tooth. After all, he had no X rays to guide him. He would then stop the bleeding by placing against the gum a small piece of cotton soaked in iodine. The pain would be excruciating; people would leap out of the chair. The poor peasant, screaming with pain, would not even be certain that the right tooth had been extracted. The dentist assured him that he would feel better the next day. If he didn't, he couldn't complain to the so-called dentist, because the dentist would be off to another *yerid.*

Saturday, the Sabbath, is, according to the Torah, a day of rest. It took God six days to create man and woman and the universe. On the seventh day, according to the Scriptures, He rested, and, as a consequence, we were obliged to do likewise.

That's why we prepared the *cholent* on Friday, so we would not have to toil away on Shabbat to make a meal. In our town, it was customary to enjoy the *cholent*, perhaps take a nap, and then, weather permitting, to go *shpatziring*; that is, take a stroll, an aimless, relaxed, easygoing walk about town, such as God must have taken after his six days of intense labor.

Right after the Saturday prayer session in *shul* was done, people would rush to our home to pick up their *cholent.* Our house, as earlier noted, was a depository for all the cooked goodies for Shabbat because we had an oven that we used for baking and, therefore, available on a Friday to handle the *cholent.* Our oven was made available to all my mother's clients, to those who would buy bread and cakes and the like from her, but it was also available to friends and neighbors as well. The sense of community in our shtetl was built into our circumstances: we needed and counted on one another.

Needless to say, this nonritualistic ritual kept my mother busy on the day of rest. Seeing to it that the pots were properly placed and removed in a timely fashion kept her quite busy. But, as is the custom in most civilizations, housework was not considered "work," and so it was permissible on Shabbat. Every week the same routine was repeated, whether in winter or in summer. Shabbat was Shabbat and did not change with the seasons.

After we had partaken of the *cholent,* some of the older folk would take a nap, a very proper thing to do on the day of rest. After some twenty or thirty winks, they would go *shpatziring,* not as lonely walkers but, in the spirit of the *shtetl,* with their friends and neighbors, as part of a community. They would stroll less as individuals than as an assemblage of associates on a symbolic wandering, whose essence was less where they were going than the fact that they were going wherever they were going together. They were reenacting, on a Saturday afternoon in Kavarsk, the story of the wandering Jew over generations, undoubtedly unaware that they were doing so.

My parents, together with the Shmucklers and some friends and neighbors, would walk to the town square, where they would be joined by my mother's cousin Zelda and her husband, by Chana Rachel and her husband Chatze Dilatski, and by other relatives and guests. All came in their Saturday best. They would start out by walking up Wilkomer Street; then they would walk to the *krenitzeh,* on church property, a short and pleasant walk through an arcade of overarching trees. The spot was called *krenitzeh* because it had bubbling cold springs at the bottom of a hill. Wooden troughs carried that water to the road where other troughs, about six feet high, had been installed, enabling us to get at the water that was in continuous flow. To capture the water for drinking purposes, enamel cups, attached to chains, were made available for our use. This refreshing spot was our "pit stop," an oasis for us, the ever-wandering Jews.

If you stood at the springs and looked upward you were treated to a truly picturesque panorama. At the top of the hill was the residence of the priest, a beautiful spacious house overlooking the countryside and the river. Leading to the top of the hill were steps with benches located at the half-way point to give the climber a chance to relax. Past the roadway and the drinking fountain was another fountain in the form of a showerhead spraying water. The water would, from that point, flow into a large concrete reservoir and would be fed downhill in pipes to a turbine engine, where it would generate enough electricity to light up the church and the residence of the priest.

This *krenitzeh* was the high point of our ritual wanderings for most of the townspeople on a Saturday afternoon—after *cholent.*

When we ended the walk, where there was always a lively discussion about everything, whether personal or communal, we would retire to someone's house and partake of a hot glass of tea served from a samovar. The usually steaming hot beverage was flavored with strawberry or cherry preserves, which were stirred into the glass. The tea was drunk through a lump of sugar held firmly in the mouth between the upper and lower tiers of teeth.

Our town in the Wilkomer (*Ukmergas*) district was known for its liberal thinking. It was also known to have a goodly number of Communist sympathizers. They were not as organized a group as the liberal-minded Zionists, but we knew who they were. Some of them were serving time in jail for belonging to the Communist Party, which had been outlawed.

I shall never forget the morning when we were told that during the night the police, without legal search warrants, had rapped on the doors of several homes and had arrested several of the young people who lived there. The youths were charged with being Communists. Some twenty-five to thirty Jewish youths were hauled away to jail. To the best of our knowledge some of them were not Communist sympathizers at all, and none were card-carrying members of the Communist Party, since there was no such underground outfit in Kavarsk.

After spending a night in jail, they were taken off to Kovno in my father's bus to face trial. There they were held in jail for several months before being tried, at which point most of them were found not guilty and set free. Three or four were found guilty of being Communist Party members and were sentenced to lengthy prison terms. Later on we found out that a Jewish man who worked for the town government had fingered the arrested youths. He was awarded a fee per person for each one who had been tried and found guilty.

After this experience, we were supercautious. We'd never carry red handkerchiefs, and women would never wear red scarves, for fear that the simple wearing of the red might make you a suspected Communist and put you in jail.

Our town had a very active and talented dramatics group, comprised of young people, which would regularly put on plays. While a performance was still in rehearsal stage, notices would be distributed in Kavarsk and surrounding towns. Sizable audiences came by chartered bus or by horse and wagon. The performances took place in the only playhouse in town, belonging to the church. The so-called director and leader of the group was a very talented young lady from somewhere outside Kavarsk. She was also the town photographer.

For us, as children, to see a play was truly a treat. It was a big event in our small town, but rarely did we have a chance to go. We just did not have the money to buy a ticket. I do remember one time, however, when, in rehearsing for a play, the troupe looked around for a child to play a rather simple walk-on role. I do not quite know how it happened, but the group asked me to play the role of that child. I was endlessly elated and thrilled at the thought that, after I learned the part, I would actually be on stage as one of the actors. There was also a fringe benefit; I could see the entire play without paying for it. (It must be remembered that the live play we were occasionally privileged to see was the equivalent, at that time, of our modern movies, videos and TV.)

By the 1930s we were exposed to a glimmer of the cinema. There were men who travelled from town to town by horse and wagon carrying equipment to project silent movies, and one day two such entrepreneurs came to Kavarsk. They went from door to door to announce the time and place—a designated home—where a movie would be shown. Those who came would be charged, of course, and children also had to pay, although a reduced price. We were bursting with anticipation at the thought of seeing a "real movie."

Bear in mind that this movie was to be shown sometime in the early 1930s, at a time when there was still no electricity in town. We were filled with wonderment, not only about the forthcoming film, but also about how the miracle of a movie on a screen could be made possible.

So, there we sat with our eyes glued to a small screen. The men set up a hand-operated generator. By cranking it, electricity would be generated, thereby setting in motion the machinery to project the film on the screen. The process was, to say the least, primitive.

I do not know what the movie was all about, and I am certain nobody else knew either. All we saw were faint figures flitting here and there with the light from the projector going on and off, with uncertain images moving fast or slow, depending on how fast or slowly the hand crank was spun to generate the needed electricity. That was my initiation into the fantasy world of the "flick." That disappointing episode may explain why, for the rest of my life, I have been turned off by movies.

My great-uncle Ruvin Jaffe was one of the two butchers in town. And by the standards then prevailing in Kavarsk, he was considered to be well-off. As a butcher, he and his family were indeed well fed; they never ran out of meat, and meat was a rarity in most Jewish homes in town. Few families could afford to have meat more than twice a week. And some could only indulge on the Sabbath. In Uncle Ruvin's house, it was part of the daily fare.

My uncle did not operate alone. He had plenty of help—a family of six boys and one girl. The boys were, off and on, brought into my uncle's butchering business.

One son, Morris Jaffe, left for America. Another son, Israel, went to the *yeshivah* to prepare for the rabbinate. The youngest son, Baruchke, also went to a *yeshivah* briefly, then returned home. He joined his older brothers in the butcher trade. As a consequence, there were always three or four children in the family business.

The only daughter, Baske (Bessie), who left in 1939 for South Africa to marry her boyfriend Morris Goldman, who had gone there much earlier, was treated like a princess in the house. She was, after all, the only girl in a family with six boys. I was very close to all of them and spent much time in their home.

By town standards, their house was very large. It had six rooms, with the butcher shop in the center and three rooms on each side. One side was known as Bessie's apartment, set aside for her and for special guests. It was tastefully decorated with beautiful furniture and papered walls.

Bessie would spend lots of time in our house as did our cousins Rochke and Hashke, who were all about the same age. Her visits to us became more frequent after her boyfriend left for South Africa. Our home was a sort of social center for the girls, a place where they could meet some boys from our town. This was particularly true in the winter months.

My uncle's house was, for our town, very much up-to-date. The family had the latest English-made bicycle. And it had the latest forms of entertainment equipment—a gramophone and even a radio with attached earphones. (I will have more to say about this later.)

In summer on Saturday evenings after *shul*, the boys would open the windows of their room and play the latest cantorial records sung by Yosele Rosenblatt, Hershman, and other world-famous *chazonim* (cantors). Some of those returning from *shul* would pause to listen. While they may have been attracted by the music itself, what seemed to fascinate them most was the *vox humana* coming out of the horn of a hand-cranked machine. Later, some of the younger folk would gather around the record player to listen to waltzes and tangos and the like.

Although Bessie was much older than I, I found myself spending a great deal of time with her. Neither of us had a job. We would, now and then, have time on our hands. We used to play cards. She was fairly literate and literary, having spent some time in the *gimnasie* (high school) in Wilkomer. She would recount stories she had heard, or about which she had read. At her house, I would repeatedly put on the earphones and tune in the radio, which miraculously carried words and music from far away into this house in our little town.

I would also occasionally help out with the slaughtering of an animal. On a Saturday night, right after *shul*, I would join the *shochet* to slaughter a cow. This took place Saturday night because on the next day, Sunday, the farmers and peasants would come to church and would buy their meat after the services. Also the day after that was Monday, market day, and once more there would be a demand for meat. So, to accommodate the double rush on Sunday and Monday, we did the slaughtering on Saturday night.

Although I helped with the slaughtering, I did no slaughtering myself. My job was simply to provide light by holding up a kerosene lamp that illuminated the spot. The area consisted of a stable and a small yard, part of which had a shed. After the slaughter animals would be hung in that shed, their insides and skin removed.

My cousins, Simon and Hertzke, who were strong and well-built, would spread straw over the ground of the yard where the animals were butchered. They would lead the cow from the stable; they would tie rope around the legs of the cow. At a given signal, one of them would pull the rope and the other would grab the head by the horns, the idea being to throw the animal to the ground. The cow would struggle to get loose, and it would take some time before they were able to topple it on its side. Then they would tie more rope around the cow's legs so that it couldn't move. Then they'd twist its head in such a manner that its mouth faced straight up and its neck was stretched out. At that moment the *shochet*, ready with his *chalef* (long knife), slit the animal's throat in two or three sweeping strokes. The blood would gush into a bucket that was held in readiness; within minutes, the animal was dead. It all seemed so painless.

After the blood stopped spurting, they would drag the animal to a spot where a special rig was located. They'd use the rig to lift the animal by the hind legs until the head was off the ground and the animal was suspended in midair. Then they would open its belly and remove all the insides. They would remove the hide with a sharp knife, ever careful not to damage the hide because to do so would lower the price of the precious skin.

The beef, cut horizontally, would be distributed along religious lines. The upper half was sold to the Jews as kosher; the lower half was sold to the gentiles because it was not kosher. In my role as bearer of the lamp I was really more a spectator than an actor, as I stood there in mute admiration of the skill involved in pulling off this tricky operation.

Among his many talents and pursuits, Uncle Ruvin was a master bricklayer. I recall his building the stove in our house. He was often called upon by the wealthier families in town to do their brick work. Aunt Goldie used to make soap for washing clothes and helped supplement the family income with her sales.

Although Uncle Ruvin derived much joy (*shep nachos*) from the exploits of all his children, he took exceptional pride in his son Israel, who was officially ordained as a rabbi. An especially great occasion took place when Israel came back to Kavarsk to join the family. That Saturday, the rabbi introduced Israel as a distinguished scholar and called upon him to deliver the sermon for the Sabbath.

I believe I lack the words to describe the glorious feeling my uncle must have felt that Shabbat as he sat there in his usual place on our bench, surrounded by family, as we all listened intently to every word of Israel as he stood there in front of the *oren kodesh*, the holy ark, delivering the sermon.

I have often wondered what the deep inner thoughts and feelings of Uncle Ruvin must have been as he, a devoutly religious man, sat there watching his son deliver a sermon that, in turn, would be followed that afternoon by a *musof* service conducted by Uncle Ruvin himself.

There were several people whose livelihood revolved around the synagogue, either directly or indirectly. There were the two butchers, my uncle Ruvin being one of them, who sold kosher meat. There were the two *shochets* I mentioned earlier, one of whom also ran a piece-goods store and the other a grocery store. There was the *Bal Kriah*, who was the Torah reader and *hazan* on holidays. He was compensated for his services.

We also had a full-time rabbi, who derived a livelihood from certain assigned concessions that were given him. If you needed yeast for your baking, for example, you had to buy it from the rabbi. The price was set by agreement with the congregation. Sales were dependable, since just about every Jewish family baked *challah* for Shabbat. If you wished to slaughter a chicken, you had to get a ticket from the rabbi. The price, again, was set by the congregation. Unless you had a ticket, the chicken would not be slaughtered by the *shochet*, whose fee was also set by the congregation. In addition to fee-for-service per client, the *shochet* also received a payment from the congregation itself.

We had several Jewish shoemakers. One, a younger man who lived right across the street from Uncle Ruvin, used to make our shoes. Whenever I had some spare time, I would drop in on him just to observe how he applied his skills. It was all done by hand, using very simple but effectively designed and crafted instruments.

To me, the making of the shoe was a mechanical miracle. Every detail was a delight to watch. What intrigued me most was how he joined the upper portion of the shoe to the inner sole. He would use an awl to puncture holes in both the top section and the sole. Then he'd use a pig's bristle as a needle, with a sturdy thread attached, to stitch the top and bottom parts together. Next, he'd cut the hard leather for the sole, joining inner and outer soles together by piercing holes in both and attaching them with wooden nails.

We had three tailors in town, two Jews and one Lithuanian. The Lithuanian was a young man who had learned his trade in the big city of Kovno. He returned to our town, where he enjoyed a reputation as a fine modern-style tailor. He made the suit I eventually wore to America.

We had one *kirzner* (hat and cap maker) who made our velvet caps. His son was graduated with me from elementary school. We had one *volikes* maker who manufactured our woolen boots, described earlier.

We had quite a few seamstresses. The best known was Dobke, who lived close to our school. Her brother, Arke, was a friend of mine. Working for Dobke as learners and full-fledged seamstresses were several girls including my girlfriend, Yochke Shmuckler.

We also had two blacksmiths to shoe the many horses in town. One of them was both deaf and dumb, but he knew how to shoe a horse.

We had one furniture maker, who doubled as a carpenter. His daughter, Keilke, was graduated from the public school with me. We had one glazier; namely, my uncle, Yankel Hoichman.

We had one chimney sweep. He would come to the job with a long rope attached to a special broom with a weight attached to it. He would climb to the rooftop, drop the broom down the chimney, and proceed with the cleaning. This was a job that had to be repeated quite often. We had wood-burning stoves and ovens, which gave off an awful lot of heavy black soot. The chimney sweep was readily detectable. He walked the streets dressed in a black jacket and pants covered with soot. Around his waist was a *gartel* (girdle), a heavy black rope with a broom dangling from it at his side.

We had one small tannery owned by my father's close friends, the Garber brothers. The tannery, one small building, was located near the brook below the flour mill. To drive the turbine, little rivulets were dammed up and then released; the water would empty into the brook. (I will have more about the flour mill later.)

We had one *vapneh*, a lime-processing plant, owned by a cousin-in-law who was married to my mother's cousin Channa Rochel. Small lime stones lying around the countryside would be collected by people who'd bring them to the *vapneh.*

The plant was basically just a great big hole in the ground; upon this ground, grates were erected. Underneath the grates firewood was piled up and ignited, generating a high heat. On top of the grate were placed the pieces of lime. During the process, the light cast by the fire gave one the feeling of being near an active volcano. This illusion of a volcano was created because the *vapneh* was located on a hill and, at night, the flames lit up the sky. After the firing was completed, the *vapneh* would lie cool and dormant for many weeks.

The processed lime was in great demand. It was mixed with sand to provide plaster for walls, and was also used as whitewash for the same walls. My friends and I would earn a few pennies searching the fields for the raw limestone and cashing it in at the *vapneh.*

The town had one government liquor store and one government-owned cooperative store.

There were a few commercial bakeries, two barber shops, one photographer, one pharmacy, several textile stores, and many grocery and general stores. We had one Jewish bank called the *folks bank* (people's bank), which was a branch of the major Jewish People's Bank of Lithuania headquartered in Kovno. It had its own building on Laisves Alleyia Street, a tree-lined boulevard with a median planted with more trees and flowers.

The town had one police station, three police officers, and a small wooden building that housed the jail.

We had one post office and one telephone, which was housed in the post office building. To make a call, you went to the post office and gave the postman the calling number and information. The postman would crank the telephone by hand to get an operator, to whom he would give the number and other relevant information. You would then stand by and wait for an indefinite time, depending upon the place to which you placed your call.

Getting a phone call from outside the town was a complicated process: The postman would get the call. He would then fetch the party for whom the call was intended. That party would then have to make his or her way to the post office phone to take the call. During all this coming and going, the phone line would be tied up. (I knew of only two Jewish families in town who had private phones in their homes.)

Mail would arrive once a week at the post office. It was brought to our town by horse and wagon from Wilkomer, twenty-four kilometers (fifteen miles) away. The local postman would deliver the mail on foot. If he had a package he would so inform you, and it would be your responsibility to go to the post office, get the package, and carry it home by yourself. The postman would deliver mail to nearby villages by horse and wagon. It took about a week for him to cover his route.

If you wished to send mail, you had to take it to the post office. If the office was open, you brought it in; if the office was closed, you deposited it in a mailbox outside.

There were a variety of orchards in the town and vicinity bearing apples, pears, plums, and cherries. The land was generally owned by small and large landowners who rented it out to Jewish fruit or general-interest merchants.

There were certain unwritten rules that governed the process of renting orchard land from a landowner—a speculative act that might involve considerable losses. In the spring, when the trees were in full bloom, the merchant negotiated with the orchard owner to purchase the forthcoming produce. If the owner accepted, they would close the deal with a handshake; no written contract was involved. If no mutually satisfactory agreement could be reached, the merchant would leave, and the landowner would then try to get a better price from someone else.

In any agreement, there was a certain amount of risk incurred by both parties:

1. Once an agreement was signed, the renter was obliged to pay the orchard owner whatever the stipulated sum might be, and to pay it on time.
2. The payment had to be made regardless of what ensued after the agreement was concluded, whether it be a windstorm, hail, drought, or any other "act of God." If the renter failed to honor that agreement, he would be blackballed by all the landowners and would never again be able to rent land in that vicinity.
3. The orchard owner also ran a risk. If he held out for his price too long, he might be stuck with the orchard and run the same risk as a renter in the event of some natural disaster, so he would try to reach an agreement with a renter as soon as possible in order to avoid unnecessary risks.
4. Some landowners preferred to exercise another option. Rather than rent the land when the orchard was in its blossom cycle, they would wait until the fruits were in full bloom; then they would try to sell the ripe or near-ripe fruit with the expectation that they'd get a better price this way. This option was also risky for the landowner, because he could not know in advance what the weather would be or what he might get for the fruit in the final sale.

I remember Father renting a small orchard of apples and pears, which was then in the blossom cycle. I worked alongside him for a whole summer, picking the fruit from the trees and placing it in the wagon. Once it was filled he would take the wagon to Kovno, but instead of trying to sell the fruit at retail he would sell it to wholesale distributors who, in turn, would sell most of the produce for export to foreign markets. At each stage, the negotiated price depended upon the supply and demand.

That year, Father's venture did not prove to be very profitable. The fruit was plentiful, but it may have been too plentiful to command a good price. I do not recall his renting another orchard after that first experience. What he did do was buy wagons of fruit and transport it for sale in Kovno.

There was a woman in town named Nechame Ettel Orzan who was a fruit merchant. She had two sons. One, named Moishke, was a barber; the other son was named Leibke. (She also had other children in America.) Nechame used to rent orchards from farmers. I remember her as a small woman, slightly built, but a very competent and clever fruit dealer. She was a close friend of my father, whom she held in high esteem and often consulted for advice on various matters.

I was also quite close to that family. The son, Leibke, who, like his mother, was of slight stature, was often my partner as we picked apples in the orchard and loaded them onto the wagon. The apples were then sold in town at retail, or on market days in other towns.

I used to help them a great deal in the summer when it was time to pick the cherries. I would mount the trees on a ladder in order to pick the fruit from the higher branches; we could pick the cherries on the lower branches from the ground. I have a suspicion that, when I first embarked on this tasty adventure, I ate most of what I picked on the spot. I would come home with a bellyful and a bellyache.

The family emigrated to America about 1934. They settled in Cleveland, Ohio, where Nechame Ettel had brothers. (The late Herb Kravitz's father was her brother.) Since our family moved to Boca Raton, Florida, I have seen Moishke (Morris) and Leibke (Louis) there quite often. We love reminiscing about old times in the old town.

This picture was taken in Kavarsk in 1928. At the left of the picture is the flour mill. The water was the reservoir that powered the mill. When I returned to Kavarsk in the summer of 1991, what remained of the town seemed ancient, predating 1928 by half a century.

A wedding picture of my father and mother who were married in 1920 or 1921.

The first bus service in Kavarsk, initiated by my father and his three partners in 1930. It operated between Kavarsk, Ukmerges, Wilkomer, and Kaunas (Kovno). The bus was a Chevrolet.

The only Jewish elementary school in our town (1930). I am the fourth from the left in the front row.

My parents, my sister, and myself (1930). I am eight years old and my sister is four years old.

Dinner on this occasion of my aunt's visit from America with her youngest daughter, Margery (1931). It took place in Uncle Ruvin's house (Morris Jaffe's parents). The girl with earphones is tuned in to the improvised radio service we had in Kavarsk.

Aunt Lena and daughter Sandra with Shrolke and Dovidke.

Cousin Sandra and myself (1937) in a boat on the Shventa River. In the background a raft is being negotiated through the dam by a *plitnek*.

Aunt Lena with my mother behind her (at right), and Sose with aunt Elke behind her (at left) at the grave site of my grandmother Neche Minna.

At the *Krenetze.* From left to right, my mother, cousin Esther, cousin Hannah Rochel, some relatives whose names I can not recall, and cousin Zelda Rapshonsky, Esther's sister.

Cousin Simon Jaffe (at left) with uncle Shmuel Norwitz (mother's brother) in the middle and a friend.

My sister, Neche Minna, at the *Krenetze* in the winter of 1940 when she was 14 years old.

The Shmucklers, their relatives, my mother and sister behind our house. The girl kneeling and holding a little girl is Yochke.

On the occasion of my cousin Sandra's visit from America, (from front to rear) cousin Hirshka, Sandra, myself, Simchke, Chaim Osher, Minka, my sister Minna, and Beilka.

End of the ORT (Kovno) school year term (1936), a class photo of pupils and teachers. At left is Director Jacob Oleiski; at right is Engineer Nomberg.

Overlooking bridge at Alexsoter (a suburb of Kovno) with my roommates. I am "pilot," my cousin Yakov Jaffe is "co-pilot," and Tzalel Dilatsky is the "passenger" (December 1937).

Saying good-bye to my cousin Yakov Jaffe in Ponevez before my departure to America (July 1938).

With Alex Weiner aboard the *Normandie* crossing the Atlantic Ocean (July 1938).

My father's four brothers and myself at a cousin's wedding (January 1942). Reading from front to rear—Sam (Shmulke), Joe (Yoshka), myself, Louis (Leizke), and Irving (Shrolke).

My first week at Coney Island (August 1938) with my aunt Lena, my uncle Irving, and his wife Florence.

Our wedding picture (September 1, 1946).

Cousin Leizer (Eliezer) Heiman.

After 53 years, our first meeting with cousin Yakov Segal in Vilnius, Lithuania (June 1991). Outside of those who had come to America, he was the sole survivor of our extensive family. He lives presently in Kazakhstan.

Yakov, Trudy, Janet, and Leo Rubin (left to right).

Myself at age four.

Myself, Yakov, and Leo (left to right).

The clay tablets inscribed in the "house of death" by Eliezer Heiman.

My father's sister Peshka and family in Vitebsk, Russia.

About to leave for America are my father, his brother Irving, cousin Morris, with friends from our town. Photo was taken in Berlin, 1925.

Wedding of Sore to my great-uncle Simon.

My sister, Neche Minka, 14 years old, with my aunt Keilke's daughter from Kupishik (1940).

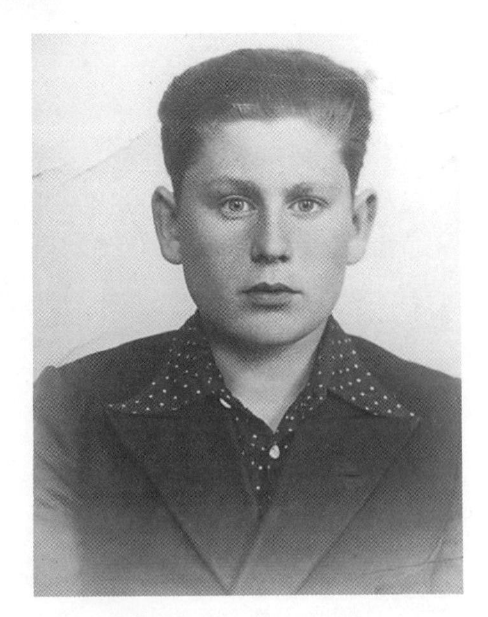

My passport picture when I left for America.

My uncle Louis and my aunt Lena who brought me over to America (1944).

Dinner on the occasion of my aunt Lena's visit from America with her youngest daughter Margery in 1931. It took place at the home of Dina Segal, my father's sister, who lived in Roguva. (She was well-off, as may be seen from the papered walls.)

My cousin Hirshke Hoichman in the Lithuanian army (1940).

Nechamke Shmuckler (July 23, 1938).

Berl Shmuckler, at left in white shirt (July 23, 1938).

Nechamke Shmuckler (at left) and Soske Gander (December 3, 1938).

Pesach Sigalski (July 12, 1937).

My father (Shiya Leib) on horseback at age 19.

A 1937 photo of myself with Berl Shmuckler seated on the ground surrounded by members of the young Zionist organization in Kavarsk. The man standing with the girls was a "sheliach," a representative of the Zionist agency from Palestine.

Aunt Dinah, Uncle Refoel and four of their seven children (Roguva, 1935). Yakov, sitting on the chair (second from right), now living in Kazakhstan, is the only survivor of the family.

My sister, Neche Minka, with Nechamke Shmuckler (August 8, 1939).

My sister, Neche Minka (at left), with cousins (1940).

Hayim Shmulke and his brother Henechke Rapshansky on their tricycle that I rode and mention in the text.

This is where my mother and her parents were born.

This is the town (shtetl) where myself, my father and grandparents were born.

This is where I would spend many summers with my grandparents and Uncle Shmuel.

Memorial for "four mass graves of Jews from Panyvez and the surroundings who were murdered by the German-Lithuanian fascists in August 1941" (inscription).

Memorial for 10,239 Jewish men, women and children who were murdered by the Nazis and Lithuanian sympathizers in September 1941, in Pavonya Forest, Ukmerges (Wilkomer).

FOURTEEN
More about Our Town

In the late 1930s, my father established the first and only link by auto-bus and truck transportation between Wilkomer (Ukmerges) and Kovno (Kaunas). In this pioneering venture he was joined by his partners, Alex (*Alliyahu*) Hoichman (my uncle Yankel's brother), Pesachke Weiner (the late Sadie Jaffe's brother), and a third partner I recall only by his first name, Yudke.

The coming of this "modern" form of transportation transformed our town economically and culturally. It expanded our business opportunities and extended our intellectual horizons. We were no longer strangers to the "outside" world.

In an earlier chapter I described how one could leave our town at 6:00 A.M., make a trip to Wilkomer and then to Kovno, and return home to Kavarsk by 7:00 or 8:00 P.M. In the course of this lightning-speed journey, you could pick up the daily newspaper in Kovno, read it on the bus on the way back, and then complete the reading at home. Thus filled with information, you could become the local fountain of knowledge for family and friends, an informed purveyor of news about what was going on in the world. That bus revolutionized life—materially and spiritually—in Kavarsk. It not only carried passengers and goods from place to place, it carried our town from the past into the twentieth century. Interestingly enough, there were towns that were bigger and better equipped than ours, with paved streets, sidewalks, running water, and electricity, that, nevertheless, were far more isolated from the evolving world than we were. They lacked a vital ingredient; namely, swift transportation. They lacked my father's vision and the bus that was born out of that vision.

Our town set the pace in this respect, and in time other towns followed in our footsteps, setting up their own bus lines and truck transportation.

At about the same time that Father was introducing us to a bigger world through his bus, another resident of Kavarsk was introducing us to that "outside" world via sound—by means of a miraculous machine called a radio.

The young man who introduced our town to this contraption must have been something of a genius. Although I can not recall his name, I remember that he was the son of one of the blacksmiths in town. Although no one in town had ever listened to or even seen a radio, the blacksmith's son seemed to know what radio was all about. He set up what we would now call a radio station, and for a fee he would see to it that your household would, at certain stipulated evening hours, receive radio broadcasts.

We knew that there were radio sets in large cities, where they had electricity; we also knew about sets that operated with earphones and a crystal receiver, but these were alien instruments in our town. Despite this our young man, who'd had no formal education or any prior experience in radio communications, succeeded in bringing radio to Kavarsk.

He might not have been another Edison, but he was exceptionally creative and enterprising. Who can say what inventions he might have brought into the world had he been given the opportunity? Instead, he, like the others, was one day to have his life cut short by the murderous marauders who overran our Jewish communities in Lithuania.

Our unheralded town genius lived in a house on top of a small hill. In back of the house his father's smithy was located. The young man built a tall antenna on top of the straw roof. From his antenna he ran a double wire, similar to a telephone wire, from roof to roof, servicing those homes that subscribed to his service. Then he would run wires into the interior of the homes, connecting them up with a set of earphones. In effect, he set up a primitive version of a modern cable system. How he managed to tune in to radio signals emanating from places outside our town without electricity or a battery is still a mystery to me—but he did it.

My uncle Ruvin subscribed to this radio service and occasionally I would listen to the music that came from Budapest or Bucharest. Mainly it was gypsy music. Incidentally, this improvised system served still another purpose, in that it was possible for you to communicate with your neighbor if that neighbor was also wired and one of the subscribers. In short, our young man had created a homespun network in his own backyard, and had hooked into it radio signals coming from distant places. We were taking our first feeble steps into the age of telecommunications.

While our town was, in many ways, changing with the changing times, there were some practices that continued down the time-honored paths of the past. One such revered occasion was the wedding.

A wedding in Kavarsk was far more than an event attended by family and friends; it was a public occasion. The whole town was welcome, and without written invitation. (The only exceptions being those with whom the bridal families were not on speaking terms.)

Mother would prepare for the marriage moment by making a sponge cake (*tort*). She would break the eggs and separate the white from the yolk. She'd stir the yolks by hand while adding sugar, and then she would whip the whites with a fork. After adding the other ingredients, she would bake the mixture in a round pan. When it was removed the fun would begin, for we'd all pitch in on the decoration. We went at this bit of artistry as if we were in a competition with all the other cake makers in town. When you entered the home where the wedding was to take place, you'd search out your particular cake, which, you'd hope, would outshine all the others.

The decorations often included inscriptions such as *mazel tov, chatan khala* (good luck, groom and bride). There might also be a star of David and the like. These cakes were much more than food for the body; they were nourishment for the spirits of the husband and wife to be. They were brought to the bride's home the night before the marriage.

By that time, the family of the bride had been busy all week preparing for the big event. They cooked and baked day after day. The delicious aromas emanating from the house would spread through the town, especially delighting those who were favored by the winds. The festivities surrounding the wedding would generally run from Friday through Sunday; in some cases, they might run for a whole week.

The *chupah* would be raised on Friday in front of the synagogue. Everybody walked from the bride's house, where the wedding took place, through the town streets. At the head of the parade were the *klezmer* (musicians) playing their lively tunes. Many in the procession would carry candles. The formal blessing and exchange of vows would take place under the red velvet *chupah*. The four poles holding the *chupah* aloft would be kept in place by members of the marital families. The ceremony would begin with the bride circling around the groom seven times, followed by the customary blessing (*bruche*) and prayers. The finale would be the breaking of the glass under the groom's heel.

The meals on Friday night and at noon on Saturday were attended by close family members and invited guests from out of town. Yet everyone who came to the wedding felt like part of a big extended family.

The *klezmer* were present at each and every wedding in our town, and at many weddings in other towns. They had a fairly standard repertoire. They provided music for a *kadril*, for a *sherarle*, a waltz, a polka, and the highly stylized and traditional *baroiges* dance.

After synagogue services on Saturday we would come, dressed in our finest, to the bride's home, where the tables would be set for the wedding banquet. Upon entrance, everyone would be formally announced by Moishe the Klezmer, who served as the MC. A typical introduction would go this way: "And now, in honor of Mr. and Mrs. So-and-So, we will play a *kadril* [quadrille]." The honored couple would, of course, give Moishe a tip.

All night long, people would eat and dance. I can still taste some of the things they'd prepare for the wedding feasts. I am not thinking of the heavy foods, such as the meats and kugels, although they were delicious; what I remember most are the desserts, the *teiglech* stuffed with raisins and nuts soaked in honey, *angemachts*, candied carrots, and a variety of other sweets whose ingredients I did not know but whose flavors I still can savor. And then, to top it off, there was always the *tort*. For me, a wedding was always an occasion to fire my mood and fill my mouth.

Although all weddings were memorable for me, there was one that had special significance. It was the wedding of my cousin Simon, Uncle Ruvin's second-oldest son. He had served in the Lithuanian army and had come back to Kavarsk looking for a girl to marry.

Normally the marriages of young people in our town were preceded by courtships that started at an early age. Boy and girl would repeatedly be seen with one another, and it was simply assumed that, when they reached the proper age, they would get married. The "proper" age was determined, in part, by how old the young man and woman were, and, in part, by how well they could manage financially. Generally, the marriage would be consummated without the help of a matchmaker. Indeed, Hertzel, uncle Ruvin's third son, married a girl from our town without benefit of a *shotchen* (matchmaker).

Simon was seen as a good catch: He was a good-looking guy and he came from a respected family. Unfortunately, however, his stint in the army had disrupted his life sufficiently that, upon his return home, there had been no childhood sweetheart waiting for him he could claim as his own. The matchmakers, ever on the lookout for business, approached him with all kinds of proposals involving girls from other towns.

Finally, an arrangement was concluded. As usual, the girl came to our town to spend some time with Simon's family; and, vice versa, Simon went to spend some time with the girl's family in her hometown of Malat, about twenty-five miles from Kavarsk.

After the exchange of visits, it was decided that the marriage should take place. A date was set and we all got ready for the coming event. Needless to say, with my appetite for weddings I looked forward to this trip, an excursion we would be making in my father's bus.

Early on a summer Friday morning we set out for Malat in the heavily loaded bus. There were Simon's parents; his brothers and sister; my father, mother, sister, and Aunt Elke; Yankel and his four children; and a few other close relatives. (Simon was not on the bus because he had left for Malat some time earlier and was now awaiting our arrival.) I was elated when my father allowed me to share his seat up front where the chauffeur sat. Needless to say, I resolved then and there that when I grew up I would be a chauffeur.

Mother had a problem travelling on the bus, in that occasionally she would suffer from motion sickness. Sure enough, half way there she took sick. We stopped the bus, got out, and let Mother rest on the wayside. She threw up and then began to feel better. We subsequently resumed our journey to Malat, and all arrived safe and sound.

In this town of Malat, the *chupa* was not placed outside the *shul*. It was located outside the bride's house. And, quite unlike the weddings held in our town, there were no *klezmer*.

We spent Friday and Saturday night with the bride's family. Being among the honored guests on the groom's side, arrangements were made for us to stay with relatives of the bride Friday and Saturday night. On Sunday, we departed for Kavarsk. This time Mother sat near an open window and did not get "seasick."

This was the first out-of-town wedding that I'd attended. It was interesting to see how Jewish marriages were the same everywhere, yet at the same time, were different—even in a town only twenty-five miles away.

Meanwhile, back at the "ranch," there was tragedy in the making—one of those unexpected things that one, in time, comes to expect.

It happened during my summer vacation from the ORT school, a year before I left for America. I was sitting on a bench atop the hill at the *krenitzeh*. I have described the beauty and tranquility of this spot, with its bubbling brook, its running water, its lovely languid landscape. My soul was soaking up the scene. I was there with Sorke Ziskind, chatting and petting a bit. Berke Shmuckler was sitting near us. Suddenly we were startled to see the sky turn red.

We knew what it meant. Someone's house was on fire. We ran down the hill to the town square, where we saw a house burning on Mizraim Street. (Mizraim means Egypt. The street was so named because the new cemetery was in a field just past this street.)

We ran to help extinguish the blaze. There was no fire department, nor was there any pumping apparatus to spray the flames with jets of water. Our only resource was a well, a *broonem*, nearby; we could fetch water with a pail at the end of a rope. People lined up to form a bucket brigade, passing the pails of water from hand to hand.

Despite our efforts, our little pails of water were no match for the roaring blaze. We kept passing the buckets while helplessly witnessing the total incineration of the wooden house.

It was a sad feeling to see a home reduced to ashes. It was even sadder to feel that there was nothing one could do about it. There we were, helpless amidst the havoc. One moment, the joys of petting on the *krenitzeh*; the next moment, the coming of the fire.

Our cousin Sore was our grocer. We ordered all our supplies from her. She entered the charges in her soiled soft-covered paper notebook. To do so, she would moisten her pencil with her tongue and press down hard on the paper. She entered the items we bought in Yiddish, and how much we owed her.

I do not know how often we settled our accounts with her. I do recall that we always owed her money.

I would be the one who ran the errands—placed orders and carried the foodstuff home. My mother needed this assistance, since she suffered from rheumatism in her legs, and I was always pleased to be helpful. Actually, I kind of enjoyed going to the grocery. It was a place I could buy my favorite sucking candy. The other reason I liked to go to the grocery was Simchka, Sore's daughter.

Her presence sweetened the sweets; I really enjoyed seeing her and chatting with her. So I was drawn to that grocery by several strings: by blood, through my cousin Sore; by my love for the candies; and by my friendship with Simchka, who was named after her father, Simon.

Simon died prematurely and tragically. I was never told the true and full story directly. Maybe it was not told to me because I was too young. Maybe adults believed that kids were not really interested in stories of people who came before us. The truth is, as I think about it, in retrospect I was always interested in what had happened to my parents when they were young, but they'd never satisfied my curiosity or interest. Whatever information I was able to accumulate had been acquired through eaves-dropping. When, on some occasions, the family would get together and the adults would speak with one another, they would talk about various events in the past and I, as a bystander, would pick up a few words here and there, pasting them together to reconstruct a story of what had happened some time ago. It was in this hit-and-miss fashion that I picked up the story of what had befallen Sore's husband, Simon, my grandfather Yankel's brother.

It wasn't long after their wedding. (I have a photo of their wedding ceremony.) He was accidentally killed in what we would now call an industrial accident. He operated or leased a flour mill, located outside of town across the river. The mill was driven by water power, and farmers would bring their corn or wheat to be milled.

The process of milling was three-tiered. At the top level, the peasants would unload their raw grain. It was then carried by chute to the second level, where it was ground to flour by rotating stone wheels. From there it was delivered to the third level, where the ground grain was emptied into waiting bags.

To make sure that the peasant or farmer who brought the grain to the mill got all that was his, the miller would scrape his hand across the rotating stone wheels to clear away any stray grains that might have been clinging to the wheel. In that way he could guarantee that whoever bought the grain would get his full share.

While pushing a few stray grains into the rotating stones, Simon's arm got caught in between the stone wheels. He struggled to get loose but he could not escape the powerful, water-driven grain crushers. The machine mutilated and mauled and murdered the man. This was the tragic story of Sore's husband. Sore never remarried. She ran her grocery until the day she was liquidated by the Nazis—Lithuanian as well as German—in the little town in which our family had lived for hundreds of years.

Simon's mill was not the only one in the area. There was also a mill bordering on the old Jewish cemetery. The water power for the mill came from several brooks in the neighborhood. In anticipation of the time when the summer heat and drought would either reduce or eliminate whatever water we had, rainwater would be accumulated in a seminatural reservoir. The water accumulated in this way was controlled through a series of gates. When the water was exhausted, the mill closed down.

This mill was operated by the Berzon family—a mother and her son. There was also a daughter, known to be a Communist, who emigrated to Birobidzhan, an autonomous oblast designated by the Soviet Union for Jewish settlement. I never knew what happened to the father of the family, or whether there were other children.

The mill was the only life that this woman and her son knew. She and her son did not associate with anyone in town. Needless to say, they did not attend services at the synagogue. There was, despite this, a fairly close relationship between that family and my father. It may have been that they needed him in the pursuit of their business.

I suspect that he may have had some kind of equity in the business, based on an oral, unwritten, agreement. The Berzons had plans to set up a new modern mill, to be operated all year round by a water-driven turbine when there was an adequate supply of water. They also planned to accumulate a reservoir of additional water by building a dam and to install diesel engines to power the entire operation. This modern mill was intended to do more than just turn the raw grain into flour; it was also to separate out the wheat intended for "white" flour from that intended to be dark flour. This was done by running the former, the "white," through a bleaching process.

The family's ambitions went beyond this, however. They were also planning to install machinery to process textiles handwoven by the local peasantry. Since my father was one of the most knowledgeable people in town in such matters, it would have been natural for them to turn to him to assist in their project.

Before they could proceed with their plans, however, they had to acquire the property on which the operation would be located. There was some question as to whether they were truly the legal owners of the land on which they operated. A court action was initiated against them. My father, together with some lawyers, represented the family in court in Wilkomer. The court decided in favor of the family. They laid out their plans for the construction of the new mill. Father joined in the work, literally lending a hand by physically engaging in the undertaking. I saw him there, shovel in hand, mixing sand, cement, and water for the dam.

He put in many hours without pay, along with others who were paid. My father was both a worker and the supervisor of the dam project. When it was completed and the new mill was in operation, outfitted with electric lights that replaced the old kerosene lamps, Father demanded what had been promised him. It seemed, however, that the Berzons refused to acknowledge their debt to him. He was disappointed and hurt and, for a while, his unhappy mood affected the atmosphere in our household.

Outside the mill, close to the cemetery fence, there was a large pile of birch wood that had been cut up for winter use. Father borrowed my uncle Yankel's horse and wagon and asked me to go with him to help load the wagon with these logs, which we would use in our house. He must have felt entitled to tap this supply.

We drove to the mill and began to load up the wagon with wood. No sooner did we have the wagon about half loaded than we saw Mrs. Berzon in the distance running wildly toward us. Cursing my father, she jumped on to the wagon and began to toss the logs out of it onto the ground.

I was amazed to see how my father maintained his composure. So far as I, a teenager, was concerned, I was quite ready to lift a log and let her have it over the head. It killed me to see how she was paining and humiliating my father after all the work he had done for her. And now, here was this old bitch refusing to let him have some wood to keep our home warm in the winter.

She and her son were also murdered by the German Nazis and their Lithuanian collaborators. When I returned to Kavarsk in 1991, there was not a trace left of the mill or of the old Jewish cemetery.

I've mentioned my aunt Elke's involvement in the ice cream business. She was as industrious as the other two sisters I knew. I am thinking of my late aunt Frieda, who lived in Passaic, New Jersey, and ran a candy store to maintain a family with a chronically sick husband, and of my aunt Dina from Roguva, whose husband was a blacksmith; she helped him actively in his trade, a heavy hammer in her hand. As a secondary occupation, Dina also ran a store that sold metal products.

As you can see, these sisters were real doers, hardworking entrepreneurs. In the case of Aunt Elke, she was so driven that she tried to launch a business to compete with my father's bus service—a mistake, as it turned out. But there could be no mistake about their drive to do, to get out there and get things moving.

Aunt Elke learned the tricks and trade secrets of the ice cream business from a family that came back from Israel, then called Palestine. In 1933 this family, the Bernsteins, returned from Israel to Kavarsk, which had been Mrs. Bernstein's hometown. After a short stay in Kavarsk, the Bernsteins decided to move on to Kovno with their family of three children. Before they left, however, they decided to sell (or give) my aunt the formula for making ice cream.

At first, there were only two flavors—vanilla and chocolate. I didn't know the formula but, for the performance of my part in the making of the ice cream, this arcane piece of knowledge was not necessary. My basic job was to twist a galvanized container from right to left and back again. That container had a lid on it and a handle with which to twist it. It was inserted into an ice-packed wooden barrel. Coarse salt was poured onto the ice.

Grabbing the handle of the galvanized container in both hands, I would turn and twist it from side to side. Its contents, of course, would begin to gel as the sides of the container rolled around in the icy wooden barrel. From time to time, I would remove the lid to scrape the congealed ice cream from the sides of the barrel and mix it with the remaining mass in the container. By repeating this operation over and over, the entire mass within the galvanized container was sufficiently hardened to be removed and placed between two wafers and then sold to the public. I was not paid for my labors, but I was rewarded with some ice cream.

On market days, my aunt and her two sons, Hirshke and Hayimke, would travel to town and peddle their delicious delights in two or three locations.

On one occasion, the country decided to celebrate the birthday of the Lithuanian President, Antanas Smetona. He was to dedicate a newly built school in the town of his birth, about ten miles from our town. For my aunt, this was a rare opportunity to sell ice cream. I joined in. We prepared an extra heavy load, since the day was hot and the crowd was expected to be large. We set out very early in the morning so we could get a favorable spot. We arrived early and, with each passing hour, the crowd swelled. I was impressed by the town itself, with its well-swept streets and cement sidewalks.

About noon, I saw what looked like a huge mechanical bird hovering overhead. It was my first glimpse of a helicopter. It circled above the newly built school and then, its rotating blades kicking up a little storm around us, it came to rest on a grassy parade ground in front of the school. Soldiers ceremoniously surrounded the helicopter. And there, climbing out of the helicopter and waving to us, was the president of Lithuania.

For us this was an incredible experience. Here I was, personally seeing the president of Lithuania—in the flesh—coming to us out of the sky, mingling with us, then taking off like a bird through the summery heavens back to the capitol city of Kovno. I could not wait to get home to tell everyone what had transpired. When I did get home, I talked and talked and talked.

One day when I was about ten years old, I began to run a fever that refused to go away. What to do? Our town had no doctor. It did have a pharmacist, who prescribed aspirin that was sold in powdered form in a small envelope decorated with a red rooster, the trademark of a superior product. I took the aspirin but the fever hung in there.

My father sent me, along with Mother, to Ponyvez, about twenty-five miles away, to see a well-known doctor, a "professor." We made the trip in my father's truck. I was placed on the outside on the truck's rear deck, covered with a blanket, and given a pillow to rest my head. My mother sat alongside me holding my hand as we rode the bumpy road to Ponyvez.

In Ponyvez there was a special sort of inn (*achsanya*), where merchants and other travellers would put up for the night. My mother and I were ushered into the room we'd rented. Later the doctor came and took my temperature. He must have noticed that my mother was worried, for he gave her a prescription for me and assured her that, in a few days, the fever would break and the crisis would be over.

I don't recall how many days it took for the illness to run its course. I also do not know just what the ailment was. I do recall, however, that when the fever subsided and I returned to normal my mother was so elated, kissing and hugging me over and over, that she forgot to notify my father that all was well. The next morning, however, she did call the bus office to tell him the good news. Father came to fetch us and to carry me, now fully restored to health, back home.

The most elementary things that we take for granted in twentieth-century America were not readily available to us in our town in Lithuania in the 1930s. Life was a struggle at every step. I think it important to record that mundane fact as I think back now about my life. It suggests how much strain, even suffering, went into the simple effort to exist from day to day. Yet, despite these difficulties, the families in our little town survived. They endured and continued to strive for a better life for themselves and, most importantly, for their children.

I realize that I am a product of that culture. My parents worked very hard, both of them, to provide me with an education and to teach me a trade in tune with the times. They aspired to do the same for my sister. For them to send me to the ORT school was a great sacrifice, a costly luxury that was, in fact, a burdensome necessity.

When I say that every detail of living was a headache and a backache, let me tell you what I mean. Take the simple need to wash or clean clothes. We had no electricity and no running water. Even those more advanced cities that had water and electricity had nothing resembling our modern-day washing machines. Yet washing clothes was imperative: dirty clothes smelled bad, looked bad, and attracted bad little parasites, so they had to be cleaned or washed regularly. Yet there was no formal facility for doing so. We had to improvise, and we did so in bits and pieces.

To begin with, we had limited wardrobes. There were very few who could boast a new dress, or a woolen suit or coat made by one of the seamstresses in town. This was all dress-up attire, intended for Saturdays and holidays. Those who had such fancy clothes would generally have one such and would wear it for a lifetime. If it ever got real dirty, the likelihood that it would be cleaned properly was zero. If there was an occasional stain, we would labor to remove it with soap and water or with kerosene. In dealing with a very stubborn stain, I noticed that my mother would apply some special chemical and then rub the soiled area repeatedly with a brush.

Our everyday clothes were made almost exclusively out of a rough washable cotton made in town. Until I was a teenager of thirteen, I would wear a long white linen shirt that was tucked into my short pants. I wore the same thing all day long and, when nighttime came, I went to sleep in the same shirt. I did change it once a week. On Saturdays, the Sabbath, I would wear a special shirt and shorts.

I wore no underwear; neither did any of the other boys. The adults did have underwear, known as *gotkes*. My mother would have our clothes washed once a month. The first time in my life that I wore anything other than my cottons was when I left for ORT, where I was introduced to underwear and imported cotton.

To wash the clothes my mother would hire a peasant woman, who would come to our home early in the morning. She would get a few buckets of water from the well and empty them into large, heavy aluminum pots. She would boil the clothes for a long time. When the clothes had been cooked long enough, she'd carry them to the brook nearest our house. At a spot behind the building where the lemonade and seltzer were bottled, she would rinse the laundry in the running water of the brook.

The rinsing was no simple process. The individual pieces were taken one by one, whether a shirt, towel or tablecloth, rubbed with soap, then placed in the running stream, and swished back and forth. They would then be removed, dripping wet, and draped over a rock, where the woman would then pound them with a large flat wooden paddle. Then she would rinse them all over again, wring them out, and place them on another rock. When she was done with all the rinsing, she would throw the washed and rinsed laundry over her shoulder and carry it back to the house.

In the summer she would hang the wet wash out to dry on a line. In the winter the process became more complicated, since the brook was frozen over. But she managed somehow; and of course the drying had to take place indoors.

When it came to ironing things, the chore, again, was much more difficult than it is today because we had no electricity. The irons we used in Lithuania were all made of cast iron. To heat the iron, it was necessary to insert a burning coal into the iron itself. This was done by lifting the movable top of the iron to allow the coal to be placed inside the iron. About an inch from the bottom of the iron, there was a grate that would allow air to enter and keep the coal burning. On top of the iron was what amounted to a small chimney, shaped like a tuba, that provided a vent to keep the air circulating. To make certain that the person who was doing the ironing would not be hit with the hot blast, this was turned sidewise, away from the ironer.

The coal that we used to heat the iron was quite different from the coal or charcoal that we use in the United States. We had no commercial coal. We used a sort of charcoal that was made from a wood-burning log. We used that fuel to heat the house and cook. When the log was burned about halfway, we would remove it from the fire, set it aside, and let it cool. This was the "coal" we would turn to when we needed it for ironing. We would put it into the iron and then ignite it by placing thin slices of wood underneath it in the iron. When the kindling caught fire, the coal would begin to glow. In short, we treated the inside of the iron as if it were a miniature fireplace.

As you can see, almost every detail of the housework that may seem like such a chore to us today is as nothing when compared to the laborious and complicated procedures we had to resort to in our town during my years there. Before applying the first stroke of the heavy iron we had to work our way through many, many steps.

Difficult as life was, we did not curse our fate, perhaps because we did not know any better. So far as we knew, if you wanted to iron something there was only one way to do it, so that was that. While the chores were truly physical chores, psychologically they were just run-of-the-mill, normal acts to carry us through our days.

The streets in our town were dirt roads that, in wet weather, turned into muddy roads. But there were some streets that were paved with cobblestones, and thereby hangs a story.

The streets in the town itself were all dirt roads, but outside the town limits a road that ran up a hill leading to Anyksht was paved with cobblestones. To me, this was a puzzlement. Why should the streets in town be dirt and mud and this other street, outside of town, be paved with cobblestones? It seemed to me to be illogical and unfair.

In due time, a decision was made to convert the dirt roads into cobblestoned streets one by one, and sometimes half a street by half a street. The obvious question was Why, if cobblestoned streets were preferable, was the first such street outside our town?

The answer was hidden in history. During World War I, when the Germans occupied Lithuania, the military issued an order to cobblestone their street; they needed it for their purposes. In time, however, it was decided that cobblestone was better than dirt and mud. Step by step and street by street our town brought the roads up to date.

The authorities, whoever they were, decided to begin with the town square, the marketplace. Frankly, whoever made this decision and why they made it is still a mystery to me. But it did happen, and, as a consequence, anyone who owned a house was now assessed a tax. If you did not have the cash, you were obliged to provide a stipulated number of stones to be used for the cobbling.

The amount of stones you were to provide was measured by the wagon load. You were obliged to go out into the fields and search about for the stones and deliver them as ordered.

My father was ordered to deliver cobblestones. Once more, he borrowed Uncle Yankel's horse and wagon to gather and deliver the stones. He and I started out early one morning to a certain field where we picked up stones, placed them in the wagon, and delivered them to the site where they were needed. Having made the delivery, we were also obliged to unload the wagon.

I do not recall how many wagonloads we delivered to bring our dirt streets into the twentieth century. I do remember that it took many, many hours of back-breaking work.

I was hypnotized watching the way the cobblestone setters went about their work. They would study the stone; they would dig out a hole in the sand to accommodate the stone; they would set the stone in place. To do this, they would have to scoop out the sand just so in order to create a cradle to hold the stone. I was astounded to see how neatly the stones fit into their cradles.

But that, apparently, was only a rough and temporary setting. After the stones were allocated to their assigned spots in the sand, a man would follow up with a wooden hammer in his hand. It was very flat, about three feet long by four or five inches wide in diameter. This instrument was used to align the stones, so that they would make a reasonably traversable flat surface for what would otherwise be an unpredictably precarious road.

By the time I left for America the market square was completely paved with cobblestones, as were about half the streets in town, including our street.

As I think back about my life, I sometimes wonder why certain episodes lie hidden until certain other recollections trigger their recollection, and why certain other events stand out so strongly that they are always, so to speak, immediately before your eyes. I don't think I have the answer, but I do know that this is so as I recall a melancholy moment when my mother wept and wept all day. It was a day I shall never never forget.

Our cousin Hashke Levitt, who was not married and who lived with her mother Sore, was very close to my father and mother. She would spend a great deal of time at our house, together with cousin Bessie and cousin Rochke. Sometimes, boys would join them. One of these was a young, good-looking Lithuanian lad who worked as a chauffeur on my father's bus. He seemed to enjoy the company of the young ladies at our home; he also made passes at them, trying to pat their behinds and kiss them, and the girls would, in a pleasant sort of way, push him away without any display of anger.

Father used to borrow money from Hashke, how much and whether he paid interest on the loans I do not know. But I do know that he was often in debt to her.

One summer morning, when I was on vacation and Father was not at home, Hashke demanded that Mother repay her the money Father owed her. Mother told her she did not have any money, and that she would talk with Father about it when he came home that evening. But Hashke was unrelenting; she wanted to be paid immediately.

Mother was terribly upset. She burst into tears and wept uncontrollably. I was deeply pained. And I was truly angry with Hashke.

When Father returned, he knew that something was wrong. All he had to do was to look at Mother's eyes, which were red from her crying. He asked what had happened. Mother told him what had taken place with Hashke and that I had witnessed the embarrassment. He did not doubt her account of the encounter, but he was, indeed, surprised. He consoled my mother and told her not to worry. He would borrow from some one else to repay Hashke, and then he would never borrow from her again.

Both Hashke and her mother, Sore, were murdered in the Holocaust.

As noted earlier, the only medical facility in town was the pharmacist. He was neither Jewish nor Lithuanian; I believe he was German. If you were sick, you went to the pharmacist and described your symptoms—fever, headache, stomachache, backache, cough, and so on. The pharmacist would then prescribe.

I recall our cousin Rochke's mother, Sosa, who was on in years and, so long as I can remember, was constantly coughing. In the last few years before I left for America, she would lie in bed and cough her lungs out.

She undoubtedly had TB, tuberculosis. The pharmacist prescribed a cough syrup that, at best, was only a palliative. Her daughter had to be at her side all day and night. After I left for the United States, the aged Sosa passed away.

My father had a close friend in town whose name was Leibke. He was married, had kids, and lived in a house just past the post office on a street that led to the river and the forest. He had a horse and wagon and made a living by buying things from the farmers, such as wheat or flax, and then selling his wares in Kovno or Wilkomer.

He would sell to merchants who, in turn, would have contact with domestic or foreign markets. On his return from the big cities, he would bring back supplies for storeowners in our town.

When our Young Zionist club dissolved, after a number of members had left town, his parents moved into our house to occupy the space that had been our clubroom.

Leibke's wife got sick. As time went by, she got progressively worse. Her body broke out in sores and she ran a high temperature. The word was that she had an infectious disease that was highly contagious. She had to be taken to the hospital in Wilkomer. No one offered to help her for fear that, if they came near her, they, too, would contract the disease. The rumor was that her husband, Leibke, liked to frequent the Kovno brothels on his journeys there and had contracted a venereal disease, which he had passed on to his wife.

When the time came for her to be taken to the hospital, my father performed a simple but courageous act that added to his repute as a good man, for which he was already highly regarded by his friends and neighbors. But when they learned of his "noble deed," his *bikuach nefesh*, he rose even further in their esteem.

When the time came to take Leibke's wife to the hospital, my father volunteered to help carry the patient to the waiting wagon. He made her comfortable on a straw mattress. He covered her with a blanket. He stayed with Leibke for the fifteen-mile trip and was there when the sick woman was admitted to the hospital in Wilkomer.

After a long period of illness, she did recover. Both Leibke and his wife were wiped out in the Holocaust.

FIFTEEN
Other Towns

My grandmother Etta, my mother's mother, together with her second husband, Shiya, and her youngest unmarried son, Shmulke, moved from Gelez to Subatz (*Subacius*), a larger, more prosperous, more modern town. It was blessed with a station stop on a major railroad that ran from the western border of Lithuania eastward through many major cities, such as Telz (*Telsias*), Shavel (*Shiauliai*), Panyvez (*Panevezys*), and Rokishok (*Rokiskis*). The line terminated at the eastern border of Lithuania.

The family moved to Subatz some time between 1930 and 1932. They took with them the machine, used to process raw wool for use as thread, which was the means by which they made a living.

My uncle Shmulke would have nothing to do with this business. Although he lived with my grandmother and her husband, Shmulke conducted himself in a very independent fashion. He looked upon himself as a "merchant," and therefore as someone with higher social standing. He bought wheat and flax and arranged to have the products shipped by train to companies that would, in turn, generally export the product for sale outside Lithuania.

In Subatz there was a prominent and wealthy Jewish family named Schneider. They were wholesale suppliers. Their volume of business was sufficiently large so that their property was connected to the main railroad line by a special siding. The wares they received were delivered directly in boxcars that unloaded the cargo into their backyard.

They might be described as distributors. They would receive bulk shipments of steel products, glass, salt, sugar, and other items, and would then distribute these wares to retailers who were located over a wide area. I had a very good-looking cousin, also named Ruvke, who lived in Subatz and worked for the Schneider company. When I would visit Subatz he would take me to his place of employment and show me around.

So far as I was concerned, I thought that this must be the biggest business operation in the whole wide world. There were these mountains of burlap bags loaded with salt and sugar. There were all these people, scurrying from here to there and back, loading and unloading wagons destined for different towns, some of which were one or two days' journey from Subatz.

When my cousin Ruvke left for South Africa I missed him badly. We were never in touch again.

In the summertime I looked forward to going to Subatz. I'd have a chance to do so whenever my uncle Yankel, the glazier, would go there to buy glass for his own use and for others in our town.

We would go by horse and wagon, departing from Kavarsk after *shul* on Saturday night. As often as I took this trip, it was still always an adventure to me. We would bounce around in the wagon over dusty, bumpy dirt roads, through forests that scared me enough to give me the shakes. I imagined a robber would leap upon us from behind every tree. The stories of such holdups were many. We'd drive through the night. It was not possible to sleep with the wagon rattling, banging, and tossing about, its passengers completely at the mercy of the rutted road.

In retrospect, I've often thought that if we'd had enough milk to drink before embarking on the journey it would have been churned into butter by the end of the voyage. We were truly shaken up, physically and psychologically. Although the total distance was only thirty-five kilometers (about twenty-one miles) it seemed much, much longer to me. When we returned with a loaded wagon, the trip felt (and, actually, was) much longer, not in distance but in time.

When we arrived at my grandmother's place, I was certain that I would get a warm greeting. I was, after all, her oldest grandchild; I suspect I may have been her favorite. I was also the only grandchild who would regularly spend my summers with her. I've previously related the joys of summering in Gelez, and here now were happy days to spend with Grandmother Etta in Subatz.

Grandmother exuded a special kind of warmth I never encountered with anyone else. At home, in my own house, there was no lack of love and warmth, but with Grandmother there was just another quality. I knew in advance that with her, it was always "yes" and never "no."

My stepgrandfather, Shiya, was a warm nice man who, I believe, was somewhat older than my grandmother. (It may be that he really wasn't older but simply seemed to be so because he had a beard.) As I noted earlier, I used to work with him at the wool-processing machine and would enjoy the work.

Grandfather used to make his own cigarettes. He would pour the shredded tobacco carefully into a specially treated, very thin paper he'd hold stretched between his fingers. He would moisten the paper with his tongue as he rolled it around the tobacco. A few more touches here and there and he had a cigarette ready to be lit.

When I was about thirteen years old I was curious to find out how a cigarette tasted. When Grandpa was not around, I would take some tobacco, some cigarette paper, and a box of matches to the outhouse. There, in secrecy, I would imitate Grandpa and make a cigarette. Then I'd light it up and try to smoke. When I'd inhale I'd almost cough my insides out. I hoped that no one would hear me choking or would see smoke coming out of the outhouse. I didn't like the taste at all. Yet, I repeated the unpleasant prank several times during the summer I was with my grandparents in Subatz.

I spent most of my time with my Uncle Shmuel. I loved him dearly, and I know that he reciprocated. Thanks to his good looks, he was probably the most popular bachelor in town. He had many friends in town and used to visit many families, on which occasions he'd take me along.

There was one family we visited where there were three daughters. The oldest was my age and the other two were younger. Shmuel would always kid with me about my marrying one of the girls. Why not? They were nice looking and they were rich. He would show me off. Why didn't I deserve the best? After all, I was not bad to look at either, even if I had to say so myself.

On Saturdays, we would go out into the forest outside of town where people from nearby towns would rent a dacha, a bungalow, for the summer. The place was popular, and so was my uncle.

My uncle decided to build a house for himself next to my grandmother's house. Perhaps he was planning to get married. If the many matchmakers who were trying to "make him a match" had their way, he was certainly well on the way to marriage.

One year after he'd made his decision the house was completed. I was a welcome guest and would spend my nights sleeping there. Uncle Shmuel would arrange to have a small bathhouse, owned by a Lithuanian, made available to us. We would frequent it quite often.

The last summer I spent with him he was married to a woman from another town. I remember that she was pregnant, but I don't recall her name; neither do I know how he happened to get married, or when he got married, since none of us ever attended any wedding. (As I said, Uncle Shmuel was a very independent soul.)

When I left for America he gave me a watch, the very first watch I had ever owned.

We had a cousin who lived near Grandmother; her family name was Segal. This Segal woman had a son, who was a watchmaker, and a daughter. This woman I believe, was a sister to my late grandfather Ruven.

I liked my cousin, the watchmaker, very much. His name was Pesach Sigalsky. I spent much time with him, continually intrigued at the way he could disassemble and reassemble a watch. When I left for America he gave me a picture of himself.

His young, good-looking sister, whose name I cannot recall, decided to go to Palestine. In those days, there were two ways that a young girl could go. One was to be a member of some Zionist organization that would prepare you to make the trip. The other way was to engage a young man who, for a fee, would get papers establishing that the young man and the young maid were husband and wife. They would also carry with them another set of papers showing that they'd been divorced.

These shenanigans stemmed from the fact that Britain had a mandate over Palestine, making it necessary to comply with certain regulations in order to get a certificate of admission. I recall that, on one occasion when I was visiting Subatz, I met this alleged "husband," with whom my cousin was "eloping" to Palestine.

While I was always curious about what was happening to our extended family, there were many things that I did not understand about relationships within the family, especially where the persons involved lived in another town. Although the twenty-one miles separating us from my grandmother would be like nothing today, at that time even such a short distance was considerable in the absence of a phone or a car.

I do not recall any time when my mother made the trip to see her mother, my grandmother, or her sister. They did correspond now and then. We did see Uncle Shmuel quite often, because he had developed a friendship with some of his contemporaries in our town. He was our line of communication between Mother, Grandmother, and Aunt Keilke.

I was the other connection, thanks to the visits I made to and from Subatz.

One of the great attractions for me in Subatz was the railroad station. I was thrilled to see a train arrive, puffing smoke as it rolled into the station. I was fascinated to see the passengers get on and off. As the train departed, I would wait for the jet of steam that the engine would spout from its sides. As this snorting dragon would roll on its way, the air would be pierced with a shrill whistle that sounded like a pained and mournful farewell. My eyes would be glued on the last car until it disappeared somewhere beyond the horizon. To me the sight of a train was the sight of a new world, since it was in Subatz that I saw my first steam engine, a noisy mechanical "horse" towing its many "wagons" across the landscape.

Subatz was one of the other towns with which I had some acquaintance; Roguva was another. It had about as many Jewish families as Kavarsk. It was northwest of our town, about ten miles away, halfway between Kavarsk and Panyvez. It was a more prosperous town than ours. It had electricity, which meant that every house had at least one bulb hanging from a wood beam. This beam served a double purpose. A bulb could be hung from it, and in addition the beam also served as a reinforcement, supporting the floor for the attic above the room.

The ceiling of the attic was determined by the pitch of the roof at the top of the house. It was possible to access the attic directly from outside the building. There was a wood ladder on the outside leading up to the attic, which had its own wooden door.

The attic was used primarily for storage, for laying away hay to feed the horses or cows in the winter. It also stored fruits such as apples, pears, and plums. Some of the apples were stored there over the winter so they would freeze, because they tasted so delicious after the thaw.

The presence of electricity in Rugova also meant that they could light up the streets and the town square. More of their streets were cobblestoned than in our town. Whenever I went to Roguva I felt that it was a wealthier town than ours. The houses looked better, appeared bigger. I was impressed by the houses around the marketplace that were surfaced with red brick. Some of the streets were quite wide and lined by trees on both sides, with houses set back from the streets. There were also wood sidewalks and lawns.

To get from Kavarsk to Panyvez we had to pass through Roguva.

Roguva benefitted from the fact that it was so close to Panyevez, with its great *yeshivas* and its commercial activities.

My father's sister Dina Segal lived in Roguva with her blacksmith husband. You will recall that they had seven children. Their house was beautiful, both inside and out. They even had a telephone. Our family visited them only on special occasions, such as the time that Aunt Lena came to Kavarsk. On my own I visited more often, spending a day or two with them each time.

There were other relatives who lived in Roguva. There were cousins on my mother's side. My mother's father's brother, Itzik Norwitz, lived in Roguva. He had a married son, Rachmiel, who lived in Roguva with his family. He had a daughter, Esther, who died while giving birth to a second child. He also had another daughter, Zelda Ropshanski, who lived in Kavarsk and a daughter called Chayke (Ida) Rabinowitz (Rubin), whose husband went to America. She moved in with her two children, Leo and Rita, to live with her parents.

Ida and her sister Esther were close to my mother. They used to come often to stay with their sister Zelda in Kavarsk.

As Mother did, so I also felt closer to them than to my uncle Rafael and my aunt Dina. I was particularly fond of Leo, who was my age, and of Rita. They would come quite often with their mother when she'd come to stay with her sister in Kavarsk. I used to play with them and with our cousins Haim Shmulke, who was our age, and his younger brother Henechke. Rita would play with my sister, Necha Minke; they were of the same age.

I must say that Leo was really something. He could never stand still. His mother, Ida, would holler at him to quiet down, but to no avail. He wouldn't or couldn't stop. We nicknamed him Mercury (quicksilver). Despite this, we always got along with each other.

At one time, after I'd already settled in the United States, Ida told me that there had been a period when my mother lived with her family in Roguva, and it had been her father, Itzik, who'd made the wedding for my mother.

Ida's husband, Benzion Rabinowitz, lived in another town in Lithuania. She lived in that town after he and Ida were married, and that is where Leo and Rita had been born. In 1930, Ida's husband left for the United States. He had brothers in Philadelphia. The plan was for him to come over first, accumulate some money, then bring over the rest of the family. When he left, Ida and her kids went to live in Roguva with her parents. In 1937, the year before I left for the United States, they left for the United States.

When they departed, I said good-bye to them at the train station in Kovno. Little did I know that I would be saying hello to them the next year in Philadelphia. I was in Kovno at that time, attending the ORT school.

SIXTEEN
A Turning Point

In 1937, the political kettle in Europe was about to boil over. Hitler was on the move.

In our relative isolation in Kavarsk, we really knew very little about what was going on in the world. No radio, no TV, no daily contact with what was happening outside our customary circle. I, at the age of fifteen, had no notion of the true dangers facing us. We were, of course, not alone. A storm was brewing, but we had no way of knowing it.

As Hitler undertook his aggression, England was busy signing all sorts of agreements with him. One of these agreements revolved around Hitler's claim to a part of Czechoslovakia that was heavily inhabited by Germans, and which had been taken from Germany after World War I. It was called the Sudetenland. Hitler threatened to take this area by force if no peaceful settlement could be reached.

The Prime Minister of Great Britain, Neville Chamberlain, flew to Germany to discuss Hitler's claims and demands. The newsreels showed Chamberlain returning to England after signing a pact with Hitler that, in effect, legitimatized the rape of the Sudetenland. As Chamberlain was shown exiting his plane, he waved to the cameras and proclaimed, "Peace in our time."

The newspapers the next day echoed that proclamation in their headlines. Hitler had promised that there would be no war. It was at this seemingly happy moment—a time of peace—that we got ready to welcome Aunt Lena on her second visit to us. She was coming with her second daughter, the seventeen-year-old Sandra.

This time, Aunt Lena was no stranger to us. She had, as you know, paid us an earlier visit. She had grown quite close to us, perhaps even closer to us than my parents' very own brothers or sisters. Although she was an in-law, we all felt about her as if she were a blood relative. We had never met Sandra, of course, but we could recognize her instantly from the many pictures we had received from them.

By this time we were living in a larger house, which we shared with two other families. It was much more modern than the old wood cottage with the bare dirt floors. We were able to accommodate our guests with real spring mattresses instead of strewn straw. A bedroom and two beds were reserved for them. My parents moved in temporarily with the Shmucklers. I slept at Aunt Elke's house. And, once again, we took special care in spiffing up the outhouse.

The two weeks that followed were the most memorable moments of my life as a teenager. I thought Sandra was the most beautiful girl in the world. My sister and our friends went wild over her. It wasn't her physical features that made her so attractive; it was her personality—the aura of friendliness, warmth, caring, and concern she projected so winningly.

I just loved everything about her. By now, of course, I was a grown-up young man of fifteen years and six months who had been polished in the urban ways of Kovno. I was no longer some yokel from a small town. There was no problem communicating with her. As none of us spoke English, we would simply converse in Yiddish, a language in which both she and we felt at ease.

We all had a real ball with Sandra. Every teenager in town, ages fifteen and up, gathered around her. We went swimming together, especially on Saturday nights, a popular moment for folk to gather at the riverside. There was one fellow, in particular, who seemed to be drawn to her. His name was Itzky Dubovski; he was about nineteen years old, tall, handsome, and blond. He was looked upon as belonging to the "upper class" in town; his father owned a flour mill on the Shventa River. He lived in an attractive, above-average house. He was quite a talented violinist. He had a bike, a camera, and everything else that a young man's heart might desire.

He and Sandra took a liking to one another. They spent a good deal of time together, but I was present just about all the time. Together we visited his father's mill, which was about five miles away. He took us on one of his boats and had us watch the rafts of floating logs as they were maneuvered down the flowing waters.

During these many activities revolving around Sandra, there was a festive atmosphere in our town. Every night we were guests in someone else's house, chatting and chattering away. In homes where they had a gramophone, we listened to the music. At Uncle Ruvin's home we had specially prepared dinners, with all the young folk in attendance. Professional photographers came to take pictures. They used the old-style flash, with the inevitable consequence that half the people in the photo seemed to have their eyes closed. We loaded up Father's bus with family members and drove to Roguva to spend a weekend with Aunt Dina.

Finally the hour had come when Aunt Lena and Sandra had to return to America. We were all heartbroken. We had, in a short time, developed an incredibly close relationship, closer than most folk might be able to establish in a lifetime. I was saddened by the thought that I might never see Sandra again. I'm certain my parents felt the same. Frankly, we had fallen head over heels in love with Sandra.

The last letter I received from my father was mailed just before Hitler took over in Lithuania. It was the letter in which he wrote about my sister's recuperation. The first things she'd asked for when she'd come out of her paralysis were pictures of Sandra. She kept kissing the photos over and over again.

What I did not know when Aunt Lena left is that she had indicated to my father that, after returning to America, she would make every effort to bring my family to the United States. (On this trip, as on her first trip, Aunt Lena visited her mother, brother, and married sister with her children in Milatucze, Poland. They, too, were consumed in the Holocaust.)

During these crucial years of the late 1930s, I was to spend most of my time in Kovno at the ORT school. Right after the high holidays I was to depart from my beloved little town and my loving family and set sail into the unknown. There, at the tender age of thirteen and a half, I would have to face an uncharted future. Although Kovno was only sixty miles away, it seemed to me it might as well be on another planet. I felt lost in outer space. How would I find my way from place to place? Who would wake me in the morning? Who would help me prepare my supper? Take me to the public bath? Wash my clothes?

These and similar fears raced through my mind as I was readying myself for school in Kovno. They were days of doubt filled with question after question about who, what, when, and where. The only question to which I seemed to have an answer was—why? I knew the answer to that:

I was going to the ORT school in Kovno to prepare myself for a career for which I could not be trained in Kavarsk.

Mother packed the wicker basket with the clothes and underwear one was expected to wear in the big city. The basket was to be my chest, my vault, and my pantry. For the next three years, I lived out of a piece of woven wicker.

When the hour of departure came, friends and family gathered around to bid me good-bye. Mother wept while holding my sister's hand. As father closed the doors and sent the chauffeur on his way, I waved them a fond farewell.

You must understand that my going to the ORT school in Kovno was a milestone in our town. I was the first young person from Kavarsk to attend the ORT school. Up until the time of my enrollment in ORT, no family had had the foresight to have their youngsters learn a modern trade that would equip them for the world outside our town. My father and I were somewhat ahead of our time in our town; we thought not only about what was, but also about what could be and what should be.

When we arrived in Kovno, my father took me to the apartment where I was to spend my first school year, at 25 Dukantos Street (*Yatkever* Street). The apartment was on the ground floor facing a courtyard. It consisted of four rooms and a toilet (a water closet). It had a tiny kitchen, a coal stove, a sink, and cold running water. Two of the bedrooms were rented out. One had been rented to two brothers; another tiny bedroom had been rented to another cousin of mine, who was Sosa's second daughter. Her name was Chayke; she had been married and divorced, and was then working as a salesgirl for a wholesale textile company.

The owner of the apartment was a widow who slept in the third bedroom. One of her two sons worked in a store where they sold all kinds of metal and hardware products. The other was a third-year student at our ORT school.

I slept on a couch in the combination living and dining room. My rent included lunch, which was our main meal. We all ate the same food, except that the dessert, which was a fruit compote, was not served to me. The widow also ran a small grocery around the corner from our dwelling.

Before I started school I went to the store where my landlady's son worked to purchase some tools that were essential for my training. My father showed me how to get to the school, which I would be attending six days a week. It was about three quarters of a mile from my residence.

The school itself was new and still in the process of completion. It was a three-story brick building, with large windows facing in every direction; as a result, the rooms were all very bright and light.

After my father had showed me the way to school, we returned to the place where I was to be a tenant for the coming year. Father bid me good-bye and told me not to worry: He would try to see me as often as he could.

It wasn't until my father left that I realized the great burden of responsibility that had been bestowed upon me. I was now on my own. Here I was, at the age of thirteen years and six months, still a child who should be going to some school for teenagers and occupying his spare time playing with friends. Instead, I found myself scared and alone in this vast city, not knowing anyone and still not fully aware of all the obligations I'd assumed. From that moment on, *I* had to make the decisions about my life, whether in matters small or large, without the advice and consent of my parents. I had to stand on my own feet. The first year would prove to be very difficult for me. I suffered acutely from a disease called homesickness.

My ties to home, of course, were not totally severed. Every two weeks my mother would send me a large loaf of her famous sweet-and-sour-dough black bread and some Danish. That would sustain me for two weeks. Every morning I would have a slice of that bread and butter with hot tea, or a Danish with tea. For lunch I would eat whatever was prepared by my landlady, and for supper I would, once more, have my mother's bread with butter, or a Danish with tea.

That was my ordinary routine for the three years I spent in Kovno. There would, however, be one notable exception: On Friday nights I would have dinner at my Uncle Itzik's and Aunt Vichne's apartment. (I will talk about them later.)

The ORT school in Kovno was considered to be the best vocational and technical school in Lithuania. Upon graduation, just about everyone was guaranteed a job with good pay. But, as a young kid of thirteen and a half, I did not understand all this and I wasn't looking that far ahead into my future. I went to the school on the advice of my father, whom I loved and revered. I was eager to comply with his wishes at all times, and rarely said no to him. I did what he suggested not out of fear, lest I be punished, but out of respect for his judgment and for his concern about me. Indeed, I can recall only one occasion when he spanked me, and that was with good reason. It was to warn me never to pull the hairs off the horses' tails because they might kick me and cause me great harm.

In my eyes, Father could do no wrong. Even if I didn't like some of the things he wanted me to do, I did them anyhow, confident that he knew better than I that these were the right things to do.

As I said earlier, Father was always ahead of his time. He foresaw what economic circumstances lay in the years ahead, and he wanted me to be ready to fit into the changing scheme of things. (The one thing he did not foresee, lamentably, was the onrushing Holocaust, perhaps because, to a man of his sensitivities, it would have been unthinkable.)

At school, I studied hard. The program was rigorous. School ran five and a half days a week—full days from Sunday through Thursday, and then half a day on Friday. The vocational classes ran from 8:00 A.M. to 4:00 P.M. Academic classes followed from 5:00 P.M. to 8:00 P.M. every day except Friday. We had a one hour lunch break, which included the time it took to get to and from our eating place.

The vocational and technical part of the curriculum was quite comprehensive. We learned how to do tool and die making, how to operate a lathe, how to do milling and welding, and so on. Although my grades in the academic area were just average, in the technical and mechanical courses I shared the number one spot with another student, whose name was Poochert. In our third year at ORT, the school got an order for a fireproof vault. The project was given to the two of us. We had to start from scratch and build a vault with a combination lock. We did it and took great pride in our accomplishment.

The Maccabee sports grounds were located right opposite our school, alongside the Vileiya (*Neris*) River. The Maccabee soccer team and the Kovno Hapoel team were rivals. They were also part of a national league that involved Lithuanian and Polish clubs. To a small-town kid like myself, watching two top teams play against each other was a super-thriller. Ordinarily, I would not have had the opportunity to witness such an exciting contest, but being in Kovno and so close to the playing fields, I did, indeed, have the good luck to see the Maccabees engage some of the best teams in the country.

In my first year at school, my cousin Naftali Heiman was a player on the Maccabee team that won the national championship. He was also on the Maccabee junior soccer league team and would even play as a substitute in the major leagues. He was an all-around athlete who, as a member of the Maccabee club, won the national Lithuanian amateur boxing championship. Need I tell you how elated I was when he first escorted me into the stadium to see the top players in action?

In that first game I attended, my cousin's team played against the anti-Semitic Polish Spartas; the Maccabees won. I was overcome with joy at seeing our Jewish Maccabees, my cousin Naftali (*Tolik*) playing a pivotal part, defeat the anti-Semitic Spartas.

After the game I visited Naftali's parents, whom I would join for an occasional tea on a Saturday. I assumed that after the game the players would retire to their locker rooms, change clothes, and depart peacefully to their homes. But that was not the way it went. As the Maccabee players started to return home to celebrate their victory they were ambushed by the members of the losing Polish club. A fistfight ensued. The "sportsmen" on both sides were quickly bloodied.

When Naftali came home and opened the door, he looked a frightening figure; his shirt and pants were covered with blood. My aunt was shaken. What had happened? After changing his clothes, Naftali told us. I asked him what had happened to the Polish boys. Tolik grinned. They had been shellacked. I believed him because he was a rough, tough fighter. I also learned that our boys had not been taken by surprise: The Spartas had a reputation for seeking "revenge" whenever they lost a game. Our boys had been ready for them.

Had I known what was going on in Europe at that time I might have looked upon this spat between Jews and Polish anti-Semites as a foreshadowing of darker days ahead. When, six months later, Tolik left for Israel, I was saddened. I would miss him, and I would miss the free passes to the soccer games.

(In 1944, as the Second World War was coming to a climax, I encountered Naftali in Palestine. It was the first time our paths had crossed since his departure for Israel. I was there recuperating from my service as a soldier in the American armed forces. I saw him again, together with Trudy, in 1963. From that time on, we related to each other as if we were brothers.)

Back at ORT, I just could not wait for the first term to end. I packed my old belongings back into my wicker basket along with some handmade tools and other mechanical contraptions I had devised. They were my "trophies," my own creations; I wanted to show them off to my family and friends. But the object of which I was most proud was for my sister, a shiny, highly polished brass pin in the shape of an M, the initial of my sister's name.

I was so pleased to be home again with my father, mother, and sister. I think my mother, especially, was happy; she catered to me as I had never been catered to before. How do they say it? "Absence makes the heart grow fonder."

I was back to "home sweet home" again with family. And then there were the friends, the forest, the swims, the noshing on the fruit of the vine, the overeating of still unripe berries and cherries and the customary stomachache. In the process, we were also able to collect a bit more than we could devour and sell what was left to earn a few pennies.

My friends looked upon me now as a worldly man, coming from the big city, exposed to an education, and worthy of real respect. Kovno made me, in their eyes, more than just another commoner: Now I was a somebody.

While at home, I would help Mother with a variety of chores. One of them was to help make butter, a process that involved several steps:

Step Number One: Once a week, I would take two gallon-size clay jars, outfitted with a rope handle, to a nearby farmer, a trip of some two miles.

Step Number Two: The farmer would milk some cows on the spot and fill my jars with fresh, warm milk.

Step Number Three: I would rush home with the milk, unpasteurized and, surely, unhomogenized.

Step Number Four: My mother would pour a portion of that milk into other jars and cover it with cheesecloth. She would let it ferment for several days.

Step Number Five: Mother would, in time, remove the cream from the top of the milk and pour it into a tall wooden vessel. The top of that vessel had a removable round cover with a hole in the middle of it.

Step Number Six: A round wooden rod would be inserted in that hole. At the bottom of the rod we attached two square pieces of wood at right angles to one another. I would move the pole up and down, churning the cream until it turned into butter. The vessel used for the churning was, in Yiddish, called a *kaleteika*.

My first summer back home raced by very swiftly. There were the usual rites and rituals, the cakes and victuals, the public baths and their hot *pleitzes*, the usual rounds with family and friends. I was back in the groove and loved every second I spent in the old familiar ways. Part of that pattern was, of course, a visit to the *shul* to purify our souls after we had purified our bodies in the bath. Somehow, when I went to the services after my first year in Kovno, I felt grown-up, a man among men.

I was struck by the fact that the *shul* seemed much better lit than in the past. It was not due to the introduction of electricity—that we still did not have. It was due to a large paraffin lamp made of metal and glass. The most significant part of this lamp was a small asbestos part that looked like a sock. When heated, it glowed and cast a blindingly bright light. I was entranced by this new fixture. And, in my vainglorious imagination, I fantasied how proud I should be that this lamp had been erected to cast its glow throughout the synagogue in honor of my return.

Sooner than I would have wanted, Rosh Hashanah and Yom Kippur were upon us. The high holidays had come and gone. It was time for me to depart for Kovno again. Mother packed my wicker basket and I was off to face my second year. I was now fourteen and a half, a "veteran" in the war to survive and make it in Kovno; but, I must confess, once I was actually in Kovno again I was gripped with homesickness. I yearned for the solidity, serenity, and certainty of my *shtetl*. Kavarsk was still in my bones.

The next year, and in the subsequent years I spent at the ORT school, I lived in a new apartment with my cousin, Yakov Jaffe, and with another fellow from Kavarsk whose name was Tzalel Dilatsky. Both were a little older than I. We lived on Mapu Street, about fifty feet off Vilnius Street.

The apartment consisted of three rooms plus a small grocery. The owners of the apartment were a couple and two children. The father was legally blind. The daughter, about twelve years old, and her younger brother shared one bedroom. The three of us—my cousin, a friend and myself—slept on high sofas in the combination living and dining room. In a small kitchen, the landlady did her cooking on a Primus.

My dinners were not covered by my rent, as had been the case in the place I'd rented my freshman year; I had to prepare my breakfast and my supper by myself. Once more I fell back on my bread and butter washed down with hot tea. To allow me to sleep a little later in the morning, Father brought me a thermos bottle so I could prepare the hot tea the night before.

The toilet was outside in the yard and served several apartments. In the winter it was bitterly cold. In the morning, I would try to contain myself until I got to school, where the toilet facilities were nice and warm.

In my second year, as I began to adjust to the new environment and mature as a person, I found life in Kovno more interesting and fulfilling. I began to leave my small-town ways behind me and to take on the attitudes of a more cosmopolitan life-style.

Slowly, my dress, too, began to change. For the first time in my life, at ages fourteen and fifteen, I began to wear a ready-made pair of shoes and a winter coat. I engaged in window shopping; I would pause at the shoe shop, admiring the well-built, well-styled footwear. I'd dream of owning a pair, or several pairs. I'd peer through the door to see who was buying what.

I was particularly allured by the "in" shoes that were quite popular with the students. They were low lace-up boots with heavy leather soles studded with special nails. The charm of these shoes was that they made a distinctive noise when you walked in them and, because of their structure, you could wear them for a long time.

When my father, on one of his regular visits to Kovno, broke the news to me that he was going to buy me a pair of these shoes and an overcoat, I could have jumped into his arms, embraced him, hugged him, and kissed him, had I not felt somewhat embarrassed to do so. Although I did not openly display my joy, whatever my inhibitions, inside I was bursting with glee.

When I entered the shoe store, sat down, and removed my home-made shoes, the clerk measured my feet for size with a wooden ruler—not with a strip of paper, as in Kavarsk. When he brought out a suitable pair of shoes, I slipped my feet into them, laced them up, stood up, and took a little walk to see how they felt. Frankly, I did not really know how they were supposed to feel. I was in seventh heaven, walking on clouds. If the shoes did pinch, I don't think I would have noticed. I was beyond pain. When I removed the shoes, my eyes and my heart remained fixed on my rare new acquisition. When they put the shoes in a bag, they added studs for the soles. These had to be properly nailed to the sole by a shoemaker.

In the beginning I used to reserve my newly bought shoes for Friday evenings, when I'd go out to visit with some friends. I also wore them on Saturdays, when I would march on the cement sidewalks or the cobblestone streets to the music of my studded shoes as they struck the hard surfaces.

As to a coat, the most popular and stylish winter coats worn by the young people were made of a light pepper and salt blue-grey colored hairy cloth. After Father and I were done with our shoe shopping we walked, packaged shoes under my arm, to a store where they sold ready-to-wear men's clothing. This was the first time I had ever been in a shop that sold ready-to-wear clothing for men.

I had seen such clothes on display in a store on Laisves Alleiya, the main boulevard in Kovno lined with stores selling expensive items, but I had never been inside one of these attractive shops. Now here I was, no longer an outside onlooker but an inside buyer. A clerk brought us coats of various sizes, designs, and colors. I tried them on, standing in front of a mirror appraising how I looked with this one or that one.

I could hardly believe what I saw in that mirror. Here was this one-time local yokel, with his small-town vision and limited exposure to the world, parading back and forth before a mirror making an aesthetic judgment about which coat would be to his liking. My father looked on, beaming with pride. He made a few adjustments here and there, tapping the shoulders, tugging at the front to make sure that it was the right fit and allowing some extra space for this growing lad of fifteen. We finally decided on a blue tweed coat. Father paid a price for this ready-made overcoat that was, as customary, more expensive than a coat made to order.

What a wonderful feeling it was when I walked out of that store with my precious shoes under my arm and my father at my side! I could sense his pride in me. He would let me walk ahead so he could size me up from the rear. Then he would catch up with me and match me stride for stride. We were not just walking; we were parading—just the two of us—in celebration of a marked moment. I had arrived at another one of those turning points in my life. And to top it all off, we had a meal of soup and some specials at the Rosemarine restaurant on Vilnius Street.

I realize that it must be difficult to imagine that so insignificant an experience as buying a pair of shoes and an overcoat could have been such a great event in anyone's life—but it was. It was something that ranked with other turning points, such as coming to Kovno and going to the ORT school. I was now grown-up, grown out of my parochial provincial image of myself as a kid from Kavarsk. I got a great psychological lift from the new status I acquired by joining the other students in their manner of dress.

The next two years at the ORT school in Kovno were most enjoyable. I was particularly pleased with the vocational training that, I felt, was conducted on a very high and comprehensive professional level. I looked forward to my graduation, to a good job, and employment in Kovno in any one of the many modern plants that welcomed students from ORT. (Through all these years, I had no inkling about what was brewing in Europe to shatter our hopes and dreams.)

Through these years, a sort of feeding routine was established. From home, every two weeks, I would receive mother's sweet-and-sour dark bread and a batch of Danish pastry (*bulkalech*). I would have dinner between one and two at the *Folk's Kitchen* (the People's Kitchen). As a student I would pay twenty-five Lithuanian cents (five U.S. cents) for a dinner consisting of a bowl of soup and a *kotlet* (meat loaf) with mashed potatoes and bread. These were my staples for the next two years while at ORT.

On most Friday nights, I would have dinner with my granduncle Itzik and aunt Vichneh Heiman (Naftali and Yakov Heiman's parents). My late grandmother, Neche Minna, and Itzik Heiman were siblings.

My father and my *fetter* (uncle) Itzik were very close. My father's recurrent trips to Kovno gave him the opportunity to spend lots of time with Uncle Itzik and Aunt Vichneh at the textile and piece-goods store they owned and operated. The close relationship between my father and the Heimans came naturally to include me as well. I felt especially close to their older son, Leizer (Eliezer). Their other sons, Yakov and Naftali, and their daughter Ziporah, had by this time emigrated to Palestine.

Leizer, who was not yet married when I was in Kovno, was a university graduate and became a Hebrew teacher in a Hebrew high school in Wilkomer. He became part of a literary circle of Jewish and Hebrew writers. He distinguished himself by his contributions to Jewish newspapers and by writing a book on the life and works of Abraham Mapu. Mapu (1808–1867), who was born in Slabodka, a suburb of Kovno, was known as the creator of the modern Hebrew novel.

During my days at ORT, Leizer was the curator of the Jewish museum and archives in Kovno. He also had quarters there. On Friday nights, he would join us for dinner at his parents' place. After dinner, he'd give me a private Hebrew lesson. Quite often, I would accompany him back to his quarters at the museum, not far from his parents' home, and would spend the night sleeping over. Leizer married a girl from Roguva, whose name was Ziporah. This happened after I left for America.

During the Holocaust, they were all burned alive in their bunker, their hiding place, a cellar in the Viliampole–Kovno ghetto. In 1973, when Trudy and I were in Israel, Leizer's brother Naftali obtained two clay ceramic tablets, found by Lithuanians who had scavenged the ghetto after the war and came across these remains in the bunker where they'd all perished. These tablets are now on display in Israel, in the museum of the ghetto fighters (*lehomei hagetaot*).

I have a photo of the tablets. The words are written in Hebrew. The following is my own English translation:

Tablet I:

Eliezer Heiman, my wife,
Zipora, my father Yitzhak,
My mother Vichneh and my mother-in-law
Pese Feige
The remaining Jews
In Lithuania
We are sitting in the house
Of extinction, in this Jewish
Ghetto in Viliampole
A suburb of Kovno.

Tablet II:
I Eliezer
Heiman
From the remaining
Young Jewish writers
In Lithuania, I have inscribed
These lines with my own hands
On these tablets
For the future generations to remember
This day in the
Creation of the world
Corresponding to the 22nd of September 1943

According to the Christian calendar.

An article on this subject appeared in the *Jewish Forward.*

Eliezer Heiman was born in Kavarsk and had written a book in Yiddish about his birthplace. He would visit Kavarsk quite often. We were not his only relatives in Kavarsk; he had an uncle on his mother's side who had a very lovely brick house, perhaps the most attractive house in town, located adjacent to the marketplace. Eliezer would stay there when he visited Kavarsk. He had many young friends and loved to get back to the simpler ways of our town. He wrote about nature, life in the village, the peasants. He painted word pictures that brought all the natural beauty of the shtetl to the mind's eye. His tablets were his parting words to the world he'd once embraced.

Uncle Itzik and Aunt Vichneh treated me royally whenever I visited them. Uncle was a religious man. He carried himself in a distinguished fashion, his neatly trimmed Vandyke beard adding to his bearing. Aunt Vichneh was a good-looking woman, a bit on the heavy side. She catered to Uncle with the highest love and respect.

When I visited them on Friday evenings, she would treat me with great courtesy and concern and make sure I was well fed. I think she knew how I felt as a young person away from home. She tried hard to fill the void of homesickness with all the attention she showered on me.

My uncle and aunt were always together, never apart from one another through all their married years. They ran their business jointly. It was a prosperous operation. Up until the Great Depression of the 1930s, my father would tell me how well they did in their store with its several hired hands. Their residence overlooked the River Neman, and they were able to afford a sleep-in maid.

After the crash, unfortunately, they lost their store. Ziporah and two of the boys left for Palestine. My uncle and aunt moved into an apartment, where they shared kitchen and dining room with a young couple who had a small child. What I remember most about that couple is really a matter of no consequence that, nevertheless, has left a lasting impression on me: They used to cut an orange in half, squeeze the juice out of it, and then have the child drink the juice. That was the first time in my life that I had ever seen that done.

After they'd lost their store, the Heimans opened up a small booth in a marketplace near the president's house. They peddled textiles, of course. They would stand there outdoors all day long trying to make a sale. I would go out of my way occasionally just to pass by their stand and say hello. I have a remembrance of them in winter, standing there in the cold all bundled up, holding their hands over a kerosene lamp to keep their fingers warm. They wore knitted gloves cut away at the ends to allow them to handle piece goods and money. They were wonderful people, true survivors—though they were unable, lamentably, to survive the man-made calamity of the Holocaust.

When I came to Kovno, I was introduced by my father to a family who were related to us. I never really knew their name, but it was something like Tzuckerman or Tzuckernick. They had two beautiful daughters. To me they were very elegant, the sort of women you see as French models in magazines. There was also a son, my age, whose name also eludes me. He was in my freshman class at ORT. The family had a butcher shop, a *yatke*, close to my place.

The wife, Reizel, would stay in the shop and sell the meat, while her husband would tend to the slaughtering and preparation of the meat for sale. Their son became a good friend of mine; proximity helped make it so. Their house, with its nearby butcher shop, was close to my residence.

I was occasionally invited to their home for dinner, but somehow I felt out of place. It probably had less to do with them than with my own lingering feeling that I was inadequate, as a small-town kid, to fit into this big-city company.

Here I was, surrounded by beautiful dishes and furnishings, by a maid who served us, by two stunning ladylike girls, without any ability on my part even to make the necessary small talk. The circumstance was just too fancy for me.

Yet, when I encountered Reizel in her shop, I would spend some time conversing with her. In that shop we were on common ground; in the house I felt that I just did not belong. I thought to myself that they were too stuck up, although they were not.

When my Aunt Lena and Sandra visited us in 1937, they spent a few days in Kovno with this family and hit it off perfectly. They talked endlessly about how great they were and how much they were enjoying one another's company. Sandra was completely at ease with the two girls. To me, this was a case of the big time meeting the big time. I still felt like an outsider from the sticks.

In one of the last letters I received from Father in 1941, just before

Germany launched its war against the Soviet Union on 22 June that year, he mentioned the fact that Reizel had come to Kavarsk to get a birth certificate. He wrote: "You would never have recognized her. She became very skinny. One should never be envious of the old once-rich people today."

Lithuania had become, in 1940, a "republic" under the heel of the Soviet Union. As a consequence, all the rich people were sent to Siberia, put in jail, or assigned to some work without their consent, and all their tangible wealth had been confiscated by the government. I do not know what ultimately happened to them. I believe that they were exterminated during the Holocaust. I've had no word they survived from them or from anyone else.

In my second and third years at the ORT school, I began to develop a sense of self-esteem and self-confidence. I rejoined the Zionist youth organization which I had been a member of in Kavarsk.

Although I was not yet fifteen years old, my exposure to the school and to Kovno made me feel older than I was. My social life expanded in several directions. In addition to my friends at school, I became friendly with other young men and women, some of whom were older and more mature than I. Then there were some boys and girls who had come from Kavarsk to seek work in Kovno—a trend common at that time among small-town youth, who were drawn to the big cities with their greater opportunities. We naturally gravitated toward each other.

Friday evenings were a time to get together. The older boys would do a bit of drinking and smoking. There would always be music via a record player or the radio. We would dance a polka, a waltz, or an abbreviated version of the tango. I was picking up a bit of sophistication. I danced with girls and came to enjoy them.

The most beautiful time in Kovno was during the Christmas and New Year holidays. Although homes were not lit up and decorated, as is customary in the United States, the main street was beautifully adorned and illuminated. The opera house was likewise spruced up and glistened like a multicolored gem. A tall evergreen, which had been erected in front of the national museum, dripped with shining electric bulbs. Although the air was bitter cold, it was dry and crisp. Outfitted in my new shoes and fashionable overcoat, I liked to walk along the main drag. I would pause to peer through the store windows at the glamorous displays.

Now and then, if I had some cash on hand, I would venture into a famous dairy restaurant known as the *Pieno Centras*, a government-owned cooperative. I would order boiled potatoes with sour milk, a very special treat to me. And then, to top it off, I would have a cup of hot chocolate, cocoa.

For me, the sights and smells of the season were something very special. What a panorama: the broad main street, glistening in all its glory; the long line of trees, branches heavily laden with blankets of pure white snow under a gray sky always threatening to burden the branches with more—truly a winter wonderland.

One event I experienced at winter's end I really have to share with you. It was a Saturday afternoon, sometime in March or April. We had a gathering of boys and girls from our Zionist group on a corner outside the well-known fish market located at the point where the Vilaye River flows into the Neman.

During the winter, both rivers would freeze, of course. While we were standing there, involved in our group discussion, somebody noticed that we were being surrounded by water bubbling up from the sewers and pouring in from the side streets. Our meeting broke up as we all started to run for an elevated dry spot.

What had happened was this: The Vilaye River had begun to thaw. Ordinarily, it would flow into the Neman, but the Neman was still frozen. Since the water from the Vilaye could not penetrate the solid blocks of ice of the Neman, the melting waters of the Vilaye began to back up and flood the city streets.

The street that we traversed to get to school—Janover Street, which ran along the river—was totally submerged. The waters did not reach our school, since it was on higher ground, but to get to school we had to take a detour. We got to school via the *greener barg,* (green hill) that rose above the waters. The flood lasted for about three weeks.

Uncle Itzik had a second-floor apartment overlooking the fish market. The floor below him was half flooded. In order for my aunt and uncle to get to work, they had to be transported in a rowboat. When, as usual, I went to have dinner with them Friday nights, I had to be taken there by boat.

I was informed that such flooding was not uncommon, but normally the water did not rise enough to cause great inconvenience. When it did, the army would come to the rescue with explosives to blow apart the ice blocks and speed the thaw.

Our ORT school was, in its time, considered to be the most modern vocational school in Lithuania. It was stocked with the latest technical equipment available for use in the teaching and training of the students. During the years I attended, enrollment reached its peak. There were some four hundred students, plus an extra contingent of adults who'd enrolled for night classes.

Although there were a number of ORT schools in many cities in the 1920s, by the time I enrolled the Kovno school was the only vocational high school left in the ORT system. To be a student there was a rare opportunity, both for the superior training offered by the school and also for the guarantee of employment after graduation.

Earning a diploma and certificate from the school was no simple matter. There were very extensive examinations, conducted in the presence of official testers who represented various departments of the government's educational system. The elaborate procedure made the student feel a sense of pride and importance.

As I noted earlier, the director of the school was Jacob Oleiski. He survived the Holocaust and became the director-general of ORT in Israel. I developed a close relationship with him that lasted until his death.

He was a tall, distinguished-looking man who always carried a pipe in his hand or in his mouth. He radiated a sense of authority and confidence. I respected him and, at the same time, feared him. In my eyes, he was the ultimate authority in the school—if you did something wrong, he had the power to discharge you. I may, however, have had an exaggerated notion about his role and his personality, because I was this young student from a small town with its primitive system of elementary education.

When he arrived at the school in the morning he did not go directly into his office, which was located in the front section of the building where offices were situated. He preferred to come in through a back door of the building to an area where there were automated lathes, die presses, milling drills, and similar equipment. He would look around, making sure that all was in order, and then he'd proceed to his office. It seemed to me that he wished to establish his presence in the flesh, to let us all know that he was a real person, right here, and not just a name out there.

When he entered, his eyes would sweep around the room. He would take a few steps and then walk down the center of the workshop in the general direction of his office. On one side of his path were the freshmen working away at long tables equipped with vises; on the other side were second- and third-year students working on their assigned projects.

As he walked, he stood tall and erect with pipe in hand. He'd turn his head left and right without saying a word. We would continue busily at our work. I do remember one occasion when another student and I were making a wall safe, the project I mentioned earlier. Our usually silent director stopped and asked us what we were doing. We told him, and then, without saying anything or even nodding recognition, he continued his routinized walk, or should I say inspection, of our workroom.

For the Passover holiday, the school would be closed. The students who lived in Kovno would go to their homes. Those of us who lived in other towns or cities would leave a few days before the holiday. I had a particular problem every year, because I was needed back home far in advance of Passover to help my father and uncle bake matzos for sale to the townspeople.

To depart that early I had to get permission from the director, and to do so I had to go to his home. He and his wife lived in an apartment house on a street near the Neman River, called *Klein Vilner Street* (Little Vilnius Street). I would climb the stairs to the second or third floor, scared stiff and shaking like a leaf. As I pushed the bell and the door opened I'd continue to quiver.

If Mrs. Oleiski opened the door, I'd ask for Mr. Oleiski. He would enter, pipe in mouth, and say, in his strong voice, "What can I do for you?" I'd beg him, "Please, let me go home for Passover three weeks in advance to help my father with the matzos." I would explain that we needed the earnings to pay for my tuition at the ORT school. After a brief exchange, he would grant me the permission to leave two weeks early. I would leap down the stairs feeling very much relieved.

I encountered Oleiski after the war in 1969, at an ORT conference in Canada. I reminded him of the incident related above. He said to me, "Jaffe, I remember when you would come to me to let you go home early to help bake the matzos."

The head of the vocational and technical departments of the school was an engineer whose name was Nomberg. He had a staff of highly competent and dedicated instructors; a few of them were recent graduates of the school. Upon my departure for America, my schoolmates and friends paid me the honor of posing for a photograph with me. It was a memento I treasured.

I would meet with Oleiski on my annual visits to Israel. On one occasion, he asked me whether I had any pictures of the years I'd spent at the ORT school. I told him that I did. He wanted to use them in some publication with which he was involved. I gave him the pictures. After he had used them, he returned them to me—all except the one photo of myself and my friends. He said that he had somehow misplaced it and could not find it, for which he apologized profusely.

In my last two years in Kovno I was living on Mapu Street and at the corner of Mapu and Vilnius was a coffeehouse where people would gather to play dominos, smoke cigarettes, drink coffee, and devour Napoleons. I would pass this spot every day and, in the evening, I would stop and peer through the window to feast my eyes on what was going on there.

After making a move in their domino game, the players would dig into their big Napoleon, slicing it with a spoon and conveying the rich dessert to their lips; then to be washed down with a cup of coffee. My mouth would water, and I would be whispering silently to myself, *I would give anything for a piece of that delicious-looking Napoleon.* And I would wonder whether a day would ever come when I would be able to walk into this place, get seated, and then order a Napoleon with coffee.

In 1991, when I went back to Kovno, I made sure to visit this shop. The building was still there; by now, I probably could have bought the place. But the coffee shop was no longer there. When I looked through the window I saw an office with people at their desks, pens and pencils in hand. But, believe it or not, my mouth watered again in remembrance of the Napoleon I had yearned for a half century earlier.

My roommate, cousin Yankele (Yakov, or Jacob in English), worked in the back room of an ice cream parlor, where his job was to make the ice cream. Whenever I had the time, I would drop in to watch him at work. As someone who had firsthand knowledge of how we made ice cream in the *shtetl*, I was entranced by the mechanical methods used in Kovno. My second reason for going was Yankele's decision to use me to taste the many flavors of the delicacy he was producing.

Aside from my personal involvement, I mention the parlors because they became a craze, the "in" thing, throughout the larger cities in Lithuania. Suddenly, these urban centers were seized with ice cream mania. And what town, do you suppose, was responsible for this? The answer is—Kavarsk, not directly but indirectly.

In Kavarsk there was a shoemaker whose family name was Komas. Some of his several sons emigrated; two remained in Kavarsk. All the boys were quite bright and creative in their own way.

One of the émigré sons went to Germany. When or why or even whether Shlomo Komas, the shoemaker who lived on *Mitzraim Gas*, even had a son in Germany was something I did not know. It does appear, however, that this son had lived in Germany for a number of years. He was married and had children, but in 1933, when Hitler came to power, he and his family decided to leave Germany. In 1934, they came to Kavarsk. One of their children, a boy about a year older than I, became one of my friends. Once back in Kavarsk, the question was—how to make a living?

It seems that when this scion of the Komas family fled Berlin and returned to Kavarsk his eye was on the big city, on Kovno. He had apparently invented an ice cream machine that could turn out the product without the use of ice. He opened an ice cream parlor in Kovno. It was more than a place to consume a delicacy; it was a social center. He offered a variety of flavors, served at tables in a glass dish. At his cafe, especially in the summer, friends would gather to partake of the sweets and one another's company. There were tables on the outside as well as on the inside. The shop was located on the main street of Kovno and was known as the Komas Cafe. It was an instantaneous success.

That success became a model for a chain of outlets throughout the big cities in Lithuania. They became a sober, well-savored, socially acceptable substitute for the saloon.

The entrepreneur Komas would supply the machinery, provide the formula, and set up the parlor. He also placed people he could trust in management positions. First he placed his brothers and other members of the immediate family in such posts; then he reached out to cousins and other relatives. He also reached out to young people from Kavarsk who might not be relatives but who, as small-town neighbors, were as close to kin as one can get without sharing blood lines. And that is how my cousin Yankele got his job in Kovno and how ice cream mania overran Lithuania.

Whenever my father came to Kovno, he and I would go to the cafe, where we enjoyed the ice cream and the company of the man who made ice cream famous.

I must confess that, although I took great pleasure in spending time with my cousin Yankele in the back room of the cafe, the crowning moments of my involvement with the ice cream parlor were those that I spent with my father and the owner of the chain.

SEVENTEEN
Farewell to Kavarsk

My personal observation about the emergence of anti-Semitism in Lithuania in the last two years of my life there was that, while there were no openly anti-Semitic laws enacted against the Jews by the Smetona government, as there were in Germany, and there were no anti-Semitic acts condoned by the government, there were many actions that were indirectly bound to affect the Jewish community negatively. While there were no overt actions that might invite the opprobrium of the outside world, there were many acts that did direct harm to Jews yet would not invite negative criticism from outside Lithuania. For instance:

Jews were very prominent in the import and export business. What the government did was to establish a government-run agency with exclusive authority to handle import and export transactions. In effect, Jews were shut out. The government set up and owned cooperative stores, which drew much of their business from clients who had once patronized Jewish stores and were now exhorted by priests to patronize the government stores.

One of the casualties of this policy of establishing government or cooperative monopolies in certain areas, where, in the past, Jews had predominated, was my father. He ran a bus. Others ran a variety of other transport operations. Jews had originally gotten into the transport business because they'd been excluded from other trades. So they got a horse and wagon and served those who wanted to move products or persons from one place to another. Jews were known as the *ba'al agoles* (the teamsters), always ready to convey whatever or whoever it might be from here to there. Now, however, in the late 1930s the government was stepping in to reorganize the industry and squeeze out the nongovernmental operators who, in the main, were Jews.

The government decreed that the number of buses was to be limited, and each bus had to be authorized by the authorities. Originally

Jews were included, since there wouldn't have been enough buses to carry on essential operations without them. But step by step, the government tightened its grip on the industry. Both drivers and conductors had to be licensed by the authorities and were required to wear a prescribed uniform. Fares were set by the government. To be admitted to the government "cooperative," it was necessary to use the latest equipment only. Approved buses were given a distinctive marker, a red cross that indicated that this bus was allowed to travel on the major thoroughfares.

When Father's second bus was denied permission to carry the red cross, he also lost the right to use the highway. The government made an annual decision as to which buses might or might not carry the red cross. If they found that our old bus was no longer acceptable, we could not replace it with a new bus. The government would make the replacement with its own bus. They were pushing the old fleets off the road and out of business.

In effect, the government was transforming an industry started by Jews into an industry without Jews.

I was an eyewitness to this tragedy. Step by step the Jews were eliminated from the intercity bus service they had initiated in Lithuania. Thus did a silent, but sinister, anti-Semitism work its wicked ways in Lithuania, even before the Nazi and Communist invasions.

While in my third year at the ORT school, I received a notice from the post office that there were two dollars awaiting me. The money had been sent from America. It was a gift from Aunt Lena. I exchanged it for ten Lit in Lithuanian money, which was for me at that time a meaningful sum. Obviously, Aunt Lena had not forgotten us. I certainly had not forgotten her, or, of course, Sandra.

Shortly thereafter, when it was my father's turn to be the conductor on the bus, he came to my place in Kovno. He was already there awaiting me when I got home. He'd bought some salami at the famous Rosemarine Restaurant. I prepared some tea. Mother's homemade bread was served. After this little meal my father addressed me in a grave manner.

He told me that he had received a letter from Aunt Lena, in which she said that she would like to sponsor one of us to come to America and that, at a later time, she would like to bring over the others.

I told my father that this was great news. "Father," I said, "you will go to America. I will finish school. And then we will join you."

His reply was, "No, Ruvalle. *You* will go first. It will be easier for them to bring you over. We will come later."

I was shocked. I never expected that Father would even *think* of sending me first. I told Father I would not go. I was too young; I wanted to finish school first; I could not go all the way to America by myself.

He said to me, "Listen, Ruvalle. You will go first and then we will follow you. You are not to be afraid. There is a man from Kavarsk by the name of Alex Weiner who, with his family, is going to America. I will make arrangements for you to go on the same ship with them."

I was devastated. I didn't want to leave my father, mother, sister, and all my relatives and friends and go to such a faraway place across a vast ocean. I wasn't quite sixteen yet. I really did want to finish my schooling at ORT.

My father was sympathetic to my feelings—my fears and my friendships—but he felt that for me to be the first to go to America was the right thing. As you know by now, I revered my father and his judgment. If he felt that my going was the right thing, who was I to question his opinion? (It turned out later that his plan was almost realized. I will talk about that later.)

The one thing that gave me the courage to face the challenge ahead was the knowledge that I would not, in America, be alone among strangers. I already knew Aunt Lena and Cousin Sandra. I assumed that I would be staying with them when I got off the ship. The thought that I would be with them was a ray of sunshine in a future that otherwise suddenly looked very dark to me.

I didn't tell any of my friends about the impending revolution in my life. I figured that I would wait until it happened. I would then be discussing something that was a fact and not just some fantasy about the future, and that would be the time to break the news.

I was certain that Father and Mother had jointly made the decision that I be the first to go to America. I thought often of my mother; I wished that I could be home with her in these last days of mine in Lithuania, rather than in school. I felt I knew how she felt as the time approached for me to depart, perhaps never to see each other again.

In due time, the necessary papers and affidavits from America arrived. They were furnished by my Uncle Louie and Jack Levine, owner of J. L. Plumbing Supply Company in Brooklyn. My uncle and Levine had a business relation, but they were also good personal friends. The affidavits confirmed that I was a close relative and that I would not be a burden on the American society. They further affirmed that I was going to America to further my education and that Uncle Louie and Jack Levine would see to it that I did not become a public charge.

I took these papers to the offices of HIAS (the Hebrew Immigrant Aid Society) in Kovno. I wanted to know what the affidavits said, as I was not able to read the English in which they had been written. The HIAS people translated the documents for me and then referred me to the American consulate. I was advised to tell the consulate that the affidavits were executed by my uncle and cousin and that my object in going to America was to continue my studies.

I took the papers to the consulate. They asked the expected questions. I gave them the answers I had been told by HIAS to give them. Shortly thereafter, I received the notice of approval and was advised to come in person to get the visa. But to get the visa I would first have to get a physical examination by a doctor designated by the consulate. Since I was then at school in Kovno, I was able to handle all these details by myself. I got the visa. Everyone was happy except myself. I was doing what I was expected to do, but my heart was just not in it.

There was another small but crucial matter involved in my getting a visa. I needed a birth certificate. Luckily, I was able to get one. I say, "luckily," because if we had had to depend upon the notoriously inefficient Lithuanian bureaucracy to furnish the necessary certificate, we might never have found one. Fortunately, when I was born, Jewish communities enjoyed a semiautonomous status in Lithuania. They were run by *kehilas*. The rabbinate in our *kehila* kept a record of my birth.

To get a passport, there was one more detail: I had to show tickets for both train and ship—tickets that were paid in full. As it turned out, Alex Weiner, who was fairly well off, was emigrating to America with his wife and three children, two boys and one girl. His wife, Leah, had several brothers living in Illinois who were sponsoring the Weiners.

The Weiners had booked passage for the last week in July 1938 on the French liner *Normandie*. (During the Second World War, the *Normandie* caught fire and was destroyed in New York harbor.) At the final moment some complication arose about my getting on the ship with the Weiners, but my father managed to set things straight and I sailed on the *Normandie*. Needless to add, I felt a lot better knowing that I was making the voyage in the company of people from our town who were older than I.

The time had finally come when I had to inform my friends and schoolmates that I was to leave for America. In the light of the world situation, with Hitler on the march, my departure was seen as a great piece of good luck for me. Many of my acquaintances were envious. They wished that they, too, were going off to the New World. They all wished me the best of luck.

At the time when I gathered with my friends, I had all my papers ready. The only things I lacked were the ticket for the ship and my passport. They were slated to arrive two weeks before my departure.

I decided to come home early to spend some time with my mother, sister, relatives, and friends. Father was on the road most of the time. I did, as noted, have numerous opportunities to spend time with my father in Kovno.

Mother was in charge of getting ready the clothes I would have to take with me. The first step was to buy some bolts of good-quality imported woolen cloth out of which to make a suit. Mother purchased a green striped fabric in one of our two textile stores. It was then hand-tailored by a young Lithuanian tailor who had been trained in Kovno. He lived on a hill right above the house of one of my girlfriends, whose father was a *shochet*. She and I were slightly intimate. So going for fittings for my suit was a double pleasure, a chance to do both business and a little monkey business.

I drove to Subatz with my uncle one night. He was going there to buy some glass from the Shneider brothers; I was going to say good-bye to my grandmother and my stepgrandfather, as well as to my uncle and his wife. As a going-away gift, my uncle gave me a wrist watch. It was a first for me and I was thrilled. I returned home with Uncle Yankel. We travelled through the night and arrived home early the next morning.

Then I went to Roguva to say good-bye to my Aunt Dina and her husband Rafael and my cousins.

Time was rushing by. My hour of departure was drawing close. I still had to get my tickets and my passport. I travelled to Kovno by bus to get the tickets. I then went to the government offices with passport pictures, birth certificate, ship and train tickets in hand. After a few days of rushing hither and thither, I did manage to get everything in order and was ready to return home.

Father gave me a complementary pass for the bus back home. As a member of the "cooperative," he was privileged to provide such passes to members of the family. Unfortunately, the bus for which I had the ticket did not go to Kavarsk. It did, however, traverse the highway off which there was a dirt road leading to our home. So I got off the bus at the point of intersection; removed my good shoes; and, barefoot, I plodded for five miles over the dirt road to my home.

In my last days at home, my mother pampered me as only she knew how. Her specialty was making the foods that I liked best. One of my mother's specialties was a jelly doughnut without the jelly, deep fried in butter. We called them *puntzikes*. She made them for home consumption and for sale. There were a few people in town who had a real love affair with this piece of pastry. My mother knew that she could count on these people to buy her *puntzikes* whenever she made them. So she made them, notified the devotees, and they would come flocking.

How, you might wonder, did my mother know how to make these deep fried doughnuts way back in 1938 in an out-of-the-way town called Kavarsk? I don't think that, at that time, there were any Dunkin' Donut shops in the United States. However, Mrs. Bernstein, whose family had moved to Kovno, ran a small business built around these doughnuts; her husband would peddle them out of a basket which he carried around the marketplace. This Mrs. Bernstein gave my mother the secret formula for *puntzikes* and taught her how to deep fry them in butter.

While in Kovno, I would visit the Bernsteins. They had several children, the oldest of whom, about three years my senior, worked in a place where they made leather wallets. Their second child, a daughter, Rivka, who was my age, was the sole survivor of the family in the years of the Holocaust. She had gone to Israel, which was where I met her.

When I came to America, the taste of my mother's doughnuts still lingered in my mouth. When I ordered my first doughnut in the United States, it looked so appetizing that I could hardly wait to take my first bite. I sank my teeth into it, only to be deeply disappointed: It was nowhere as good as Mama's mouth-watering morsel.

The Weiner family, with whom I was to make my passage to America, had liquidated its business before departure. They also sold their house, which had doubled as both workshop and residence. Alex Weiner was a *kamasen shteper*, a craftsman who specialized in making the leather upper part of a shoe. He had machines to sew leather and a few people working for him. He was a supplier to shoemakers in our town and in neighboring towns.

Their house was a modern wooden dwelling with a galvanized tin roof, polished floors, and plastered walls. They had no problem selling it, especially since it faced the market square, a choice location.

By Kavarskian standards, they were well-to-do. They did not leave Lithuania for economic reasons; they left because their family in America advised them that Hitler was a real threat and they should get out of Lithuania as soon as possible.

The date on which we were to depart depended more on the Weiners than on myself. If the Weiners were not involved I would have left much earlier, since I had no business and no home to liquidate. But Father insisted that it would be better and safer for me to go with them.

Actually, I had a ticket for a ship that left earlier, but when my father found out that the Weiners were leaving on a later ship, he changed the date of my departure and arranged somehow to get me on the same ship as the Weiners. The rescheduling of my departure entailed an extra charge—after all, next to the British ship the *Queen Elizabeth*, the *Normandie* was "it."

We were to go to Kovno from Kavarsk on a Sunday morning in my father's bus. From there we were to travel by train to Paris and then to Le Havre, where we would board the ship for America.

Saturday evening I went through the streets bidding good-bye to most of the families that lived in our town. This was customary whenever anyone who was single left for another country. If an entire family was leaving, people would come to visit them.

The next dawn, the crowing of roosters behind the house was like a trumpet call proclaiming the arrival of a new day. This raspy wake-up call was accompanied by the pealing bells of the church summoning the faithful to gather and hear the voice of God, to which the peasants responded, tumbling out of their straw mattress beds. Dressed in their finest, they recited prayers in the Latin they did not understand and listened to a sermon by a priest whose preachment invariably resounded with anti-Semitic overtones.

Not far from this church was a small wooden house with a thatched roof. Shutters protected the windows against anti-Semitic rock throwers and burglars. I always felt this "protection" was less real than imagined.

On this particular Sunday, when the shutters were thrown open and the morning sunlight poured into the house, its rays fell on a wooden sofa covered with a colorful homespun burlap sort of material filled with crushed straw. Lying on top of this heap was a lad of sixteen and a half who had spent the whole night wondering and worrying about what lay in store for him in the days ahead. I was scared and I was shivering as if I were running a high fever. My worry was that I would show my fear, so I made up my mind not to reveal my panicky condition to anyone. But the tension and trembling were there.

True, I had been separated from friends and family before, for example at the time I'd left Kavarsk for Kovno, but I'd always known that I was close enough to those I loved that I could (and would) see them again from time to time. But the separation this time was different. The distance between Kovno and Kavarsk was a mere stone's throw when compared with the distance between Lithuania and the United States. I was not simply going to another town; I was going to another universe.

I really was at the point of panic. Wild thoughts kept popping into my head. Perhaps I should change my mind and not go to America. To whom would I turn in that alien land when I felt lost or fell sick or fainted from fear?

All these frightening thoughts within me were joining together with one voice shouting, "Don't go!" But there was another voice within me—the voice of my father. I had made a commitment to him. How could I renege on my promise? I knew there was a dark cloud over my future, but I resolved to look for the silver lining. I thought about the positive things, about the *goldene medinah*, the "golden land" where anyone and everyone enjoyed a measure of plenty. I thought about some future time when, through hard work, I could make some money to help my parents back in Kavarsk. I thought of the time when I would be able to bring them to America. I would shower them with sweets for their mouths that would bring sweetness to their hearts. To escape thinking about what would be, I fantasized about what could be.

These imaginings, these dreams, are what gave me the strength to overcome my fears, to rise from my straw-filled mattress one last time. Yes, I would miss that crude, rudimentary bed where I had been content to sleep for so many years. It was the only way I knew and I had become attached to it; it was part of our household, and part of me.

Ours was a household drenched in love. It was a love that penetrated everything, including inanimate objects like a wooden couch and a straw-filled mattress. I was too young to know this at the time. It is only in retrospect that I realize what the unseen power was that so profoundly endeared to me the people, the objects, and the intangible atmosphere around me. It may all sound corny, but it was love.

Yes, it was time to go. Dreams were deluged in details. My father, mother, and sister were up and dressed. Mother was preparing breakfast: hot tea, her wonderful delicious yeast dough Danishes that she always baked on Friday for Shabbat. While preparing the table she would cast glances at me, still in my bed. Through the corner of my eye, I could see the tears rolling down her cheeks.

I got up, washed, and got into my new green-striped suit. Proudly, I put on my good shoes and a new dress shirt. This was no normal day, and I had to look my best.

When Father had finished his breakfast, he took my suitcase to the marketplace whence, at 6:00 A.M., the bus was scheduled to leave. Father would be there at an earlier hour, selling tickets to the passengers destined for Wilkomer or Kovno. He handled the luggage, which he would place on the roof of the bus.

Back home, I had my tea with Danish. My sister had something to eat. My mother did not eat.

I told my mother that it was time to go. She asked my sister to start walking up the hill and that we would follow. As soon as my sister left, my mother took me into the room between the combination living/dining room and her bedroom, which was usually quite dark and that was furnished with the tub she needed to relieve the aches from her rheumatism. In that room she embraced and hugged me tightly. I could feel her heart pounding fast and heavy, and I felt her golden wet tears flowing down my face as she kissed me for the last time before we parted for an unknown and fateful future.

I believe that Mother took me to the dark room to spare me the pain of seeing her tears, but she was too overcome to contain her weeping. I didn't have to see her tears; I felt them. At the time, still a teenager, I really did not fully sense the anguish she must have been enduring as she held her son tightly against her bosom for the last time. Only now, years later, do I fully understand how she must have felt.

We left the house to ascend the hill to the bus. My sister was halfway there; she stopped and waited for us to catch up. She took Mother by the hand and the three of us, together, walked to the bus in the marketplace.

It was packed with people. This came as no surprise to me. It was customary for many to gather in the square when someone in our town was leaving for another country. In my case, there was an unusually large family, an extraordinary number of friends, and even some Lithuanian neighbors who had come to say farewell.

The bus was ready to depart. Father told us to say good-bye and take our seats. I said my farewells to a few late arrivals. I kissed my sister and mother again. I sat myself near a window in the bus so I could get a last glimpse of my mother, my sister, and all the people I knew and cherished. Through the window I waved my hand.

As the bus moved slowly away from the marketplace, the people began to disappear. As we left the last house in town and moved on to the street that fed the road to Wilkomer, I looked back at the wooden houses with their thatched roofs. One of my last sights was the yellow and white painted church with its lofty steeple and clock gradually sinking and falling below the horizon. That was the last I saw of my *shtetl*, my birthplace and the birthplace of my father and of his father.

We arrived in Kovno about nine in the morning. I spent most of the day with Father. We had a good dinner in our favorite eating place, the Rosemarine Restaurant on Vilnius Street. I said good-bye to *feter*, my uncle Itzik and aunt Vichney, and my dear cousin Eliezer. I bid good-bye to Reizel, the cousin who had the butcher shop not far from where I'd lived in Kovno. I also managed to get around for farewells to my old friends in Kovno who were home on their summer vacations. Then Father took me and my suitcase to the train station, where we met the Weiners.

EIGHTEEN
To the Golden Land

According to the American immigration law at that time, I had to have at least seven American dollars in my possession to be cleared for entrance. Father gave me ten dollars and cautioned me to watch it carefully, and to make sure not to spend or lose it. In effect, my future hung suspended on ten dollars.

We boarded the train at the Kovno station at a late hour. I was assigned to a compartment that I was to share with the Weiners and a few strangers. I remember a woman who befriended the Weiners and became part of our new "family" all the way to America.

At the Kovno station, my father and I spoke our last words together. He kissed me as we embraced, but neither one of us shed a visible tear. Once more, my father asked the Weiners to keep an eye on me. Weiner told my father not to worry; the Weiners would watch over me.

The conductor signalled the usual, "All aboard." The whistle tooted its melancholy moan. The locomotive hissed steam from its steely sides. I waved and waved again to my father until he, like Kovno, Kavarsk, and my youth, were no longer before me.

I settled down in our compartment, right near the door. As we sped toward the German border, it suddenly hit me that this was the real thing. I was leaving my parents and my ancestral home and there was no turning back. But even as my sense of insecurity returned, I was able to beat it back with the euphoria that came from the immediate excitement of travelling by train through strange lands and then by ship to America. I was torn between my attachment to the past and my attraction to what was to come. Reality had not yet really set in, the reality that I was now on my own in soon-to-be faraway, unfamiliar places.

Our first stop was the Lithuanian-German border. My initiation into the Germany of Hitler was soon to be administered by the German conductor with his swastika-decorated uniform, pistol in his holster. He came to our compartment to check our tickets. Methodically, he checked the passport and rubber-stamped it. Then he punched the ticket. Putting passport and ticket together in formal fashion, he returned them both to me.

While punctiliously performing his function, he noticed that I was reading a newspaper, and from the Hebrew lettering recognized that it was a Yiddish publication. He ordered me to give it to him. I was startled, having no idea what it meant to be reading a Yiddish publication in Nazi Germany. He grabbed the paper out of my hands, threw it violently on the floor, and then proceeded to crush it under his heavily heeled boots. He left shouting, "*Du, verflichte Jude,*" a German expression that, in English, means, "You damned Jew." And with that, he gave me the look of someone ready to kill me.

I sat down quietly in my corner near the door, my head lowered, while he checked the other passengers. When he left, I sighed a sigh of great relief. I had just experienced my first personal encounter with the spirit of Hitler.

The next stop was at the border of Germany and the Polish Corridor via the cosmopolitan city of Danzig. The corridor had been negotiated by the Allies in the Treaty of Versailles, signed at the conclusion of World War I. In order to give Poland access to the sea, and also to punish Germany for having started World War I, the Allies carved out a "Polish" corridor separating East Germany from West Germany. The chief port of the corridor was Gdansk.

Our next stop was Berlin, where we spent a full day. Alex Weiner and I had the time to drift through the streets of Berlin in a sea of swastikas. Everywhere there were marching soldiers and police. There were no unfortunate incidents, since we did nothing but stroll about aimlessly, buying nothing, stopping nowhere—just wandering like a couple of "wandering Jews."

We returned to the station in time to take the overnight train to Paris. Upon arriving there, an agent of the French Line, which operated the *Normandie*, greeted us and escorted us to a hotel, where we spent two nights.

Paris was a beautiful city. I was impressed by its wide boulevards; by the river, with its boats for tourists; by its outdoor cafes, where people gathered amiably to enjoy the weather, as well as their food and drink. I walked past the windows and wondered how I, an outsider, somehow nevertheless appeared to be inside the stores. My wonderment continued until I realized that the store windows were not really windows at all; they were mirrors! To me, still a growing boy culturally, if not physically, Paris was a tourist's paradise. I plunged into that *Gan Eden*, Garden of Eden, by walking into a store and purchasing a handsome long-sleeved sport shirt to wear with my new suit. I was thinking of how I would look when I came down the gangplank to take my first steps on American soil.

After our second night in Paris, the French Line's agent took us to the train station and set us on our way to Le Havre. It was there that we boarded the *Normandie* for the long sea journey to the "golden land" of America.

To us, America was big, rich, materialistic, and uncultured, all of which was in sharp contrast to Lithuania, which we looked upon as a great center of Jewish learning and culture—perhaps the greatest in the world. That was our perception of America and Lithuania at the time. We truly believed that Americans were uncouth, unsophisticated, uneducated upstarts who could not even begin to compete intellectually with Europeans. Americans were cowboys—wild and wooly, without style or sensitivity.

From the Jewish point of view, Lithuania was tops in Europe and, accordingly, tops in Jewish culture anywhere. I recall having heard that no one had ever adequately portrayed the full extent of the accomplishments of *litvaks*, Lithuanian Jewry. It had its rabbis, its scholars steeped in the Torah, its yeshivas, its novelists and journalists, its artists, its Zionist youth movement, its social critics, its love for Israel, and, above all, its plain folk blessed with endless common sense.

The Jewish community in Lithuania was often compared to a tree, its roots sunk deep into Lithuania's soil over the course of a thousand years. The tree had sprouted many branches that bore millions of green leaves. The tree, its branches, and its leaves flourished in the warm and welcome sunshine. It towered over all the neighboring trees. And then, one day, came evil men who chopped down the tree and trampled on the branches and on the tender leaves.

Oh, where is the pen that may someday describe the greatness that was Lithuanian Jewry? Who will bring to life again the lost civilizations of the Kovnos and Kavarsks of Lithuania in all their multifaceted, fruitful, forgotten glory? I, who had the good fortune to have sat under a shaded spot of that great tree of Lithuanian Jewry, have a sense of its greatness deep within my heart, but I do not have the appropriate words to impart what is within me to others around me. I can only tell my small story in the hope that hidden in this microcosm is the tale of that greater macrocosm, the story of that lost civilization.

Who could have even imagined that, within three years of my departure from Lithuania, there would be nothing left of my family, my shtetl,or the land I loved? When I left Lithuania I was still wet behind the ears, with no idea at all about the fearful forces being let loose on the world. True, I had my scared moments, but these were worries about what could happen to a kid from Kavarsk trying to find his way in an alien atmosphere. Who would have dreamed that what was to be most feared was what could—and would—and *did* happen to all those I loved? Yes, we did hear something about Hitler and his wild threats to exterminate Jews and others—just about anybody who stood in his way, really—but we didn't take those menacing bits of madness seriously. Even after Hitler took the Sudetenland and Austria, we could not imagine that his poisonous plague would sweep across all Europe—a plague whose victims, first and foremost, were to be Jews. We could not think it, because it was unthinkable—until the unthinkable became a fearsome fact of life.

As I think back on my father's decision to send me to America, I feel that he knew what he was doing. He saw the dangers ahead, although even he could not have imagined the extent of the horror. The extermination of European Jewry was not the savage act of a primitive people. Germany was looked upon as the most highly civilized country in Europe. Yet under Hitler, Germany, with its collaborators in Lithuania and other countries, turned Europe into a slaughterhouse for six million Jews.

I'm sure my father felt it wiser for me to go first. I could probably find it easier to get through; I would be safe for the moment; I would be able to help bring my parents and sister over later. I am sure that when my father, mother, and sister were led to their horrendous deaths, they must have felt in their hearts a bit of relief knowing that I was alive and safe in America.

After five and a half days at sea, as we were approaching the shores of America and New York harbor, I could see in the distance the tall towers of Manhattan and, as we got closer, the inspiring Statue of Liberty, the tall lady graciously welcoming us to the Land of the Free.

I stood outside on deck, leaning against the rails and watching the wonders of the city as we inched our way through New York harbor. I marvelled at the steady stream of cars moving up the elevated West Side Highway, a sight we take for granted today but, for me at that time, a man-made miracle.

As the *Normandie*, moving up the Hudson, came to a berth marked French Line, the giant ship slipped smoothly into its destined resting place. We had arrived.

Everyone got busy collecting themselves, their family, their belongings. We were all lining up for inspection by the immigration authorities. There was also a huge hall on the ship, where people searched you out and claimed you as belonging to them. Members of the Weiner family found their relatives and guided them down the gangplank. My uncle Louie and my aunt Lena came to get me. I thanked the Weiners, bidding them adieu; we looked forward to seeing one another again in this new land—America.

Through all this hustle and bustle, meeting and greeting, I believe I was in a daze. I did not know what to expect the next moment. For instance: What impressed me most when I got off the ship was not the tall buildings lining both sides of the streets and reaching up to the skies, or even the sidewalks packed with people moving in and out at a fast pace. What impressed me most was that I was now riding in my uncle's 1937 Buick. It was the same model and year as the Buick in which the president of Lithuania rode, surrounded by his motorcycle guard.

When I arrived at my uncle's house at 811 Albany Avenue in Brooklyn, family members were there to greet me and to catch a glimpse of this greenhorn. (The term "greenhorn" was applied to new arrivals until such time as the newcomer learned to handle English and had become accustomed to the ways of the new land. It sometimes took many years before one could get rid of the tag.)

I was happy to meet my American cousins, and especially happy to see Sandra again. With the exception of Sandra and her mother, all the others were relatives I was meeting for the very first time.

Among them, besides Uncle Louie and Aunt Lena and their daughters, there were Uncle Irving and his wife, Florence; Uncle Sam, with his wife, Shirley, and their daughter, Nannette; and my cousin Morris Jaffe, with his wife, Sadie, and their daughter, Helen. Later that evening, from Passaic, New Jersey, came Uncle Joe, with his wife, Yetta, and their three children, Minna, Sylvia, and Harold. Aunt Frieda was also there, with her husband, Sam, and their daughters, Nettie and Margie.

There was much noise and talk, most of which I did not understand. I felt awkwardly uncomfortable and self-conscious, since all eyes were fastened on me.

One of the discussions taking place amidst all this hubbub revolved around my cousins deciding what my name should be now that I was in America. Obviously, neither Ruvin nor Ruvke would do. Without consulting me, they decided to give me a name of their choosing, as if I were a newborn baby. They settled on Ralph, and Ralph it has been ever since.

Uncle Louie and Aunt Lena had rented an apartment for the summer in Brighton Beach. It was located directly on the Atlantic Ocean. The morning after my initial reception, they took me to their seaside home and I spent a full week there with them.

One week after my arrival in America, I was told by my uncle Louie that I was to start work next week to begin a career as a plumber. I was not consulted in this matter; I was simply told that that was the way it would be.

Uncle Louie was a plumbing and heating contractor, but he was not the only Jaffe in this line of work. Just about all the male members of the Jaffe family who had come to America before I did were in the same business. The fact that I knew hardly any English was not to stand in the way. I was a Jaffe and hence a plumber by birth.

Uncle took me to a place in Brooklyn where there were some new houses under construction. My uncle had the plumbing contract, and he had several men there installing the plumbing and heating systems. The name of the private housing development was Halperin Homes, located near Kings County Hospital.

My uncle introduced me to one of the plumbers he employed, a man by the name of Irving Lind, giving him some instructions in English that I did not understand. And then he told me, in Yiddish, that I was to work with Lind.

Although he was American born, Lind had a smattering of broken Yiddish at his command, and he called upon me to remove some objects from the wall so that he could have easier access to install pipes. When the other workers who were nearby heard him issue the order in Yiddish, they started to laugh. They were amused to see this greenhorn in their midst being initiated into the mysteries of the plumbing craft.

After two weeks, I was introduced to Irving's brother, Sidney, who worked as a journeyman plumber for my uncle. I was assigned to him as a plumber's helper. We were able to communicate fairly well with one another. His Yiddish was not bad; my English was getting better, now that I had enrolled in a night school. We took to each other and worked smoothly side by side.

It didn't take long for the other plumbers on the job to realize that I was not exactly a beginner, without talent or knowledge of the trade. They couldn't really figure out just how I had managed to catch on and master these skills so quickly. I never told them that I came to the job with three years of both theoretical training and practical experience, acquired in the ORT school in Kovno. I took pride in my work, and I believe they were pleased to work with me.

While my work occupied my time, my mind was absorbed by a more pressing purpose—bringing my parents to America. Almost from the moment I set foot on American soil, I took steps to prepare the necessary papers and affidavits for my parents in order to obtain the visas that would ultimately get them admitted to the United States under the prevailing quota system. My being in America improved their chances of coming, since it meant family reunification.

Parenthetically, I must note that I was quite homesick. I was also disappointed with some of the things I was witnessing in the home of Uncle Louie and Aunt Lena in terms of their relationships with one another and with their children. Although they were simply wonderful to me, there were moments when I wished I had never left Lithuania and even entertained the thought that I would like to return to my old home.

Despite these occasional relapses into homesickness, I remained diligent in my efforts to get the papers in order and send money to my parents. I was now earning seven dollars a week; out of this, I was able to send five dollars a week to my parents. Whatever minor irritation or distress I had in my first year in America was pushed aside by my preoccupation with helping my family live a little better, and in making headway with the laborious process of arranging for their admission into America.

About the middle of 1939, I received the good news from my parents that they had received an American visa. However, they were still lacking a Lithuanian exit permit because they could not lay their hands on their original birth certificates. This meant delay; they would have to apply to the courts to get the proper documentation enabling them to leave Lithuania.

Here in America we were all anxiously awaiting the time when they would notify us that they had been cleared for admission to America. We were poised to prepay the ticket for the trip as soon as we got the telegram telling us to go ahead.

On September 1, 1939, Hitler's Germany and Stalin's Soviet Union invaded Poland. As part of this joint invasion, the Fascist and Communist dictators concluded a pact that turned over the three Baltic states of Latvia, Estonia, and Lithuania to Stalin. In 1940, Lithuania lost its independence and became the fifteenth Soviet "republic." The Second World War was on. The doors of Lithuania were closed. For my parents and sister, there was no exit.

In June of 1941, Hitler turned against Stalin. The pact was broken; the two dictators were now enemies. Swiftly, Hitler marched into Lithuania. The German Nazis, together with their anti-Semitic Lithuanian allies, rounded up the Jews in the small towns and villages and proceeded systematically to torture and kill them. All the Jews in Kavarsk were slaughtered and buried in a common grave just before Rosh Hashanah, 1941. Among them were seventy of my immediate family and other relatives.

NINETEEN
A Search for Family

Upon my return from more than three years of military service in the American armed forces in World War II, I left no stone unturned in ascertaining exactly what had happened to my family. I looked through lists; I chased down leads; I contacted organizations. My hope was that somewhere, somehow, I would discover that they had survived. But it was all to no avail.

Then, just a few days before my marriage to Trudy, I found out the full truth. The place where they had been taken, killed, and buried was known as the Pavonya Forest, just across the Shventa River that ran through Wilkomer. I discovered this through the Weiners, whom we had invited to our wedding and were then living in Kankakee, Illinois. Arriving a few days before the wedding, they knew what had happened to the residents of Kavarsk, including my parents and sister. However, they were not sure that they should share the information with me before the marriage, and accordingly they consulted my aunts and uncles about what to do. The consensus was to tell me before the wedding. The Weiners had gotten the information from a relative of theirs, one of the few survivors of the Holocaust, who had been in correspondence with them.

When I was informed, I was devastated. The pain was excruciating, but I resolved not to tell anyone or show my anguish. Most of those who attended the wedding knew nothing about what I had learned. I was determined not to spoil the happy mood of the moment.

I did not even share the story with my wife. It was not until years later, as I was penning these notes for my memoirs, that I disclosed the facts to her.

The wedding, needless to say, was a happy moment in my life. It marked a marriage with a woman I truly loved, with whom I wanted to share a fruitful future. While smiling and laughing on the outside, however, I was sobbing and weeping bitterly on the inside. To all in attendance, I was the happiest, most contented groom in the world; no one ever guessed at the grim gloom I was concealing from them.

Every once in a while my mind would go blank and on the empty surface would flash the faces of my father, mother, sister, and the townspeople of Kavarsk. It was a haunting tableau. Why weren't they here with us, joining in the festivities of this blessed marriage? Why weren't my parents here escorting me down the aisle? I was talking to myself, saying, *Why aren't they here? They would have* shept *such* nachos.

I asked the questions; I knew the answers. I knew they were gone. But the memory of them was still with me. I was removed from my town, but my town would never be removed from within me.

I had a need to return, to return to a part of me that, buried under the rubble of the Holocaust, still pulsated in the present with the passions of the past. I had to go back to Kavarsk to see what there was to be seen. I had to pay my respects to what once was. I had to say my *kaddish* at the grave sites of the kin and kindred souls whom I'd lived with and dearly loved. To return to my town became my compulsion, my obsession, an absolute and unrelenting necessity. I had to return to me.

I had the need to go, and the time came when the Soviet Union, under new head of state Mikhail Gorbachev, made it possible for me to do so. In the years from 1985 to 1991, as head of both the Communist Party and the state, Gorbachev introduced a series of reforms that opened up Soviet society internally and which swung open the gates of this long closed-off country to the rest of the world. (Lithuania, at that time, was still very much a part of the Soviet Union.)

I had three reasons for going: First, of course, to return to my roots; second, to go to the common grave site and say *kaddish* for my family and the others; third, to carry through on a venture that had begun in 1981, when I'd gone to South Africa in search of some of my relatives there.

When I'd left Lithuania in 1938 to go to the United States, my mother told me that she had a brother and other relatives in South Africa. I vaguely remember the family. When I was about seven or eight years old, spending the summer in Gelez with my grandmother, I met an uncle whose name was Shneika. He later married a redheaded girl, whose name was Dobka. Shortly after their marriage, he left for South Africa; she followed a bit later.

I also knew that I had a first cousin on my father's side whose name was Leibka. He'd departed for South Africa sometime in the late 1920s. He was the son of my father's sister, Dinka, who lived in Roguva and whose married name was Segal.

When I left for the United States, I had the addresses of Shneika and Leibka in my possession. For a while I corresponded with my uncle in South Africa.

When I returned from military service in 1946, I resumed our contact, but what with my marriage, raising a family, going about my work, attending school at night, I had less time for correspondence than I would have liked. Nevertheless, I did maintain some contact with him. I knew that he had two sons; he'd sent me a letter with a picture of the family.

In 1981, I decided that the time had come for me to locate my uncle Norwitz and his two sons and, at the same time, establish contact with my cousin, Leibke Segal.

To find my cousin Leibke (Leon) Segal was not difficult. My late cousin Morris Jaffe had a sister who'd emigrated to South Africa from Kavarsk shortly after I left for America; we had been quite close. Her name was Bessie, and she lived in Durban. She'd married her girlhood boyfriend from Kavarsk. (He had gone to South Africa some time earlier.)

When I wrote to Bessie, she sent me Leon's address in Johannesburg. Half my mission had been accomplished. I had the address of the cousin on my father's side, and now I needed to get the address of my cousin on my mother's side. I decided not to contact either one until I'd obtained the addresses of both.

I did know that my uncle had lived in Capetown, but since I had no contact with anyone there, I decided to get some help in the United States. I called my friend Morris Talansky, an ordained nonpracticing rabbi, who had worked for ORT. He was then the executive director of the Shaare Zedek Hospital in Jerusalem. His main office, however, was in New York City.

Morris and I had an ongoing relationship. We shared many a family *simches* together. He presided at the marriage of Rochelle and David. He officiated at the *pydion haben* for our first grandson, David, the child of Lenny and Linda.

I told Morris about my search for my South African relatives, and how eager I was to locate my cousins. He listened to my story and then said, "Don't worry. I have the right person for you. I am sure that she will be able to locate your cousins. She runs a travel agency. I will have her call you. Give her whatever information you have. Her name is Vivien Eisenmann."

A few days later I got a call from her. I told her that I had two cousins in Capetown I was trying to contact. One cousin was Morris Norwitz, whose profession I did not know, and the other was Ruby Norowitz who, I believed, was a pharmacist.

Her reply was, "Don't worry, Mr. Jaffe. I know people in Capetown who know every Jewish family there. If your cousins are there, I will find them."

A week later, I got a telephone call from Vivien. "Mr. Jaffe," she said, "I located your cousins. When I told them you were trying to locate them, they broke into tears. I broke into tears. They could hardly believe that you made this effort to find them. I gave them your phone number and they will call you."

By a strange coincidence, Rollo (Ruby) and his wife, Marianne, had been in New York City the previous year, at which time *they* had tried to locate *me*. Unfortunately, they had looked in the Manhattan telephone directory at a time when we were living on Long Island.

A few days later, I received a call from Rollo. We were both bursting with the desire to talk to each other, to reach out and touch each other, to share our mutual feelings with one another. I assured him that I would be going to see him in the coming year. The rest is history: We became very close; I feel toward him and his brother Morris as I would to brothers.

Although I referred to my South African concerns as a third reason for going to Kavarsk, this was so only indirectly, as I shall note presently.

Now that I had located my cousin on my mother's side, I decided to make arrangements to go to South Africa, but before setting any definite dates, I wrote a letter to my cousin on my father's side, Leon Segal, who lived in Johannesburg. I told Leon I was planning to come to South Africa and wanted to see him. I received a reply saying that he was very happy with the news and was looking forward to the meeting. He also informed me that his wife had passed away and he had since remarried.

I also wrote to my cousin Bessie Goldman (Morris Jaffe's sister), saying that I was planning to go to South Africa and would visit her in Durban.

Having located these long-lost relatives in South Africa, all of them living parts of my past, I decided in 1982 on an itinerary that would carry me from Israel, through South Africa, and back to the United States. I wrote to my South African relatives that I would be there sometime in August 1982, letting them know that the exact dates would follow.

A letter from my cousin's wife, Meta, unexpectedly and tragically informed me that her husband, Leon, had passed away. Meta wanted to meet with us when we came to South Africa. At that time, I knew nothing about my cousin's family, about his wife, his children, or his circumstances. Needless to say, I was saddened by the unhappy news. I wrote Meta, the second wife to whom Leon had only been married for two years, and from our correspondence concluded that she was a warm and good person, a judgment subsequently confirmed when we met.

In August 1982 we arrived in Capetown. We were met by our cousins (a meeting I will talk about at greater length later). Then we went to Johannesburg via the famous Blue Train. The trip took twenty-four hours, and we ended up in the Carlton Hotel.

I called Meta and told her that we had indeed arrived, and that we wanted to invite her and Leon's two daughters, Myra and Jennifer, and their husbands, Ivan and Ralph, to dinner along with Meta's daughter. We spent a lovely evening together.

I also found out that the daughters, Myra and Jennifer, had a brother, who did not join us. It seems that when their father passed away there was some kind of family fuss; the brother and his sisters were on the outs, and were not speaking to one another.

Before we broke up, Myra extended an invitation to us to join her for afternoon tea on the following day, Sunday. She also told us that Ivan would pick us up and chauffeur us to Myra's home. The next day everything ran as planned: Ivan picked us up; we went to the afternoon tea; we met the children. Meta was there, of course. Myra related the story of her late father and mother. She told us how hard her father had worked and how he had derived little joy from life. She showed us some pictures.

In the course of our conversation she said, "Did you know that my father had a brother whose name was Yakov?" I told her I certainly did—we'd grown up together. I told her that I also knew the rest of the family.

"My father," she said, "corresponded with him."

I turned white. "What do you mean," I almost yelled, "when you say that your father corresponded with him? Is he still alive?"

She brought out some letters that her father had received from Yakov. I copied Yakov's address.

It seems that Yakov and her father had discovered one another some time ago. They'd corresponded with one another. Her father had sent Yakov some packages. At the time we were talking about this, the correspondence had been discontinued because the Soviet Union had broken off diplomatic relations with South Africa due to its apartheid policy.

I was truly excited by the idea that Yakov was still alive. I had been looking every which what way to find relatives who had survived the Holocaust. It had never occurred to me that someday while in South Africa, chatting with cousins at an afternoon tea, I would discover the sole surviving member of our family. Regretfully, I found out that he was living far away, in Kazakhstan, a place difficult for any of us to reach except by mail.

When I returned home, the first thing I did was to write a letter to Yakov. It was a great lift for him. We were the sole surviving members of our generation in our families—he out there in Kazakhstan, USSR, and I over here in the United States. During our correspondence, and subsequently when we met, I got further details on what had happened to our family.

It appears that, in his case, when the Germans invaded Lithuania he was spared because he had become a member of the Russian army, a most incredible story that revolves around a motorcycle. Here's how it went:

A week before the Germans descended upon Lithuania, Yakov was in Roguva with his parents, sisters, and brothers. He had been graduated from the vocational high school in Ponevez, the provincial capital city about twenty-five miles from Roguva. As a graduation present, his parents had given him a motorcycle.

A high town official, who was a friend of his father, had to go to Ponevez. Since there was no bus service, and since a trip by horse and wagon would take a full day he turned to his friend whose son had a motorcycle. He spoke to Yakov's father to solicit a favor. Would Yakov take him by motorcycle to Ponevez?

Yakov's father instructed his son to do so. Once Yakov got to Ponevez, he decided to spend a few extra days with friends. He felt comfortable about it all since he had an aunt, his father's sister, who ran a bakery in that town. He felt very much at home.

When the war broke out and the Germans launched their attack, he called his parents' house to tell them that he was going to return home. A sister he was talking with told him that, just at that moment, they heard shooting. She had hardly finished telling him when the line went dead; it had been cut off.

The Russian army was in hasty retreat, but when they found Yakov with his motorcycle, they confiscated the bike and drafted him into the army. He was wounded several times and eventually ended up in a hospital in Kazakhstan. While being treated for his final wounds, he met a nurse in the hospital and married her.

The fact that Yakov was a graduate with a degree in mechanics served him well. He ended up as an auto mechanic and was subsequently placed in charge of an auto depot. He has three children, two daughters and a son, and seven grandchildren. One daughter is a doctor; the second is a music teacher; and the son is a mining engineer.

The contents of the letters I received from him were rather bland. They were pretty much limited to personal affairs—the weather, the wife's ailments, the kids, who were always doing "fine." He would also write about our youthful days in Kavarsk.

I would write to him asking whether he needed supplies or finished staples. He'd write back that he didn't need anything. His letters always required a double read: First you read the lines, then you read between the lines. He was very cautious about how he handled his and other people's money. He was equally wary when penning a letter. You never knew when your letter would be opened by the authorities, inspected, and then used in court to incriminate you.

We conducted our correspondence in Yiddish. Since my cousin had not been using this language for many years, he had difficulty expressing himself. Under the circumstances, I was surprised at how well he did and impressed by his penmanship, which was much better than mine.

For me, expressing my thoughts and feelings in writing never came easily. But over the years I have applied myself to the preservation and improvement of my *mama loshen* (mother tongue), the Yiddish language. I have conscientiously kept up by reading Yiddish newspapers, books, and periodicals. When I stayed with Uncle Louie and Aunt Lena, the household talk was heavily Yiddish. My correspondence with Yakov helped both of us polish up our traditional tongue.

In the course of our renewed kinship, I tried to extend some help to my cousin. It wasn't easy. If we sent dollars through the mail or by money order, our American money would be converted into rubles, which would purchase very little. To circumvent this system we would try to smuggle dollars in by some tourist through England. If anyone was caught with these dollars, however, he or she would be severely punished. Nevertheless, I one day stumbled, quite by accident, across a way to do it.

In January 1991, I attended the annual American ORT conference in New York City. At the gala Saturday evening dinner, I found myself at a table with a young Russian immigrant. He was one of the many new immigrants from Russia following Gorbachev's lifting of restrictions on the emigration of Jews from Russia. Like a number of others, he was enrolled in the Bramson ORT school in New York. He was at our table as a result of ORT's decision to have at least one Russian immigrant at each table in order to give active ORT members a chance to meet and speak with the new arrivals from the Soviet Union.

I told this young man that I had a cousin in Kazakhstan and inquired as to how I could get money to him. The young Russian told me that he could help. It seemed that he'd come from Moscow with his wife and child about a year ago and had been sending money to relatives in the Soviet Union. He told me how he did it:

The official exchange rate was one ruble for one dollar. In the "black market," the rate was twenty-five rubles to one dollar. He had family members in Russia who were expecting to leave for the United States. If I gave him dollars in New York, he would have them moved through the "black market" so that, within two or three weeks, the Russian recipient of the dollars would get the equivalent of twenty-five rubles for each dollar. He offered to set up such an arrangement for my cousin in Kazakhstan and see to it that he got the money.

Since this was my first meeting with this young man, I was not sure that I could trust him. I told him that I would let him know. He gave me his phone number. I assumed he would understand my reluctance to rush into his proposed arrangement, since we hardly knew each other. He must have read my mind.

"You don't have to give me any money now," he said. "Just tell me how much you want to send. Give me the name and address of your cousin. When you receive word that the money has been delivered, you may call me and you may then pay me with your check."

After returning to my home in Florida, I called him a few days later to tell him that I was sending him my cousin's address and that I wished to send him $2,000 (I tried this as an experiment) to be converted into 50,000 rubles. He told me that he would contact his people in Moscow, give them my cousin's address, and instruct them on how to deliver the 50,000 rubles to him. I was told that it would take two or three weeks before I'd hear from him and was advised to write him immediately, preparing him for the receipt of a package. I did as instructed.

Two weeks later I received a call from this young man, whose name was Leonid Polyakov, saying the money had been delivered to my cousin. I thanked him and sent him a check for $2,000.

The speed with which this whole transaction went through was puzzling. It took only two or three weeks. It normally took between three and four weeks *each way* for regular mail to get through. This meant that my cousin, in all likelihood, must have received the money even before he received my letter alerting him to the fact that he would be receiving the money. And that is precisely what happened. About six weeks after the initial phone call to me from Polyakov advising me to alert my cousin, I received a letter from Yakov advising me that he had both received the money and that he had received it some time before my letter advising him it was on the way. In a letter to me dated February 2, 1992, he described the odd ordeal he went through to get the money:

> My dear cousin Ruvka, wife and family,
>
> A few days ago, at nighttime, a man who lives in our city came to our house to tell me that he had received a phone call from his son, who lives in Siberia in a city called Tomsk. His son told him to talk with me and to tell me to call Moscow immediately. He gave me a phone number. I did not know what was going on, or with whom I was to talk. My phone had been out of commission for a long time because of severed telephone lines. I could not take a bus to a telephone station, because city buses do not run in the evening. So I had to walk four kilometers to the nearest phone station with access to other cities.
>
> You will understand how difficult it was for me to walk this distance. I have badly painful feet and I had to make the journey on a bitterly cold and windy night. The trip took four hours and I had to rest repeatedly on the way.

I must tell you that my heart was pounding and my head was filled with anxiety. I did not know what was happening, with whom I was dealing in Moscow. So far as I could recall, I didn't know anyone in Moscow with whom I should be conversing over a phone at this time. All I knew was that this man had come to our house, had given me this mysterious message, and that I was expected to make this call to some unknown person.

To add to my woes, the telephone operator rang and rang and rang and no one was answering at the other end. After each call I had to get the operator once more and go through the same frustration. This went on all through the night.

The next day, someone answered. The party at the other end told me that he had to meet with me, since he had something which he must personally deliver to me. He told me that in three days from now he would fly to a city called Kuznechk, and that he would make the trip passing through our city of Karaganda. He would stop there briefly and wanted me to meet him at the airport terminal.

I asked him to send me a telegram notifying me when he would make the trip. As agreed, he did send me the telegram; we met at the airport; he gave me the package you sent me. He also asked me to phone you immediately to let you know that the package had arrived. But, since the phone is out of order, I am writing you this letter.

My dearest cousin Ruvke, I have to tell you the truth. My heart started to ache and tears came to my eyes when I realized that in this world I have a dear cousin who remembers me and wants to help me. Dear Ruvke, I want to express my deepest heartfelt thanks to you for helping us in these hard times. I pray to God that he blesses you and your family with good things as a reward for all the good deeds you did on our behalf. I don't know exactly how this all came about, but I don't think that the people who were involved in this operation worked for nothing.

Ruvke, you should know that the airport is forty kilometers from my home. When I got the package with the money in it and had to carry it back home on the bus, I was just plain scared all the way.

The money you sent has great value for us. In the Soviet Union, there are things one can buy with dollars that one can not afford in rubles. Because most people do not have dollars or true dollar equivalents in rubles, they are not able to make any substantial purchases. The result is that the stores are empty. The only things most of them can buy nowadays are bread and milk.

I remember that immediately after the Second World War things were much better than they are today.

My dear cousin, in your last letter you wrote that you were making plans to go to Lithuania this summer. I don't know what will happen there between now and the coming summer, but I do know that right now things are not good there. Politically, things are in disorder; many people have already been killed there. I believe that before you go there you should give it some more thought and look into the situation there.

Right now, all over the Soviet Union, things are in disorder. Gangsterism is widespread. Muggings and robberies plague every street and every house. I can not ever recall such times as these. The safest thing to do is to stay home. You just can not imagine what's going on here.

Many people who go out in the streets in the evening for a walk are robbed, disrobed, and are lucky to be left in the condition in which their mothers gave birth to them. They are fortunate if they are not murdered.

Now a few words about ourselves. We live from day to day. Thank God, our children and grandchildren are well. This winter is very cold and loaded with snow.

Ruvke, I will now end this letter. If possible, please write to me and tell me how you are able to do what you did to help us. Best regards to your wife from all of us. May all of you be well, and may God give you a long life and lots of *nachos*.

Your cousin Yankele.

To travel to the countries in eastern Europe that were part of the Soviet Union became much easier after Gorbachev opened up the borders of the once-closed Soviet state. I went to the Intourist office in New York, the official tourist and travel agency for the Soviet Union. It was necessary, in order to journey through the Soviet Union, to go through Intourist, since it had total control of all the hotels in the USSR.

I told the people at Intourist what my reasons were for wanting to go to Lithuania. I told them that I would be travelling with my wife and asked them whether they could make arrangements for us to visit my birthplace, Kavarsk, and also whether they could arrange for us to visit Wilkomer, where my family and all the other Jews in town were slain and buried in a common grave.

They informed me that they could grant us a visa to Vilnius and a few other cities. There were, however, certain areas that were classified as military zones. And such "zones," which might include the places I wanted to visit, were off-limits. They suggested that I take a chance and go to Vilnius. Once there, we might get a taxi to take us where we wanted to go, which was about one hundred kilometers (sixty miles) from Vilnius.

I told them that if they could not guarantee safe passage to the two towns I wanted to visit, I would prefer not to go at all at this time.

My desire to go to Kavarsk and Wilkomer was so strong, however, that I decided to write a letter to Gorbachev in Moscow. In that letter I told him a little bit about myself and my reasons for wanting to go to the towns I had specified. I concluded by asking him to grant permission for my wife and myself to visit the two specified towns.

Not too long after that, I did receive a reply, although not from Gorbachev personally. I received a letter and a visa application from the Soviet embassy in Washington. I was asked to fill out the required form and, if I had any questions, to contact a certain person, whose name was mentioned. There was no specific reference to my request for permission to visit the "zones" where we wanted to go.

Some time early in 1990, I found out that there was a travel agency in Florida that was arranging tours to Lithuania; I contacted them. I learned that the individual who led the tour group was himself a Holocaust survivor who came from Lithuania. He had, just a few months earlier, led a group to Lithuania, and was now organizing a group slated to depart in June 1990, to be made up of about thirty people. I was advised by the agency that I would have no trouble renting a car and a driver and get to the towns I designated.

As I was making my plans, my thoughts turned to my cousin, Leo Rubin, who was now living with his wife, Janet, in Cherry Hill, New Jersey. When we were children growing up in Lithuania, Leo and I formed a close friendship, although he lived in Roguva and I lived in Kavarsk, where Leo had an aunt, his mother's sister. With his mother, Ida, and his sister Rita, who was the same age as my sister Neche Minka, Leo used to spend the summers in Kavarsk. So we found ourselves quite often playing with Leo and his two cousins, Shmulka and Henochka, his aunt's children.

When Leo was about eight years old, his father left for the United States. In 1937, when I was at the ORT school in Kovno, the family left to join him. I remember seeing them off at the Kovno station.

I told Leo on numerous occasions that I was planning to go to Lithuania and suggested that he join me on the trip. Although he did not seem to be eager to go, he finally did assent when I told him about my proposed journey in June.

So I made arrangements with the travel agent for the four of us—Leo and Janet, Trudy and myself—to go to Lithuania. By now, there were altogether twenty-six people making the journey. We sent the agent all the necessary materials—the application, the photos, the fees, and the like; Leo did likewise.

While all this was in the works, I sent a letter to my cousin Yakov telling him of our plans, noting the dates when we would be in Vilnius and the hotel where we would be staying. He wrote back that he was not feeling well, that it was a long trip to Moscow and from Moscow to Vilnius, and that he did not feel up to it. There would also be the problem of getting a special travel permit. He also reminded me that things were very unstable in Lithuania; there was an ongoing struggle for independence, as well as a lot of hooliganism and anti-Semitism, he didn't know where he would stay, and so on.

I wrote Yakov telling him I would make arrangements for him to stay in the hotel with us and would not take no for an answer; I was counting on him to join us in June. I gave him the exact date.

In March and April of 1990, there were many demonstrations for independence in Lithuania, especially in Vilnius. Several demonstrators were killed by the Soviet army. In April there was a massive upheaval in Vilnius when thousands of people marched on the TV station with the intention of taking it over. Soviet tanks rolled in, opened fire on the demonstrators, wounding many and leaving thirteen dead. I asked the travel agent how these events affected our plans; his answer was that we still would go.

In early May I received word that the tour had been cancelled. The Russian embassy would not issue visas for Lithuania. The agent said that he would return the deposits.

I immediately dispatched a letter to Yakov in Kazakhstan telling him about the cancellation. I said that I hoped he would receive my note in time, pointing out that it sometimes took two or three months for a letter to get from here to there; sometimes the letter never got through.

Two weeks later, I got a letter from Yakov in which he said he had planned to meet us in Vilnius but that, because of the violent confrontation, no travel permits were now being issued for Lithuania. I felt momentarily relieved. I wrote to him about what had happened to us. I expressed the hope that things would quiet down in Lithuania and that we would be able to resume our plans.

When 1991 rolled around, I was determined to renew our efforts, but this time I wanted to extend the scope of our tour—to start out in

Lithuania, go on to other parts of Europe, then end up in Israel. This time, however, we would not go as part of an organized tour but on our own.

I called my cousin Leo, telling him about my plan to spend about a month travelling in Europe and five or six days in Vilnius. He told me that he would talk it over with his wife and let me know in a few days. I told him I was planning to go from mid-June to mid-July, and that I would be glad to handle all the arrangements.

A week later, Leo called to tell me that he was prepared to go along, but he had to be back by the third week in July. Hence, he would not be able to go to Israel. We decided on an itinerary that would take us first to Vilnius, then to St. Petersburg, to Helsinki, Finland, to Bergen, and then by car to Oslo in Norway and to Stockholm in Sweden, to Budapest in Hungary, and to Prague in Czechoslovakia. At that point, Leo and Janet would return to the States and we would go on to Israel.

I called Vivien Eisenmann and told her of my plans, specifying that I wanted to spend five days in Vilnius. Several days later, the agency called. We made a few changes and straightened out a couple of details. We made arrangements to depart by Swiss Air on June 17, 1991; going on to Geneva, then to Zurich, and on to Moscow and Vilnius by Aeroflot. At Vilnius we were to stay at the Hotel Lietuva.

I inquired as to whether there would be any problem getting Russian visas into Lithuania. She assured me that, as of the moment, there would not, but as usual we had to fill out forms and show that we had round trip tickets. I gave her the number of my charge card and also told her to make arrangements at the hotel for my cousin Yakov, so as to allay his fears about what would happen to him if he were to go to Vilnius.

I notified Yakov of the arrangements and told him that we were expecting to see him at the hotel in Vilnius sometime between June 18 and June 23. He wrote back to me that he was not sure if he would be able to meet us there. His wife could not travel by plane; she had difficulty breathing because she had lost one lung; he had a problem with his legs, which were swollen and made walking difficult for him. He also had a problem with long flights. So, he would see.

I received his letter about two months before our scheduled departure. I wrote him again telling him that he *must* come to Vilnius, that I had to go with him to the town where we were born; it was there where we'd grown up, and there where we had to go together to say *kaddish* at the common grave of our dear ones. For fifty-three years we had not seen one another; this might be the last time we would ever see one another again.

Two weeks before our scheduled departure, our travel agency informed me that everything was in order. They were sending all the papers, tickets, and visas to us by Federal Express. I received the necessary materials, but I was still uncertain whether Yakov would join us.

Nevertheless, I simply assumed that he would show, and in anticipation of making the trip, Trudy and I discussed the kinds of things we should buy as gifts for the family and, mainly, for the children and grandchildren. This was no easy assignment, since we did not know the ages or the sizes of the young ones, but that did not deter us. We bought things and crammed them into a valise, not knowing whether Yakov would even show. If he didn't, we would give the presents to some Jewish children in Vilnius we knew.

When the day of departure came, we still had not heard from Yakov. When we returned at the end of our trip, I found a letter that had been delivered to us two days after we left for Vilnius.

I should like to share with you some of the thoughts and feelings I had on that day of 17 June, 1991. These are notes I made while in flight to Lithuania:

> Monday, 6/17/91; 9:50 P.M. It is with a heavy heart and much trepidation that I am attempting to express my thoughts and feelings while flying 33,000 feet above the Atlantic Ocean at a speed of 634 miles per hour, as just announced by the captain.
>
> We are aboard a Swiss Air plane, Flight 111 to Zurich, with an interim stop over at Geneva. Then we will be off to Moscow and, finally, Vilnius. Coincidentally, it was almost exactly fifty-three years ago that I left my home town of Kavarsk to go to America by bus, train, and seagoing vessel. We traversed three countries—Germany, the Polish Corridor, and France—before boarding ship for the Atlantic crossing. All in all, the voyage took eight days. What a contrast to my present passage. Then, it took eight days; now it takes twenty hours. The earth is shrinking.
>
> I left my home a child, scared, not certain I was doing the right thing, torn from my family, my extended family, my friends, my schoolmates, my neighbors, my shtetl. I still did not know what it was all about. I moved about in a fog—one moment it cleared, the next it obscured my view. I had no idea at all as to what to expect once I landed in America.
>
> From the moment I left I was scared by the unknown future that lay

ahead of me. I was seized by homesickness. The only thing that kept me going, which gave me strength in this venture into the unknown, was my faith that, if this was what my father wanted me to do, then it was the right thing to do.

My father spelled out my role: "Don't worry. You go first and we will follow." I also drew strength from my family's close relationship with Aunt Lena who lived in America.

Now I am here on this plane with my wife, Trudy, on one side and an Iranian doctor, who attended a medical conference in Miami, on the other, and with Leo and Janet in the two seats in front of us. The people I loved most are no longer in the town where I am flying. They are gone without a trace—not even a gravestone or a rude marker commemorating the few feet of soil containing the bodies that once throbbed with life and love in my hometown.

My other thoughts go to the long-lost relatives I rediscovered after the Holocaust, including one in a central Asian country called Kazakhstan, a distant land to which you can send mail but cannot visit.

I ask myself, "Why am I here on this plane?" And I answer, "I have a purpose. It is to return to my town and to the place where, a few miles from my home, all the Jewish inhabitants of my town were taken and shot and buried in a common grave."

I didn't know what to expect. I didn't even know whether my town was still there. It might have been completely demolished during World War II, or it might have been rebuilt as a modern city.

I interrupted my writing and closed my eyes to take a brief rest. It amazed me to see how, after more than half a century, the town came alive. I could see it all and see it so clearly. Before my mind's eye passed scene after scene, as if I were watching a travelogue. My parents, sister, friends, relatives—I see them walking and talking. I see the marketplace on Mondays, crowded with farmers and their wagons. The townspeople, bargaining and bartering and buying, a few of them staggering out of a saloon. I see the dirt streets, the wooden houses and straw-thatched roofs. The storekeepers—baker, tailor, shoemaker, cap maker, butcher. I see our synagogue, the one and only temple in town. The Sabbath and the *cholent*. I see the lovely river flowing alongside the pine forest. And there, towering over everything, stands the magnificent church with its huge clock perched on top of the steeple. I can hear the water flowing at the bottom of the hill. I feel the enamel cup in my hands as I fetch a drink from the clear, cool, comforting water. I hear the church bells ringing.

They are telling me that it is 5:30 A.M. and I must be up and about, because today I leave, bright and early, for the long voyage to America.

In condensed form, scene after scene of the drama I have been reciting in these pages raced before my eyes. And through it all, as I mused upon the past in the plane, I was both an actor and the audience and the author in this silent, stirring story.

Here in my hands was a map of Kavarsk, a map of my own making. I looked at my rudimentary drawing and saw the streets changing as the seasons pass: the spring, with its muddy streets; the summer, its roads dusty after the mud had dried; the winter, its paths swept by cold and piercing winds, its picturesque landscapes of crystalline snow.

Why, I asked myself in my quietude on this long plane ride, *do I seem able to recall these and other tableaus so clearly and sharply, while others with whom I have spoken recall hardly any of the details of their lives in Kavarsk?* Maybe it was so because I'd spent a lifetime locking up within me the emotions that I had shared with no one—not my wife, not my children, not anyone. Maybe it had been the wrong thing to do—but that's the way it had been all my life.

There were tragic events taking place around me and within me—little ones, like departures, and big ones, like the Holocaust. I did not want to disclose them to the people I knew, the people I treasured, the people I loved. I wanted to bring good cheer, not multiply melancholia. I kept the sadness locked up within me, and repeatedly mulled over scenes and scenarios, facts and faces, tears and tragedy. With so many reviews and rehearsals of happenings around me and inside of me, how could I ever possibly forget?

Enough of this musing, I said to myself at length, as I opened my eyes again to face the real world in which I now found myself. *Enough of the past. Now let's see what tomorrow holds in store for us.*

TWENTY
A Litvak Returns

At noon on Tuesday June 18, 1991, we landed at the Moscow international airport. I had been awake for twenty-four consecutive hours, flying, changing planes, walking through airports.

Our New York travel agent had advised us to take several packs of cigarettes with us. Those precious little parcels, we were told, could smooth the way in many transactions. So, we'd come prepared.

Immediately after we'd cleared customs, Leo got some luggage carts to transport our belongings, as we had to go from one airport to another to change planes. Pushing two carts, we rolled our luggage outside and found a taxi. To get to the airport we needed two taxis; both were very small, old, and decrepit. My driver, who spoke a smattering of English, told us that it would take about twenty minutes to get to the other airport and that he would take American dollars only, no cigarettes. The charge would be five dollars per cab.

We got into the taxis and started to move across roads pocked with potholes. I don't think it took twenty minutes to get to a building that did not seem to me to be a passenger terminal. In fact, it looked, from the outside, more like a place that might handle air freight, but when we entered, we found ourselves in a lovely small building with many murals, almost all propagandistic. The clerks, typically, operated out of closed rooms with at least two persons in each cashier-window enclosure. It was from this smaller terminal that we were to take our plane to Vilnius.

Leo and Janet, who checked in first, had no problem with their luggage, but when mine was weighed, I was told it was fifteen kilos (thirty-three pounds) overweight. I offered to pay for the difference. It didn't work. They brought the check-in process to a halt, informed me that I would have to go to one of the other windows, get a receipt, and bring it back to them before they could resume the check-in.

It was a very hot day; the terminal was not air-conditioned; the outstretched blades of the ceiling fans hung silent, motionless. I started to sweat profusely from all the running around, my anger and frustration mounting.

I went to the designated window to make the payment. I was informed that they could not accept American dollars; I would have to go and get my dollars converted into rubles. They all spoke English and were able to direct me to yet another window for currency exchange. By this time I had lost count of just how much I owed in dollars or rubles for my overweight luggage, so I just took out a twenty-dollar bill and gave it to the cashier, hoping that it would be enough.

In exchange I received a pocketful of rubles, which I took to the window where I could pay and get my receipt. I gave the bill to one of the girls and asked her how many rubles I owed. She told me that the total charge would be seventeen rubles, the equivalent of sixty-eight American cents.

I was ready to leap out of my skin, but I managed to contain myself. *Keep your cool, Jaffe,* I said to myself. *This is Russia.* Having gone through this utterly exasperating experience for the sake of a few pennies, I could now identify with all those poor Russians standing on their everlasting lines waiting to buy a loaf of bread, a pound of butter, or a lump of sugar.

After presenting my paid-up receipt, I was checked through and got my boarding pass. I asked if the seats were assigned. The clerk marked the tickets with a *one* and a *two* and told me that they were reserved seats.

After all this bouncing about I was finally reunited with Trudy, Leo, and Janet. We looked at each other; I shrugged my shoulders; we all broke into a long, loud laugh.

We were, we discovered, part of a group of other foreigners for whom, apparently, this part of the terminal was set aside. By now there were ten of us, and we were led to another waiting room and told that a bus would be arriving shortly to pick us up.

While we were waiting I looked around, and as I peered through the window I realized that the building we were in was really a part of the same airport we'd landed in on our way from Zurich to Moscow. In fact, I saw a foreign plane land and taxi to the same gate our plane had used when it had arrived here. I had not realized, until then, that there were two separate terminal buildings—one for foreigners, and another for Russians.

I did not know how many flights a day there were from Moscow to

Vilnius, but I kept an eye on every arriving flight, hoping that I might perhaps see cousin Yakov. Then it struck me: If there were only ten passengers on our plane, I could not count on him to make this flight with us to Vilnius.

Finally, the time had come for us to take the Aeroflot to Vilnius. The girl who had ushered us into this waiting room announced that the bus was ready. She opened the door; we followed her to the bus that was to transport us to the plane parked on the stifling hot tarmac.

We entered the plane from the rear. Inside, there was a center aisle with three adjacent seats on either side. The carpet was torn so badly that when you walked down the aisle your feet constantly kept slipping; to keep from falling, you had to hold on to the back of the seats. There was no stewardess to help or guide you. Eventually we found our places, expecting to make the journey in this sparsely populated plane of ten passengers. Exhausted, as you might expect we would be, we stretched out in our seats, drew a deep breath, relaxed, got comfy, and prepared ourselves for a nice, quiet trip.

I chose a seat near the window, primarily because the interior of the plane was so disgustingly dirty and dilapidated. I was in the third row on the right-hand side; Leo was somewhere behind me; Trudy and Janet took seats somewhat behind us on the left-hand side. We had the plane all to ourselves; if the spirit moved us, we could move around and chat with one another.

Then suddenly out of nowhere a stampede of people came dashing into the plane, pouring into every available seat. Soon there were no empty seats, but still people came pouring in looking for a place to sit. The plane was overbooked.

The foreign tourists had been given priority, as it happened; we could take the seats of our choice in the empty plane, but the Russians had to scramble. The lucky ones, the fastest and pushiest, were rewarded with seats; the others were taken by bus back to "their" terminal, and would be given a crack at making it on the next plane to Vilnius.

Our party—Leo, Trudy, Janet, and I—were now like lonely islands in a sea of strange people. We would have liked to rearrange our seating, at this point, so that our party would be closer together, but since we could not speak Russian there was no way for us to do so.

Once we were all settled in our seats, an announcement in Russian that we could not understand came over the PA. We fastened our seat belts and the engines started up.

The interior of the plane felt like an oven. It had been standing on the hot tarmac for a few hours and hadn't been air-conditioned at all during that time. Suddenly the inside of the plane filled with a thick smoke resembling a dense fog. You could barely make out objects just a few feet away. This fog, which dissipated after a few minutes, had been brought about when the air conditioner had been turned on, causing the accumulated moisture in the plane to condense.

The fog threw Trudy into a panic. She left her seat, paced the aisle, and shouted in a loud voice that she wanted to get off. I could hardly blame her, especially since I was so obscured by the fog she couldn't find me. I tried to calm her, to get her to return to her seat. I assured her there was no need for worry—the condensation would soon disappear.

Not being able to sit next to her made matters worse. As the fog lifted, I waved my hand to her across the plane.

The plane soon began to taxi around the field to position itself for the takeoff. All this time, the stewardess was on the phone making announcements. The plane took to the air at 8:00 P.M.

I left my seat and began to wander through the plane, perchance to find my cousin among the passengers. I still did not know whether or not he was coming. I was certain, however, that if he were on the plane he would recognize me, and vice versa. As I meandered through the plane, I noticed that some passengers were passing food to others. Apparently they were travelling in a group, perhaps even members of the same family; in the wild scramble for seats, however, they had not been able to sit together. This free-for-all race for seats is a scene I have never witnessed on any other airline in the world.

The smells of the food being passed about filled the plane, as did the shouting of family members trying to converse with other family members from one end of the plane to the other. And the louder it got, the louder their voices had to be raised in order to be heard above the deafening din.

At one point, a white curtain that separated the passenger section from the galley parted and a stewardess emerged. She was carrying a tray of cups filled with water. There were only six cups. Whoever was closest grabbed a cup first; the others simply had to go cupless and waterless.

This marked the only appearance of the stewardess. After that, we saw nothing of her for the rest of the flight.

Eventually I returned to my musings about the trip. Once more, I wondered whether Cousin Yakov would show up, if not on the plane then at the hotel. As I thought about our approaching arrival in Vilnius I could feel the adrenalin pouring into my body; I literally began to sweat at the prospect of what lay ahead. After a few bumpy moments before landing, we finally touched down at 10:00 P.M. local time.

As the wheels of the plane rumbled quietly over the tarmac, I was suddenly overcome with emotion—and started to cry. I was glad that Trudy was not sitting next to me. Silently I spoke to myself, *Why did it have to happen to me this way? Why couldn't I have returned to the land of my birth to find at least some of my family alive and well, people with whom I could lock arms in warm embrace?* As I started to leave the plane my body was quivering. Progressing toward the exit at the rear of the plane, Trudy joined me as we got off the plane together. (As always, I did all in my power to conceal my deepest feelings from her.)

A bus took us to a building that looked like a makeshift terminal. I noticed that a new building was under construction not far away. The building, into which we were ushered, was poorly lit by a handful of bare bulbs hanging from above. The dingy darkness cast a gloomy spell over our return to Lithuania.

As we headed toward the terminal a woman approached us and identified herself as an agent of Intourist, asking us to follow her to the baggage room. Trudy, Leo, and Janet were to stay there and wait for the baggage to arrive; I was to follow her through this dark building to the outside, where there was an old minibus waiting to take us to the hotel. This minibus would provide us with transportation for the next five days. The agent introduced me to the driver, who spoke no English. (All these services had been paid for in advance in the States.) The guide reminded me to get our baggage and bring it to the bus, and with that she left, without offering to get anyone to help; we were on our own. Meanwhile the bus driver sat there, waiting for us to bring our belongings to his vehicle.

In the baggage room our stuff had, as usual, been placed in a separate section, apart from the luggage of the native population; hence we were able to retrieve it quickly and easily. I noticed most of the "native" luggage was wrapped in heavy brown paper and tied tightly together with twine, from which I concluded the luggage must be new and the owners did not want the precious bags to be scuffed and scraped in handling.

When, later on, I shared this observation with my cousin, he laughed. The "natives" put paper and twine around their bags and valises because, he said, if they did not the baggage handlers would, as was their habit, open the luggage and steal things from it.

On our way to the hotel, we were all silent. No one spoke a word. Whether we were silenced by exhaustion or anticipation I can not say. I can only say for myself that when I saw the Hotel Lietuva sign from the distance, my heart started to pound with anticipation. I was sure that cousin Yakov would be there.

When we arrived at the hotel, a bellhop began to unload our baggage from the bus. I did not wait; I dashed through the huge glass entrance door into the lobby, my eyes wide open, darting in all directions at once, scanning every face and figure. It wasn't easy to see clearly; the lighting was poor.

My eyes alighted on a man seated on a leather couch, wearing a dark cap, staring intently at the entrance door. Our eyes met. . . . We recognized one another. . . . And, without saying a word, we rushed towards each other, embracing and kissing as we met. We wept; we held on to each other; we couldn't let go. Our hands and our hearts were reaching across a span of fifty-three years in remembrance and reunion.

I introduced Trudy, Leo, and Janet, but Yakov continued for a while to act like someone who could not believe that what was happening here was really happening—he acted like he was in shock. We exchanged few words.

By the time we got to our rooms it was almost midnight. We were hungry. Upon inquiry, we found out that on the twenty-second floor there was a disco, where food was served. Meanwhile, the driver wanted to know when he should meet us the next day and where we planned to go. I told Yakov that the first place we ought to visit was Kavarsk, and then Wilkomer. We instructed the driver to pick us up after breakfast, about 9:00 A.M.

We turned to the food. There was a limited menu of cold cuts, cheese, bread, and cold drinks. At this late hour we barely had the appetite to indulge in what looked like unappetizing food, but Yakov dug in voraciously. He had not eaten for two days. (We will talk about this later.)

We tried to talk, but the deafening music was not a conducive background for conversation. What words we could exchange were mainly about our disbelief that we were really here with one another. We did manage some conversation, however. Yakov told us that he had arrived that afternoon and had had a problem with the hotel management. I couldn't quite follow the details at that moment, but I did get the full story later.

It was now past midnight, time to retire. We agreed to have breakfast at 8:00 A.M. and then leave for Kavarsk at 9:00. We went upstairs to our separate rooms. I tried to fall asleep, but could not. I told Trudy that, since Yakov was in the adjoining room, I would like to knock gently on his door to see if he was awake.

When I did, he opened the door, saw me, and burst into tears. He, too, could not sleep. We sat down and talked and talked and talked until 4:00 A.M. We reviewed, related and, in a sense, relived the events of half a century. Yet, curiously, what had happened to Yakov in the last two days in a sense epitomized the anguish, the agony of his many hardships.

When we had entered the hotel and saw him sitting there sadly, seeming quite depressed, I'd attributed this to his general state of being—to his poor health, to his loss of family, and the like. All of these things did, of course, affect him; but as it turned out, his troubled state had been brought on by some specific events at the hotel itself.

He had left Karaganda, Kazakhstan, the day before, arriving in Moscow late in the afternoon after a five-hour flight. He'd then had to transfer to another airport for a plane to Vilnius. The cab driver insisted that he be paid in dollars, which Yakov did not have. After much begging and pleading, Yakov induced the driver to take him and agreed to pay him in rubles at an inflated price.

When he got to the airport, he'd discovered that there were no more flights to Vilnius that day, so he'd sat in the airport overnight. He'd had nothing to eat, since there was no food available.

Early in the afternoon he came to the Lietuva Hotel. At the registration desk he gave his name and inquired about our arrival. The desk informed him that they had no reservations for four Americans with the names he mentioned. He was also told that there was no registration in his name. They did, they said, expect four Americans, but with different names.

Yakov told them that I was his brother, and that I had written to him and given him the dates of our arrival and the number of days we would be staying at the hotel. He told them that I had made reservations for all of us to stay at the hotel for five days. Once more he was told that they had no reservations, either for us or for him: Perhaps we were staying at another hotel; he should try to find out. In any event, he could not stay at the Lietuva and would have to leave.

He finally persuaded them that they should allow him to stay in the lobby, where he would sit and await our arrival. In the event that we did not arrive, he would leave.

Imagine Yakov's state of mind: the anticipation of our meeting, his difficulty getting to Vilnius, and now the crushing disappointment of our not being at the Lietuva. Hour after hour these thoughts must have haunted him as he sat in that dimly lit hotel lobby, hunger gnawing at his stomach and despair at his heart.

What could have gone wrong? Had I given him the wrong dates? Had he misunderstood what I wrote? As the hours passed, his anxiety had to have mounted. As night set in, he must have given up all hope. Yet he'd mechanically kept his eyes glued on the entrance door, hoping against hope for a miracle. When we'd walked in at the eleventh hour (literally 11:00 P.M.), it was as if the Messiah had arrived.

None of us could figure out why the hotel had put Yakov through this needless torture. Why had they not given him the right information, which they'd had all along?

Upon arrival, without knowing what had transpired with Yakov, I'd gone directly to the registration desk and presented the vouchers given to me by the travel agent in New York, which covered Yakov as well as the four of us. The clerk had gone behind a closed door, returned with matching vouchers for the five of us, then checked us in without delay. Indeed, the hotel clerk had been most courteous.

I had requested adjoining rooms. "No problem," he said, further suggesting that we take a suite—the only suite on the floor—and that Yakov Segal take a room right next to our suite. Our quarters were spacious—living room, one bedroom and two baths.

After much talking amidst tears, which made us feel better, Yakov's Yiddish began to come back to him; that happy event inspired him to talk even more. By the time we gathered for breakfast the next morning, Yakov's voice was hoarse, a condition brought on probably as much by tension as by overuse, but by the time we were ready to leave for Kavarsk, he'd forgotten all about his sickness: He "felt no pain."

What was happening here was something more than a dream come true; Yakov, quite simply, could never even have dreamt that this reunion could be. He took a shine to all of us, but especially to Trudy. What kind of a woman had I married—an American girl who spoke Yiddish with him?

My cousin turned out to be a very warm personality, chock full of emotions that he, too, had kept dammed up for a long time. With all the unhappiness and misfortune he had experienced, he could never allow himself to cry, and yet now, in our presence, he could not stop himself from crying. It was as if his dam had broken and we were all engulfed in his flood of feeling. The miracle had happened and he marvelled at it all, including the fact that we had a minibus with our own designated driver.

Although the food we had for breakfast was not the best, Yakov had a chance to sample dishes he never could have in the town where he lived. There, just about everything was rationed; you got only what you were allotted.

This was true of clothes as well as food. Yakov had a total of two or three shirts, which he had been wearing for the last fifteen years. Some of the things we gave him to take back to his family he had never even seen before. He knew about them from his reading but had never actually seen them "in the flesh."

In light of his circumstances, I felt that Yakov could use some help, so before he departed for his home, I made certain he took a few dollars with him. His pension, on which he depended, was 134 rubles a month; in American currency, that would be about five dollars. Using his retirement income as a measure, I gave him enough to carry him for the next one hundred and twenty years.

It wasn't easy to do so. Yakov is a proud man. I had to convince him that this was not a handout. I explained that in normal times we would have exchanged gifts, each doing so according to his means. Since I was in a fortunate financial situation, and since I had not had the opportunity to present him with gifts before my present offering was, so to speak, merely an "adjustment," an attempt to compensate for the gifts I could not get him in the past.

We talked at some length about the future of his children. I tried to persuade him that the time had come for his family to leave the backward country in which they lived. Yakov was also having a serious problem with his house, which was located in a coal-mining area. All the digging had undermined the ground on which the houses had been erected. Some homes had already been abandoned because they had begun to sink.

In fact, his home, too, had begun to sink. How long it would be before his house collapsed no one knew, but in time it would, and there was nothing he could do about it. The government owned the mines in this largest of all coal-producing areas in the Soviet Union. To get at the rich veins of coal, it was necessary to dig ever-extended channels into the earth. Sooner or later, the natural foundation on which Yakov's house rested would be destroyed.

There was still another problem. Yakov's family lived off the land, in part. He had a bit of soil, on which he grew vegetables such as potatoes, tomatoes, cucumbers, and the like. He also had a few fruit trees. This backyard farm, if one may call it such, helped provide food to sustain the family. Yakov and his wife put in many hours working the soil to eke out enough to feed the family.

We were not unacquainted with their difficult life. Our luggage was overweight because we'd loaded it with things to help Yakov sustain his family, as well as candy, chocolates, and chewing gum for the grandchildren who had never seen, let alone eaten, these sweet bits before.

The excitement stirred in Yakov by the magic of Sanka attested to the limited level of existence in Kazakhstan. Because the coffee in the hotel was so bad, we ordered hot water and then emptied an envelope of Sanka into it. Yakov was impressed. So we ordered hot water for him, too, and gave him his own envelope of Sanka, but he refused to empty the envelope into the cup. He wanted to bring the unopened envelope back to his home, to show the folk there one of the new wonders of the world. (Needless to add, when he left for home his valise was laden with Sanka.)

There were many things, I am certain, that provided him with subjects for discussion with his family and friends back home. One of them undoubtedly had to be his encounter with Israelis.

The day we went from Vilnius to Kovno, a trip of about sixty miles, we decided that our first stop would be at the infamous Ninth Fort, about four miles from Kovno. At this site, thirty thousand Jews, Russian prisoners of war, and other "undesirables" were submitted to torture and then shot to death. Ready to leave, the Nazis decided to destroy all evidence of the atrocity they had perpetrated, so they exhumed the bodies of the Jews and incinerated them.

The Soviet government subsequently erected a monstrous monument in commemoration of the Russians who were killed, but they neglected to mention the Jews. Subsequently, those few Jews who somehow survived in that community, together with some who had gone to Israel, had persuaded the Lithuanian Republic to grant permission for a monument in memory of the Jews who had been executed, including the Jews who had been brought there for burial from the Kovno ghetto.

Our tour guide was Simon Rozan, brother of David Rozan, whom we had sponsored two years earlier as one of thirty-nine Baltic children to visit Israel. As he started to explain what this place was all about, we saw several large buses arrive under police escort. As the passengers were leaving their buses I noticed a Lithuanian woman, who represented the government, explaining the significance of the Ninth Fort. The delegation was made up of Israelis headed by Dov Shilansky, Speaker of the Israeli Knesset, a man who had been born in Lithuania and a Holocaust survivor. He and, presumably, the delegation had arrived to dedicate the monument in commemoration of the Jews who had been beaten, killed, and incinerated at this spot.

You cannot imagine Yakov's joy, although this was not a joyous moment, at being present at such a dedication, where the Speaker of the Knesset and other Israelis were to say *kaddish* for those swept away by the Holocaust. He was deeply moved by the ceremony, especially since this was the first time in fifty-two years that he had heard a cantor chant an *El-moleh Rachamim*. When he returned to his home in Kazakhstan, I am certain that he shared his personal elation with others.

He had heard many unfavorable reports about Israel and Israelis from the Soviet media, and he had heard favorable things from us. He told me that he was pleased to hear from us the good things about "our country, Israel." He felt proud to have been with the Israelis, to shake hands with them, to pray with them, to listen to the Speaker of the Knesset recite the *kaddish*.

On Saturday we went to the only remaining synagogue in Vilnius. While we were there for the Shabbat services, Shilansky arrived, accompanied by the past Chief Rabbi of the Israeli Defense Forces, by an Ashkenazi Rabbi from Israel, Goren, and other dignitaries. For Yakov, these services were something very special; this was the first time he had been in a synagogue in fifty-two years.

One man from the Israeli delegation came to me with a request. He wanted me to take a picture of him in the center of the synagogue, where the Torah is read. I told him that it would be improper to do so, since today was Shabbat. He told me that he wanted the picture because, as a young boy, he'd sung in the choir of this synagogue with a then-famous cantor. He gave me his address in Israel so I could send the picture to him. Later this man came back to present me with a beautiful Passover Haggadah, which I gave to Yakov.

At breakfast the next day, Yakov told me that he had read the Haggadah all through the night and into the early hours of the morning. For him, these pages were precious. Things were coming back to him as he recalled seders he attended at our home or at the home of his parents in Roguva. Having been deprived of such contacts over his many years in Kazakhstan, he now wanted to soak up everything he could about Judaism and Israel.

I gave him a special gold-plated key chain that had been made in Israel. It was so constructed that if you turned a part of the chain one way, you would see a Star of David; if you turned it another way, you would see a menorah. For Yakov, this toy for grown-ups was a treasure.

All these big and little episodes were clearly bringing Yakov back to his past, to his Jewish roots. We could see it happening in just a few days. His speech was changing. When we first met, his Yiddish had been halting and heavily larded with Russian; by the time we left, it was almost perfect. His *mama loshen* had been reborn, and so had his spirit, his lust for life.

Finally, the day came for us to depart. Yakov accompanied us to the airport. It was difficult for us both to say good-bye not knowing when, if ever, we would see each other again.

Yes, our reunion in Lithuania revived Yakov's spirit. But our return to Kavarsk could not revive the spirit of a town that had died. What we saw there was a corpse, without life: The shtetl was dead. Yes, the church was there, glistening and gleaming as ever, its big clock still ticking away and keeping perfect time as always. And the *krenitze,* with its ever-bubbling water, was there, although the troughs and cups intended to serve humans were gone.

There is not a semblance of anything Jewish in town. The building that once was the synagogue is there, but it has been plastered over on the outside; the section of the synagogue where our family would gather for prayer has been converted into a general store for the local folk.

My uncle Ruvin's house with its stable is there, but through the dirt-encrusted windows you cannot see a living soul moving about inside. The hill on which our house had been located is no longer recognizable. It is now a paved highway running through towns and cities to facilitate the movement of the military. The wooden cabin with the thatched roof in which I was born is gone. The house where we lived for the last eight years before my departure for America has been painted green, and is empty—a body without a soul. Aunt Elke's brick house is there, the place where we baked the matzos on Passover to supply the Jewish families in town. It looks almost exactly the same as it did fifty-three years ago, but there is no one inside.

The well behind our house, the one that I helped my father dig, looks almost exactly the same as it did the last time I visited it to fetch a welcome pail of water from its dependable depths. The only difference is a cover on top, fastened with a padlock. The water is there but no longer for human use.

The excavation where Aunt Elke used to store the ice for her ice cream business is now the foundation for a house that doubles as a bakery. The old Jewish cemetery near the flour mill, where my father's parents were buried, is no more. The plot has been bulldozed and levelled—a metaphor for what has happened to Jewish life in Lithuania.

Even the marketplace has vanished. In its place, the Russians have planted some trees and placed some benches. But there's no one sitting there, and there is no "market day" on Monday. The houses around the marketplace, once heavily populated by Jews, are still there, but there is not a Jew in sight. And the present occupants, whoever they may be, are not visible.

The flour mill, which my father labored so diligently to construct, only to be deprived of any of the benefits he might have drawn from it, is no more. The dam, bridge, and control gates—likewise. The reservoir is dried out and looks like a desert, a desert abutting a deserted town.

Most of the Jewish homes—I would say about three quarters of them—are there, and they are occupied. But you cannot see a person in or around them. It may be that when the occupants saw us coming they concluded that we had returned to claim possession of what was rightfully ours. Or, it may be that their consciences were bothering them and they were ashamed to face us. In either event one might, in our circumstance, conclude that Kavarsk had become a ghost town.

While it was, in reality, dead, in my remembrance it comes alive again. Each step and each spot, each house and each home stirs memories:

Here is the bakery where, mornings, I would love to buy a fresh sweet egg roll (*bulkale*); I can smell the aroma, and I can hear husband and wife cursing one another.

In the marketplace, I see the bus arriving from Kovno and the people gathering every night for this great event in our town. And I am there watching my father, "my hero," open the door and stepping out as the others follow.

I see my mother on Saturday morning, standing in front of the kiln with a long wooden shovel, arranging and rearranging the *cholent*. I see my sister running around the kitchen with the Shmuckler girls.

I see Aunt Elke with her boys loading the horse-drawn wagon with the galvanized iron cans of ice cream packed with ice in wooden barrels. I see the hustle and bustle of the market day. I see my friends playing soccer in the school yard. I see Uncle Ruvin and his sons in the slaughter house behind their home. I see my parents and their friends taking a stroll on a Saturday afternoon, walking and talking and telling tales of years past. . . .

These were my memories as I walked past the homes, the marketplace, past the big house where the priest lived, past the *krenitze* to the little hill lined with trees. Full of these reveries, I felt a momentary happiness dwelling in this shtetl within my mind. But then reality set in. The shtetl I inhabited existed only within me; outside of my memories, it no longer existed. My "home" was now a haunted house. The places and the plaster were there but the people were gone, the Jewish people and their way of life that had enriched our town for hundreds of years.

We returned to our minibus. As we left, I waved good-bye to the shtetl that once was.

We headed for Wilkomer, the capital city of our district and about fourteen miles from Kavarsk. Outside this city was a forest called Pavonya. This is where the Jews of the district were dragooned and murdered, among them my family and fellow Jews of Kavarsk. They were buried in common graves about 150 feet long by fifteen feet wide. I counted thirteen of them. Some 10,300 Jews were buried there. A monument has been erected there to commemorate these victims of the Holocaust.

After filming the overgrown common graves, I said *kaddish* and then broke down. It had, indeed, been a difficult day.

Before personally witnessing the graves, I'd obtained some knowledge of what had happened. The information came from people who had somehow managed to survive the Holocaust and had returned to Kavarsk. They told me that more than 10,000 Jews had been herded into the Wilkomer forest where they were murdered, their bodies tossed into the graves.

The atrocities are also recorded in a book by Masha Greenbaum, entitled *The Jews of Lithuania*, published in Israel in 1995 by the Grafen Publishing House, Ltd. An excerpt on page 306 reads:

> On June 25, Lithuanian partisans who defined themselves as "freedom fighters," began a three-day killing rampage against Jews in smaller towns and villages, during which the entire populations of over 150 Jewish communities perished.
>
> Some Jews were driven from their homes and burned alive, after having been savagely beaten and herded into synagogues, schools, and other public places that were then torched.
>
> In other instances, entire Jewish families were driven to nearby forests or riverbeds, where pits or trenches had been prepared, and were then shot. In several localities, Jews were forced to dig their own graves. Virtually all the Jews in Ukmerge (Wilkomer) were herded into the synagogue and burned alive.
>
> In Seirijai, Jews were dragged naked through the streets and then brutally murdered in the presence of cheering crowds.
>
> In Panevezys (Ponyvez) Jews, including several young women who had been raped, were hurled into burning lime.

Another excerpt, on page 307, reads:

> On June 25, partisans decapitated the Chief Rabbi of Slabodka, Zalman Ossovsky, and displayed his severed head in the front window of his house. His headless body was discovered in another room, seated near an open volume of the Talmud that he had been studying.
>
> In Slabodka (Wiliajampole) partisans went from house to house searching for Jews. The victims were thrown into the Vileja. Those who did not drown were shot to death as they swam.
>
> Most of these 150 localities became *Judenrein* some twenty-four hours

before the Germans arrived. Many of the killings and beatings were carried out in broad daylight amid acquiescing, often cheering, witnesses.

When they attended mass in church, the partisans were praised by the priests for their courage and patriotism. The Nazis were blessed and lauded as the liberators of Lithuania, worthy of the eternal gratitude of the country and the church.

On page 308, there appears the following:

College and high school students participated in the pogroms alongside the partisans and the hooligans, using every available means—rifles, guns, knives, bare hands—to maim and kill any Jew unfortunate enough to fall into their hands.

These were accounts gathered from eyewitnesses. We were spared the sight of the inhuman horrors; but we did see the graves.

The next day we went to Rugova, where Yakov had been born and where Leo Rubin lived with his sister, Rita, his mother, and his mother's parents. Leo lived there with his mother and sister until 1937, when he'd left to join his father in the United States.

The house inhabited by Yakov and his parents was no longer there. It had been demolished four years earlier, according to a next-door neighbor who now lived in the house of Yakov's aunt. However, the old stable, where Yakov's father, a blacksmith, stored his metal, was still there.

We went to the house where Leo's grandfather had lived. The house and the stable were there intact. A woman living in that house, noticing that we were foreigners looking around and feeling, perhaps, that we were there to reclaim possession, told us that the old house had been bombed and that her family had rebuilt it. Her story was untrue: Nothing had been bombed there. The house was exactly the same old wooden house that had been there when Leo lived in it. The woman had invented the story out of fear that Leo might reclaim it.

The old synagogue was there, right opposite the house of Leo's grandfather. I remembered it well. Whenever I would visit Roguva I would go to the synagogue to see the beautifully carved wooden *oren kodesh*. The building is used today as a factory to manufacture wooden kitchen cabinets.

From Roguva we went to Ponyvez, the capital of its district. We located the forest outside Ponyvez where all the Jews of that district had been rounded up and exterminated by the Nazis and their Lithuanian collaborators. Among the victims were Yakov's entire family (my family on my mother's side), including my grandmother, my uncle and his family, and my aunt and her family. They were buried, together with the others, in common graves. There was a monument here commemorating the massacre.

I said *kaddish* once more. Yakov told us that when he'd returned to this place after his service in the army, peasants had informed him that, for several days after the "dead" had been buried, the earth over the graves would rise and fall. Apparently, some of the victims had been buried alive.

After our five days were over it was time for us to leave. Yakov went with us to the airport to see us off; he was scheduled to leave the next day. Because our flight was delayed for two hours, we had another brief opportunity to talk our hearts out to each other.

He told me how hard life was for him and his family in that godforsaken place where he lived. He knew that there was no future for his children or grandchildren. I pressed him once more to start making plans immediately upon his return to leave Russia and go to Israel; I promised to help. (At this writing his daughter, Dina, her husband, Alex, and their two children have made *aliya* to Israel.)

He reviewed his hard life, his endless labors, for which he had nothing to show. The highpoint of his life, he repeated over and over again, was the five-day tour we had just completed, which had brought him a sense of satisfaction and accomplishment. He kept pinching himself to see if it was really he who was here with me. This experience had given Yakov a badly needed lift. His eyes lit up with gratitude; my heart lit up with the joy of a good deed done.

He talked on. All these years he'd had no one to confide in, no one to share his pains, no one who would understand his plight. Now, he had me; and in the few moments we had together, he wanted to cram in the whole sad story of his struggles and sorrows.

In the course of his talk, he wept repeatedly. "I don't know why," he said, "but all my life I could not cry, and now, when I talk with you, I cannot stop crying."

Our emotional exchange was brought to a halt by the announcement that it was time to board the plane for Leningrad (St.

Petersburg). We parted with tears in our eyes and a bittersweet mix of pleasure and pain in our hearts.

I knew that Yakov was not the same person on his departure as he had been on his arrival. His return to his boyhood home, after so many years of absence, and his meeting with Janet, Leo, Trudy and myself, after so many years of isolation in the backwoods of Karaganda, Kazakhstan, could not but have changed Yakov's view of the world and of himself.

This simple fact—that we, the only two survivors of our immediate family, were able to come together from opposite sides of the globe to say *kaddish*, to pay our respects to our lost loved ones, and to share our memories of a common civilization that once flourished—was an historic episode, one we shall never forget.

Yakov was very much taken with Trudy. Before he met her, I am certain he must have wondered just what kind of woman I had taken for a wife. He did know she was an American, and he must have asked himself what kind of relationship could possibly exist between the two of us and, especially, what sort of interest could she possibly have in the little shtetl we were to visit.

When, upon their meeting, Trudy began speaking Yiddish, he had been flabbergasted, and in the course of our five-day sojourn together Yakov and Trudy had come to feel very close to one another. Understandably, Yakov fell in love with her.

The days surrounding our return to Kavarsk were a totally satisfying time for me. I had, over the years, repeatedly entertained the thought of a return to Kavarsk and a reunion with my cousin from Karaganda. When Gorbachev threw the doors of the Soviet Union open, I felt that fate had read my mind and responded positively.

They say that "opportunity knocks but once." It knocked at my door; I seized the opportunity. I shall never regret it and shall never forget it.

The time I spent on my return to Lithuania was loaded with emotion, really supercharged. I believe that I shall return again. I want to revisit my town to gather more information and develop more insight, and to do so with greater objectivity and understanding. I would like to mount a retrospective and put it in the perspective of the times in which I lived.

Once I was the child of Kavarsk. Now Kavarsk that was is my child—a child I carry with me in my heart, a child who will live—and whom I will love—so long as I live.

Afterword

After I finished writing my memoirs and submitted the final manuscript to the publishers, my wife, Trudy, and I together with our children and grandchildren, on the occasion of our fiftieth wedding anniversary, started our journey in search of our roots for six days to a little town (*shtetl*) in Lithuania known as Kavarskas (Kavarsk) where I was born seventy-four years ago.

We were eleven people, which included myself, my wife, Trudy, our son, Leonard, and his wife, Linda, with their sons, David and Brian, our daughter, Rochelle Greenberg, and her husband, David, and their children, Lindsey, Evan and four-and-a-half year old son, Todd Samuel.

I am sure that our children and grandchildren will cherish this experience for the rest of their lives. I pointed out to them some of the high points of my shtetl where I was born. We walked, touched and felt the soil and places where I walked and played as a child, where my father and grandfather and grandmother before me walked and played as children, married, raised families and always hoped for a better life for their children.

Yes, we walked as a family together on the same cursed road and soil where my parents, sister, uncles, aunts, cousins, my friends and all the Jewish people of my beloved shtetl known as Kavarskas (Kavarsk) on September 5, 1941, had walked for the last time while being pushed and shoved to nearby prepared gigantic craters in the forest known as "Pavonya" to be tortured, murdered and shot by German human beings who called themselves Nazis and their Lithuanian sympathizers.

Yes, I recited *kaddish* at the memorial in front of the common graves where 10,239 Jewish men, women and children were murdered and amongst them my dear parents, sister and relatives.

I realize that this was not what my children and grandchildren had ever wished and hoped to witness however, I'm sure sometime in the future when they are asked about their roots, they will proudly be able to say, that they came from a little shtetl known as Kavarskas (Kavarsk),

Lithuania, and are proud to be a branch of that tree which its roots had produced, and they are fortunate to have had the opportunity to walk, touch and feel where their father, grandparents, and great-great grand-parents planted their seeds.